Hip-Hop en Français

Hip-Hop en Français

An Exploration of Hip-Hop Culture in the Francophone World

Edited by
Alain-Philippe Durand

Foreword by Marcyliena Morgan

ROWMAN & LITTLEFIELD
Lanham • Boulder • New York • London

Published by Rowman & Littlefield
An imprint of The Rowman & Littlefield Publishing Group, Inc.
4501 Forbes Boulevard, Suite 200, Lanham, Maryland 20706
www.rowman.com

6 Tinworth Street, London SE11 5AL, United Kingdom

British Library Cataloguing in Publication Information Available

Library of Congress Cataloging-in-Publication Data

Names: Durand, Alain-Philippe, editor. | Morgan, Marcyliena H. writer of foreword.
Title: Hip-hop en français : an exploration of hip-hop culture in the francophone world / edited by Alain-Philippe Durand ; foreword by Marcyliena Morgan.
Description: Lanham : Rowman & Littlefield Publishing Group, 2020. | Includes bibliographical references and index. | Summary: "This edited volume presents an overview of the emergence and development of hip-hop culture in France, French Caribbean, Canada, and Francophone Africa from its origins until today. Contributors discuss the artists' interactions with media arts, social media, literature, race, political landscapes, as well as hip-hop based education"—Provided by publisher.
Identifiers: LCCN 2019059476 (print) | LCCN 2019059477 (ebook) | ISBN 9781538116326 (cloth) | ISBN 9781538116333 (epub)
Subjects: LCSH: Rap (Music)—France—History and criticism. | Rap (Music)—French-speaking countries—History and criticism. | Hip-hop—France—History. | Hip-hop—French-speaking countries—History.
Classification: LCC ML3531 .H5726 2020 (print) | LCC ML3531 (ebook) | DDC 782.421649/0944—dc23
LC record available at https://lccn.loc.gov/2019059476
LC ebook record available at https://lccn.loc.gov/2019059477

For Sherri, Chloé, and Eva

Contents

Foreword

Marcyliena Morgan

In 2002, when Alain-Philippe Durand first published *Black, Blanc, Beur: Rap Music and Hip-Hop Culture in the Francophone World*, France was the second-largest hip-hop market after the United States and a leading producer and consumer of hip-hop culture (Béthune 2003; Krims 2000). What was true then remains true now. Nearly twenty years after the publication of his first collection, Durand is back with *Hip-Hop en Français: An Exploration of Hip-Hop Culture in the Francophone World*. This collection of essays continues the dialogue about the importance and independence of Francophone hip-hop and addresses a question asked by the late Adam Krims in the foreword he wrote for *Black, Blanc, Beur*: "Why did a book as important as this take so long?" (Krims 2000, vii).

While Krims's question may be predictable from the perspective of those involved in hip-hop culture, it underestimates how challenging it can be to participate in the building of a cultural movement and simultaneously appreciate and chronicle the implications of what one is actually doing—let alone know what it will mean to the world in the future! In *Hip-Hop en Français*, Durand takes the opportunity to look back as well as forward and inward in order to critique some of the research and assumptions that scholars have made about the growth and culture of hip-hop from the 1990s and into the twenty-first century. He then challenges us to continue to *keep it hip-hop* by confronting many of the same concerns, questions, and hip-hop dreams unveiled nearly twenty years ago. *Hip-Hop en Français* considers the developments that have occurred and are occurring by offering a collection of essays that provide deeper insight into the heart of the Francophone hip-hop scene and its independence and solidarity within American and global hip-hop. The result is a comprehensive, thoughtful, complex, and insightful collection that represents the dynamism and determinism of French and Francophone hip-

_ᵣ_ to uphold the fundamentals and history of hip-hop culture through hard-core questions and analyses.

As a result, the collection convincingly demonstrates that *real hip-hop* is not an American import but rather an African American ideology about freedom and justice. At the core of hip-hop is the African American protest culture and the experience of descendants of slaves in America as well as those who settled throughout the African diaspora. Consequently, the heart of this book is that French hip-hop is embedded in the creative, political, social, and cultural norms of the young African and immigrant communities, where the goal is not to simply consume and imitate but to create and participate in the growth of hip-hop music, art, and culture. It resonates with hip-hop's *get in where you fit in* ideology that considers the African American aesthetic as vanguard while not imperial. The result is a guidebook on hip-hop culture, Francophone style. This includes artistic elements, underground philosophy and ideology, language, culture, social and political activism, and the relentless quest for keeping it real (Morgan 2009; Morgan and Bennett 2011). It also confirms the centrality and "holy ground" of the cipher, hip-hop's version of the Underground Freedom School. The cipher is where artistic skills are learned, practiced, and evaluated and where knowledge and education that represent and benefit those in need—black and brown and oppressed young people—are exchanged and debated. In order to participate among African hip-hop artists in particular, there is a sustained critique of commercial gangsta rap lyrics and extreme sexualization that have been central to hard-core hip-hop culture and have historically represented (and, in some cases, analyzed) and (in too many others) glamorized the intersection of masculinity, dominance, and violence. As a result, hard-core hip-hop culture has been the historical target of global communities and has produced a contested relationship with local hip-hop cultures in the United States and throughout the world. Don't be American. *Be hip-hop. Get in where you fit in. Represent, build, come correct, keep it real, recognize.*

Hip-hop initially referred to artistic elements of (1) deejaying and turntablism; (2) the delivery and lyricism of rapping and MCing; (3) breakdancing and other forms of hip-hop dance; and (4) graffiti art and writing; and often a "fifth element"—knowledge.[1] Hip-hop knowledge refers to the aesthetic, social, intellectual, and political identities, beliefs, behaviors, and values produced and embraced by its members, who generally think of hip-hop as an identity, a worldview, and a "way of life" (Morgan and Bennett 2011). One must remember that American hip-hop began as a critique of the country referred to as a jungle with "broken glass everywhere."[2] The daughters, sons, and grandchildren of the civil rights and Black Power movements founded hip-hop in the United States. They came from the core of African American communities and social and political practice where music, critical narratives, irony, and wit are the fabric of the culture and a symbol of pride.

As hip-hop culture developed, it identified the cities and regions that it claimed as its home. Moreover, the youth who fashioned art, culture, and politics were reared on endless tales of the American Dream versus the American Nightmare. They learned early that the Black Muslim leader Malcolm X was told by his high school counselor that he should not aim too high "for his own good," that the police seem to serve and protect others, and that justice is directed at "just us" (Morgan 2009, 48). When in the early days of hip-hop, urban youth tossed cardboard boxes onto the streets of the Bronx, wrote their names in public spaces, unlaced and relaced their sneakers, refashioned their dress, reconstructed sound systems, and redefined synthesizers and mixers, they did so with the determination and creativity shared by abandoned and exploited youth who preceded them as well as those throughout the world that create with the materials the affluent discard.

Likewise, African, Arab, and Caribbean youth in Europe heard the hip-hop culture chant "get in where you fit in" that welcomes everyone who wants to participate if they understand that hip-hop culture insists that you know, understand, recognize, and represent who you are, where you are, and where you're from. As hip-hop developed into a global phenomenon, French hip-hop was already at the head of the movement. This was occurring in 2005 alongside the Paris uprisings, during which three weeks of riots of African and North African youth spread from the Paris *banlieues* (suburbs) to other parts of the country. Durand and most of this book's authors acknowledge that early research and critiques of hip-hop reflected the confusion of some writers who were caught off-guard about the nature and value of the emerging hip-hop movement. Certainly, some journalists sensationalized and stereotyped hip-hop artists and followers and described them as criminals, and their lyrics, music, dance, and art as hedonistic, misogynist, etc. Fortunately, scholarly writings on hip-hop were authored by academics that grew up within the value system of hip-hop culture and ciphers, which requires high levels of skill evaluated by others demanding the highest standards, as well as by academic institutions expecting skills and more than opinions and the sensationalizing of well-worn stereotypes. These are the conditions under which the founding of the Hiphop Archive and Research Institute became so critical.[3]

During the twentieth century, while African American bodies were segregated into restricted zones of their own country, African American music, including blues, jazz, and later rock 'n' roll and soul, traveled the world, shaping world music in ways that have yet to be fully acknowledged (Ramsey 2004; Lipsitz 1994; Mitchell 1996). Much of the world recognized that African American music and culture traveled when and where African American bodies could not. Farah Griffin argues, "Consider the ways that the American State Department selected jazz to represent national culture abroad during the Cold War, even as the government continued to deny black

Americans full citizenship at home, or the contemporary global circulation of contemporary hip hop culture" (Griffin 2004, 120). The French were well aware of all varieties of African American creativity, including musicians, visual artists, and writers who were exceptional at their crafts but had to endure racism and many forms of discrimination in America. Beginning in the late twentieth century, hip-hop music became the first African American music form to be created completely within the post–Civil Rights era. It has since continued its global journey—whose impact has been expanded and problematized in the late twentieth and early twenty-first centuries by processes of corporate globalization and new technologies, especially computer technologies—of musical production and distribution. Thus, French hip-hop is understood as vocation, lifestyle, and consciousness. It has always been about exposing and fighting injustice everywhere.

Today there are hundreds, if not thousands, of websites devoted to hip-hop in different parts of the world. Each nation, each region, even each neighborhood in the world that represents hip-hop culture does so with a unique history. Yet much of hip-hop culture remains undocumented or underdocumented,[4] including the use of hip-hop culture to engage in the exposure of injustice and, in an ironic parallel, the use of hip-hop as the political, commercial, and even spiritual arbiter of national and international cultures. The most fundamental aspect of hip-hop culture is building solidarity. It was during the "golden age of hip-hop" in the late 1980s and 1990s when America, France, and most of the world joined in confirming hip-hop's founders, who were children of the civil rights and Black Power movements, and the individuals and organizations that represented it. Historically, many in the world have supported freedom movements and defiance against injustice from their home countries. Now, there is the hip-hop notion that the fight for justice and equality concerns us all.

Today there are generations of past and present hip-hop followers, each believing that their teenage/young adult generation represented hip-hop culture at its best. These hip-hop heads are asking questions of the current generation with the expectation that there should be, would always be, change, but to keep it hip-hop. As Durand says,

> Consequently, eighteen years later, there is a definite need for another volume dealing with French and Francophone hip-hop cultures. . . . Moreover, the emergence of new scholars and artists as well as the global growth and transformation of hip-hop culture are reflected in the many changes and innovations that surfaced during the first two decades of the twenty-first century. (Durand 2002, xv–xvi)

What Durand means by this is captured in the fourteen chapters of this book that cover the foundations and growth of hip-hop in the areas of creativity, production, performance, research, and analyses that helped create and confirm that it is not only a creative, social, cultural, and political force but is changing the local and global landscape as well. There are many genres of hip-hop. They each center around style of rhyme, content, flow, location, gangsta and hard-core themes, consciousness, mainstream society, and more.

Hip-Hop en Français explores aspects and themes that have not changed and will probably always prevail because they have been at the core of hip-hop culture around the world for as long as hip-hop has existed. U.S. and global hip-hop heads have put into practice and expanded upon Frantz Fanon's theory that an individual or group that "has a language consequently possesses the world expressed and implied by that language. . . . Mastery of language affords remarkable power" (Fanon 1967, 18). French hip-hop has not merely mastered hip-hop language and culture; it has helped develop and increase its discourse and language and formed new language to redefine its many worlds. It is the essence of *WORD UP!* Through their unprecedented global movement of art and culture, the citizens of the hip-hop nation have used their unique and collective aesthetic voices to both possess and transform the world, a process that has not merely "afforded" them power but that has also enabled them to produce new forms of power, beauty, and knowledge.

Just as American rap crossed borders, French rap influenced artists in the rest of the Francophone world and inspired hip-hop scholars on both sides of the Atlantic representing various disciplines (African studies, anthropology, cultural studies, ethnology, French and Francophone studies, history, linguistics, musicology, psychology, and sociology). Contributors to this book discuss the history of French rap music from its origin to the present, the various artists and their groups, stage performances of the rap groups in Paris and Marseille, the art of graffiti, and the French public's perceptions of rap music.

In 1993, when hip-hop was in a state of growth and presence in the young world's imagination, MTV and music videos were just becoming a powerful medium to introduce a record. I stood in a friend's living room in awe as MTV Raps debuted "Le Bien, Le Mal" (The Good, the Bad) by France's MC Solaar and the late U.S. hip-hop artist Guru. In the prelude to the video, Solaar telephones Guru to arrange a meeting. Each man is filmed in separate outdoor locations while talking to the other on their cell phones. MC Solaar is in Paris outside the metro and speaks to Guru in French using *verlan*—urban French vernacular that incorporates movement of syllables and deletion of consonants.[5] Guru is in a car near the New York/Brooklyn Bridge subway stop and uses hip-hop terminology and African American English (AAE) as he talks to MC Solaar (who, of course, not only speaks French slang but is a language innovator):

Paris:

MC Solaar (in French): It's been a long time since we've seen Guru from Gangstarr. Wouldn't it be cool if he came back to Paris?

Friend: Yeah.

MC Solaar: Let's try to call him.[6]

New York:

Guru (on phone in English): Hello, who dis? Solaar! What up, man? Yeah! No, I'm comin', man. I know I'm late. Yo! Hold up for me, al(r)ight. Baby! I'm on my way now, al(r)ight! Peace!

At the end of the conversation, Guru leaves New York to meet MC Solaar and descends stairs into the subway. When he ascends the subway, he is in Paris! Then the two begin their song about injustice in their respective cities and countries and the need for unity and a determination to fight for justice. *Keeping it real!*

REFERENCES

Béthune, Christian. *Le rap: une esthétique hors la loi*. Paris: Autrement, 2003.

Chang, Jeff. *Can't Stop Won't Stop: A History of the Hip-Hop Generation*. New York: Picador, 2005.

Durand, Alain-Philippe, ed. *Black, Blanc, Beur: Rap Music and Hip-Hop Culture in the Francophone World*. Lanham, MD: Scarecrow Press, 2002.

Fanon, Frantz. *Black Skins, White Masks*. New York: Grove Press, 1967.

Griffin, Farah Jasmine. "When Malindy Sings: A Meditation on Black Women's Vocality." In *Uptown Conversation: The New Jazz Studies*. Edited by Robert G. O'Meally, Brent Hayes Edwards, and Farah Jasmine Griffin, 102–25. New York: Columbia University Press, 2004.

Krims, Adam. *Rap Music and the Poetics of Identity*. Cambridge: Cambridge University Press, 2000.

Lipsitz, George. *Dangerous Crossroads: Popular Music, Postmodernism, and the Poetics of Place*. New York: Verso, 1994.

Mitchell, Tony. *Popular Music and Local Identity: Rock, Pop, and Rap in Europe and Oceania*. Leicester: Leicester University Press, 1996.

Morgan, Marcyliena. *The Real Hiphop: Battling for Knowledge, Power, and Respect in the LA Underground*. Durham, NC: Duke University Press, 2009.

Morgan, Marcyliena, and Dionne Bennett. "Hiphop and the Global Imprint of a Black Cultural Form." *Daedalus* 140, no. 2 (2011): 176–96.

Price III, Emmett G. *Hip Hop Culture*. Santa Barbara, CA: ABC-CLIO, 2006.

Ramsey Jr., Guthrie P. *Race Music: Black Cultures from Bebop to Hip-Hop*. Berkeley: University of California Press, 2004.

DISCOGRAPHY

Grandmaster Flash and the Furious 5. "The Message." Sugar Hill Records, vinyl. Originally released in 1982.

Guru, with MC Solaar. "Le Bien, Le Mal." Chrysalis Records, compact-disc. Originally released in 1993.

Acknowledgments

I would like to thank my editors, John Cerullo, Natalie Mandziuk, and Michael Tan at Rowman & Littlefield, for believing in the project and for their advice, support, and patience. I also want to express my gratitude to the many people who contributed directly or indirectly to this teamwork: all the contributors and translators of this volume; my hip-hop studies colleagues at the University of Arizona—Jerome Dotson, Erika Gault, John Melillo, Alex Nava, Tani Sanchez, and Praise Zenenga—as well as my friend Ralph Schoolcraft III for the index, his eagle-eye editing, and the formatting; and Marcy Morgan for the foreword and for being such a strong role model to all of us in hip-hop studies. I must also acknowledge the support I received from the various institutions that gave me the time, resources, and networking I needed to complete this volume: the University of Arizona, Harvard University's Hiphop Archive and Research Institute (HARI), University of Nevada at Las Vegas, Université Paris Nanterre, Universidade Federal de Campina Grande, Universidade Federal de Santa Catarina, Universidade Federal do Rio Grande do Norte, and Alliance Française in Washington, D.C., along with the University of Arizona's Confluencenter for Creative Inquiry Faculty Collaboration Grant. Other colleagues and friends were very helpful and supportive in completing this book: all colleagues and students in the College of Humanities at the University of Arizona and Ronaldo Lima, Julie Cavignac, Josilene Pinheiro-Mariz, Alain Milon, and Seth Whidden.

Finally, I wish to thank my family for their constant support, love, patience, and nonstop inspiration. They are the most important to me, always.

Introduction

Alain-Philippe Durand

Hip-hop studies were not really a thing when I started my academic career in 1999, especially not in the field of French and Francophone studies. While specializing in the French contemporary novel, as a new assistant professor at the University of Rhode Island, I was ready to teach a wide variety of classes at all levels, most of which I had never taught before, such as French conversation. Looking for topics that would motivate students' in-class discussions, I inserted a two-week introduction to French hip-hop in the syllabus. Fast-forward a few weeks later. I am sitting in the office, and the phone rings. It is the director of the university's Multicultural Center: "Are you the professor who raps in his classes?" Little did I know that day would be the official start, not of a career in rap music, but of a new research interest in hip-hop. After I clarified that I was *only* lecturing on French hip-hop, the Multicultural Center director invited me to give a public talk on the subject, which, a few years later, resulted in a new course and a new book.

Looking back to 2002, the publication year of my first edited volume, *Black, Blanc, Beur: Rap Music and Hip-Hop Culture in the Francophone World*, one can make two statements of facts. First, as many of us already knew in those days, hip-hop culture has continued to grow and develop in a multitude of ways, to the point of becoming and remaining a true global phenomenon. It is safe to say that in 2020 there is probably not a single country on earth where at least one element of hip-hop culture is not only recognized and embraced but also practiced and adapted to local customs. Second, the field of hip-hop studies is now firmly established, for the most part respected (at least in the United States), spreading throughout academic disciplines, and generating its own derivatives, such as Hip-Hop Based Education (HHBE) (Hill and Petchauer 2013; Durand, Milon, and Norton 2018). For example, in 2013, we created a minor in Hip-Hop Studies at the University of Arizona and joined the growing ranks of American academic institutions truly committed (via specific programs and research centers) to the field, such as the Hiphop Archive and Research Institute (HARI) at Harvard University, the Institute for Diversity in the Arts and Committee on Black Performing Arts at Stanford University, the Cornell University Hip Hop Collection, or the Laboratory for Race & Popular Culture at the University of Colorado, among others (Durand 2019). Furthermore, while at the beginning of the twenty-first century it was certainly not a good idea or was highly risky at best, especially in departments of modern languages, for pretenure assistant professors to conduct research or present themselves as hip-hop scholars, it is now much more accepted and respected, and there are many hip-hop scholars working in various disciplines across the board in American universities.

I would argue that the most striking change since 2002 and the publication of *Black, Blanc, Beur*—back then the first book-length study of French and Francophone hip-hop culture written in the English language—is the dynamic development of research projects and therefore the appearance of an entire new generation of scholars (many based in the United States) interested in and actively presenting and publishing works dealing with non-American hip-hop cultures, such as Catherine M. Appert's *In Hip Hop Time: Music, Memory, and Social Change in Urban Senegal* (2018); Eric Charry's *Hip Hop Africa: New African Music in a Globalizing World* (2012); Ian Condry's *Hip-Hop Japan: Rap and the Paths of Cultural Globalization* (2006); Adriana Helbig's *Hip Hop Ukraine: Music, Race, and African Migration* (2014); Felicia McCarren's *French Moves: The Cultural Politics of le hip hop* (2013); Milosz Miszczynski and Helbig's *Hip Hop at Europe's Edge: Music, Agency, and Social Change* (2017); Halifu Osumare's *The Hiplife in Ghana: West African Indigenization of Hip-Hop* (2012); Derek Pardue's *Ideologies of Marginality in Brazilian Hip Hop* (2008); and James G. Spady, H. Samy Alim, and Samir Meghelli's *Tha Global Cipha: Hip Hop Culture and Consciousness* (2006), to only name a few examples of representative works. There are many more articles and book chapters, as well.

One anecdote can best exemplify the significant increase in the last twenty years of researchers based in American institutions of higher learning who publish studies in the English language dedicated to hip-hop culture outside of America. Out of the ten contributors to the volume *Black, Blanc, Beur*, only one was not French or Quebecois, and eight were working for French or Quebecois academic institutions. Finding contributors working on French and Francophone hip-hop based in North America who were capable of writing in English on the relevant topics was extremely difficult at the time. Accordingly, seven out of the ten contributions had to be translated from the French original. *Hip-Hop en Français*, however, is a testimony to the arrival of this new generation of scholars who are creating and growing a vibrant

French and Francophone hip-hop studies community on both sides of the Atlantic. In this volume, one finds a total of fourteen original contributions, including seven authors based in the United States and four who participated in 2002.

Consequently, eighteen years later, there is a definite need for another volume dealing with French and Francophone hip-hop cultures. Indeed, in the same way that new scholars researching hip-hop have become visible, new and upcoming French-speaking hip-hop artists have been taking center stage in all of the main elements of the culture, be it MCing/rapping, deejaying, B-boying/dancing, or graffiti art.[1] Moreover, the emergence of new scholars and artists as well as the global growth and transformation of hip-hop culture are reflected in the many changes and innovations that surfaced during the first two decades of the twenty-first century. As with their predecessors, the new hip-hop generations—regardless of whether they create, produce, perform, research, analyze, or consume—are profoundly inspired and affected by inventions, trends, and tools that barely existed (if at all) twenty years ago: music streaming; online audio distribution platforms; podcasts; high-technology wireless headphones; and affordable, powerful cell phones, minicomputers, tablets, and other high-tech equipment, such as Digital Audio Workstations (DAWs) and software sequencers, but also social media, HHBE, and urban literature, among other things.

That said, there are aspects and themes that have not changed and will probably always prevail because they have been at the core of hip-hop culture around the world for as long as hip-hop has existed. One can think of the eternal quests for identity, authenticity, legitimacy, and the dilemmas or paradoxes that reign in hip-hop culture: What is considered true or pure hip-hop? When and how does one cross the line and sell one's soul to the devil? Is signing with a record company or an agent buying into a system? Is it possible to leave one's community and still legitimately represent it? Do races, social classes, and languages or dialects play a role in consecrating and legitimizing hip-hop artists? One can also think about the common themes of social justice, migrations and oppressions, colonialism and post-colonialism/ postcolonialism, terrorism, race and gender, love and hate, and wit and multilingualism that still dominate the worlds of hip-hop nowadays.[2] Additionally, one should recall that, yesterday and today, all around the world, there is no hip-hop without a spirit of business and entrepreneurship, a devotion to high-tech innovation, battles for supremacy, and marks and defenses of territories, concrete or symbolic. Are rappers businessmen and -women? Was hip-hop better at its origins? Is French/Francophone hip-hop better than American hip-hop? Is hip-hop sexist? Who are the greatest artists of all time? All these questions and themes are addressed in this volume.

Since it was born, regardless of the country, hip-hop culture continues to reside and grow in urban environments at the margins of large cities, in what the French call *banlieues* (suburbs), a term that both urban planning and hip-hop culture have redefined and, as you will see in this volume, a term that anyone serious about the study of French and Francophone hip-hop culture cannot ignore. The lack of understanding, the mistrust, and the conflicts that predominate between the *banlieues'* inhabitants and French government authorities is something else that, unfortunately, has not changed and that even precedes the birth of hip-hop. Throughout the years, this constant, bold confrontation between the *banlieues* and the successive French administrations has regularly resulted in violent riots and mass destruction of property (with peaks in 1995, 2005, and 2017) and has continued to inspire French hip-hop artists. For example, one can cite NTM's "Le Monde de demain" (The World of Tomorrow, 1991); Mathieu Kassovitz's film *La Haine* (Hate, 1995); Kamel Saleh and Akhenaton's *Comme un aimant* (Like a Magnet, 2000); IAM's "Nés sous la même étoile" (Born under the Same Star, 1997); Sniper and Joey Starr's "Brûle" (Burn, 2006); Haroun's "Le Zonard" (From the Slums, 2007); the compilation *Écoute la rue Marianne* (Listen to the Street, Marianne, 2007); Mafia K'1 Fry's "Guerre" (War, 2007); PNL's "Deux frères" (Two Brothers, 2019); or Niska's "La zone est minée" (The Slums Are a Minefield, 2019), to name only a few representative works.

Besides these questions of urban territories that in France oppose the marginalized and diverse *banlieues* to the more economically affluent and whiter *intra muros*, there is a constant debate about the neighborhood, the region, and the country that could claim and deserve the title of "The Land of Hip-Hop" or "The Land of Rap." Thus, a simple Internet search of the French media reveals an impressive number of articles and press releases that claim such honors for the following eclectic locations in France and beyond: Abidjan, Bobigny, Brittany, Île de France, Limoges, Limoilou, Lyon, Nantes, Paris's 13th *arrondissement*, Russia, Sarthe, Suresnes, Val d'Oise, and Wallonia! That said, when it comes to numbers and data, if France was already the "world's second-largest market for hip hop musical products" (Cannon 1997, 191) in the late 1990s, it has not only reinforced that position today, but French rap has also overtaken all other musical genres in France and has shown unprecedented popularity and distribution in Europe and Africa, in spite of (in some cases) the language barrier. According to M. Oliver,

> Despite the population of France being merely one-fifth of the US, [French rapper] Orelsan from Normandy sold as many copies of his third album *La fête est finie* [The Party's Over] as Jay-Z and Beyoncé's *Everything Is Love* while Niska moved more units of his debut album *Commando* than Pusha-T, Nipsey Hussle, and Mac Miller's Grammy-nominated albums. . . . Of the 22 number one singles in France last year, over half were French hip-hop. . . . France is not only the second biggest market for hip-hop, but it's also now arguably the most prolific. (Oliver 2019)

As Oliver's figures suggest, it seems to no longer be a matter of *if* but *when* French rappers will follow in the steps of their fellow dance companies' B-boys and end up taking over the rest of the world. Instead of being a limitation, the longtime particularities of French and Francophone hip-hop—such as a propensity for language/dialect malaxations and for mixing other musical genres with rap (afropop, trap, afro trap, cloud, pop rap, reggaetón, k-pop, etc.)—have the potential to make French the respected lingua franca of hip-hop worldwide.

It was once again crucial to use an interdisciplinary approach to this volume since hip-hop culture touches on so many different topics and disciplines. *Hip-Hop en Français* gathers essays written by anthropologists; ethnomusicologists; journalists; historians; museum curators; philosophers; social scientists; and literary, language, and cultural studies scholars. In the first chapter, Karim Hammou gives a comprehensive overview of French rap music from its beginnings forty years ago to the present. In the second chapter, Jean-Marie Jacono shows the profound transformations that both Marseille, the second-largest city of France in number of inhabitants and in hip-hop, and its local rap groups have gone through since the early 1990s. Chapters 3 and 4 concentrate on the politicization of rap music. First, Samir Meghelli recounts Public Enemy's concert in Paris in April 1990 and its aftermath in order to expose the perceived growing influence of hip-hop on France's racial politics. Second, Paul A. Silverstein examines how French gangsta rappers deal with the political and ideological question of race. In chapter 5, Steve Gadet addresses the often-disregarded history of rap music in the overseas French department of Guadeloupe in the West Indies. The following two chapters pay special attention to the connections that exist between French hip-hop and other specific forms of expression. Stève Puig's chapter 6 discusses the corpus of a selection of French rappers who have turned to literature as another source of inspiration to their activism. Kathryn Kleppinger's chapter 7 looks at how contemporary French rappers use such new media as social networks to promote and circulate their creations and opinions. In chapter 8, Charles Norton explores the concept of Hip-Hop Based Education (HHBE), presenting how hip-hop cultures are implicated in education and social engagement in Paris and its neighboring suburbs. Chapters 9 and 10 focus on hip-hop dance and French B-boys. Hugues Bazin's interests lay in body politics. More specifically, he analyzes what happens when a body dancing and thinking hip-hop appears in the public sphere. For Felicia McCarren, what matters is the striking difference that exists between American and French B-boys when it comes to financial support and career opportunities; her study argues that the second are "freer" than the first. In Alain Milon's chapter 11, readers learn about French graffiti art, more precisely the anthropological and political significance of illegal mural expressions. The last three chapters return to the place of hip-hop in the Francophone world. Catherine M. Appert (chapter 12) and Maxime Delcourt (chapter 13) give an overview of the history of rap music in Dakar, Senegal, and in Quebec, respectively. In the volume's last essay, Ariane Gruet-Pelchat investigates the complex notions of authenticity and ethnicity in the case of the group Alaclair Ensemble, often credited with the revival of rap music in Quebec.

REFERENCES

Appert, Catherine M. *In Hip Hop Time: Music, Memory, and Social Change in Urban Senegal.* New York: Oxford University Press, 2018.

Cannon, Steve. "Paname City Rapping: B-Boys in the Banlieues and Beyond." In *Post-Colonial Cultures in France*, edited by Alec Hargreaves and Mark McKinney, 150–68. London: Routledge, 1997.

Charry, Eric, ed. *Hip Hop Africa: New African Music in a Globalizing World.* Bloomington: Indiana University Press, 2012.

Condry, Ian. *Hip-Hop Japan: Rap and the Paths of Cultural Globalization.* Durham, NC: Duke University Press, 2006.

Durand, Alain-Philippe. *Black, Blanc, Beur: Rap Music and Hip-Hop Culture in the Francophone World.* Lanham, MD: Scarecrow Press, 2002.

———. "'The Wind Blows in Arizona': Representing the University of Arizona's Minor in Hip Hop Cultures." In *Higher Learning: Hip Hop in the Ivory Tower*, edited by Karin L. Stanford and Charles E. Jones, 309–20. Baltimore: Black Classis Press/Inprint Editions, 2019.

Durand, Alain-Philippe, Alain Milon, and Charles Norton. "Pédagogie Hip-Hop Trans-Amérique." In *Heurs et malheurs du système éducatif en France*, edited by Marie-Christine Weidmann Koop, 95–114. Marion, IL: *The French Review* Book Series, 2018.

Helbig, Adriana. *Hip Hop Ukraine: Music, Race, and African Migration.* Bloomington: Indiana University Press, 2014.

Hill, Marc Lamont, and Emery Petchauer, eds. *Schooling Hip-Hop: Expanding Hip-Hop Based Education across the Curriculum.* New York: Teachers College, 2013.

McCarren, Felicia. *French Moves: The Cultural Politics of le hip hop.* New York: Oxford University Press, 2013.

Miszczynski, Milosz, and Adriana Helbig, eds. *Hip Hop at Europe's Edge: Music, Agency, and Social Change.* Bloomington: Indiana University Press, 2017.

Oliver, M. "The French (Hip-Hop) Revolution." *DJBOOTH*, 28 June 2019. https://djbooth.net/features/2019-06-26-the-french-hip-hop-revolution

Osumare, Halifu. *The Hiplife in Ghana: West African Indigenization of Hip-Hop.* New York: Palgrave Macmillan, 2012.

Pardue, Derek. *Ideologies of Marginality in Brazilian Hip Hop.* New York: Palgrave Macmillan, 2008.

Puig, Stève. *Littérature urbaine et mémoire postcoloniale.* Paris: L'Harmattan, 2019.

Spady, James G., H. Samy Alim, and Samir Meghelli, eds. *Tha Global Cipha: Hip Hop Culture and Consciousness.* Philadelphia: Black History Museum Press, 2006.

DISCOGRAPHY AND FILMOGRAPHY

Comme un aimant. Dirs. Kamel Saleh and Akhenaton. Why Not Productions. Originally released in 2000.

Haroun. "Le Zonard." *Au front.* Front Kick, compact disc. Originally released in 2007.

IAM. "Nés sous la même étoile." *L'École du micro d'argent.* EMI Records, compact disc. Originally released in 1997.

Jay-Z and Beyoncé (The Carters). *Everything Is Love*. Sony, digital. Originally released in 2018.

La Haine. Dir. Mathieu Kassovitz. Les Productions Lazennec. Originally released in 1995.

Mafia K'1 Fry. "Guerre." *Jusqu'à la mort*. Menace Records, compact disc. Originally released in 2007.

Niska. *Commando*. Charo Prod, digital. Originally released in 2017.

———. "La zone est minée." *Mr Sal*. Capitol Music, digital. Originally released in 2019.

NTM. "Le Monde de demain." *Authentik*. Epic Records, compact disc. Originally released in 1991.

Orelsan. *La fête est finie*. Wagram, digital. Originally released in 2017.

PNL. "Deux frères." *Deux frères*. QLF Records, digital. Originally released in 2019.

Sniper, featuring Joey Starr. "Brûle." *Trait pour trait*. Warner Music, compact disc. Originally released in 2006.

Various Artists. *Écoute la rue Marianne*. Universal Music, compact disc. Originally released in 2007.

Chapter One

Forty Years of French Rap

Identities in Crescendo

Karim Hammou,
Translated by Katie B. Angus

HIP-HOP: INSIDER MUSIC DEPENDENT ON THE CULTURAL CIRCULATIONS OF THE BLACK ATLANTIC

Three important dates mark the solidification of rap music in France: 1979, 1982, and 1984. In 1979, the single "Rapper's Delight" by the Sugarhill Gang was distributed by the record company Vogue and was a hit in discos, selling nearly six hundred thousand copies. Then, in 1982, a small group of French people living in New York City, including the journalist and record producer Bernard Zekri, organized the first hip-hop tour in France. They called it the "New York City Rap Tour" and invited the Rocksteady Crew, Grandmixer D.ST, and Afrika Bambaataa for a series of performances in both large cities, like Paris and London, and smaller cities, like Lyon, Strasbourg, and Mulhouse. Finally, in 1984, a French musician, deejay, and radio host named Sidney launched the weekly program *H.I.P. H.O.P.* on France's TF1 television channel. Over the course of a year, he introduced hip-hop dance and music to a wider audience, largely composed of children and teens (Warne 2003, 109). These founding events (Bocquet and Pierre-Adolphe 1997) made rap and its multidisciplinary culture resound in France.

The political context at the time encouraged a cultural effervescence. After François Mitterrand was elected president of the French Republic in 1981, he implemented his promise to liberate the radio waves that had previously been monopolized by the state. Opportunities to discover new music soon multiplied on the FM broadcast band. In the region of Paris, musician and fan of funk music Phil Barney rapped on the air on Carbone 14, while on Radio 7 Sidney hosted the show *Rapper Dapper Snapper*. In 1983, Marco DSL created the program *Rythmes associés* (Associated Rhythms) on Radio Bellevue in Lyon, and in Marseille during the same year, Philippe Subrini hosted the program *Prélude* on Radio Star. All these programs broadcasted the singles of New York City artists whose innovations marked a true rupture from the norm, by introducing the techniques of breakbeats, scratching, sampling, and human beat boxing.

The vocal technique characteristic of rap first attracted followers at the very heart of the commercial record industry. Recorded in 1981, the single "Chacun fait (c'qui lui plaît)" (Everyone Does [Whatever One Wants]) by the group Chagrin d'Amour became one of 1982's biggest commercial successes and inspired numerous imitations. Performers of early French rap, who were far from hip-hop culture and were more like *variété* singers than MCs, only rapped occasionally and briefly, singing most of their songs instead of rapping throughout. After the end of the program *H.I.P. H.O.P.* in 1985, the French recording industry, in the midst of a full reorganization, turned away from what it considered to be just a passing fad.

Meanwhile, hip-hop culture brought together its first followers. Throughout the 1980s, pioneers—true musical mavericks—helped the public understand the change that was happening in African American music. Some, like Dee Nasty or Philippe Subrini, were affiliated with the Zulu Nation, but its influence on most hip-hop fans in France remained limited. Many fans of soul, funk, and reggae music, who had until then been kept on the sidelines of the record industry and the dominant media (Sermet 2008), had the opportunity to travel to the United States or London, where they discovered the latest hip-hop songs. Upon their return to France, they would broadcast these songs on radio shows and at festivals in which people of Caribbean and African diasporas, driving forces of the French participation in the Black Atlantic (Gilroy 1993), played a leading role.

In the vast population of the cultural hub of Paris, the racist selection of audience members that often prevailed in nightclubs led to the creation of specific places accessible to racial minorities rather than an outright exclusion, as in most other cities (Hammou 2012). Starting in the late 1970s, Paris had a handful of deejays known for their soul and funk music shows, and it was at their parties that the hip-hop scene emerged in France. DJ Chabin brought in rap in 1983. Dee Nasty, the artist behind *Paname City Rappin'*, the first hip-hop album in France (released in 1984), organized around ten free jams in a vacant lot on boulevard de la Chapelle in 1986. Through their verbal virtuosity, rappers like Jhonygo, Destroy Man, Lionel D, and Richie proclaimed French once and for all as the preferred language for hip-hop performances in the capital. A new wave of rappers, including Saliha, New Generation MC, 93 NTM, Assassin, EJM, Destiny, and MC Solaar, came together on air on the show *Le Deenastyle* beginning in 1989, hosted by Dee Nasty and Lionel D on Radio Nova. At the dawn of the 1990s, Paris and its region were cultivating a veritable rap scene.

In other French cities, local music scenes were less specialized. Reggae, punk, new wave, and rap musicians shared venues and radio shows: In Marseille, the concert hall La Maison Hantée welcomed hard-rock musicians as well as rappers. In Toulouse, the first MCs sharpened their rhymes on Poupa Christopher's reggae show on FMR radio, *Zarmafari*, beginning in 1988, and soon the radio station organized open-mic afternoons. In Lyon, the Cool K, the first hip-hop café in France, opened in 1990 in front of Wolnitza, a cultural space where punk and anarchist rock bands performed. These musical crossovers were also reflected in the formation of rap groups with more hybrid styles. In Marseille, the members of IAM began their career within the raggamuffin posse Massilia Sound System. In Lyon, a few B-boys of the Cool K teamed up with members of the alternative rock scene and founded the rap punk band Straight Royeur, in which the future novelist Virginie Despentes would rap. In Toulouse, the rapper and beat boxer Ange B founded a rap group defending the Occitan identity and decentralization, Bouducon Productions, and the musical duo Fabulous Trobadors.

FRENCH RAP AND THE *BANLIEUES*: THE PARADOXES OF AN ASSIGNED MINORITY STATUS

From 1990 to 1991, the diversity of these musical configurations was overshadowed by the unprecedented media coverage of French rap as an "expression of the *banlieues*" (Hammou 2012), a theme that was largely absent from earlier works of French rap. Rap and its participants were now being situated in a geography of social fears linked to emerging dangerous classes.

The media fed this new visibility, marked by the success of the first compilation of French rap, *Rapattitude*, but also by the association of rap with various social problems. First, there was the issue of the deteriorated conditions in the Paris metro at the end of the 1980s, which was attributed to the development of graffiti tags. Then, there was the problem of violence attributed to teenage gangs nicknamed by members of the media "Zulu gangs" when their members were black, which caused confusion about the nature of the peaceful Zulu movement linked to hip-hop. Finally, in 1990 and 1991, there was a wave of revolts in working-class neighborhoods and vigils linked to the deaths of young people in interactions with the police or private security services, such as that of Thomas Claudio in the Lyon suburb Vaulx-en-Velin or Aïssa Ihich in the Paris suburb Mantes-la-Jolie (Tissot 2007). French rappers appeared numerous times on high-profile programs, television newscasts, or talk shows, invited to recount, explain, or answer for these events.

In addition, these artists introduced a palpable novelty. Like Sidney, who in 1984 was the first black host on French television, it was often non-white people, young and from a working-class background, who found public visibility in a media landscape lacking diversity at the time. They became symbols that the public officials themselves seized upon, anxious to use culture as a tool for social integration. Jack Lang, minister of culture and spokesman for a government that had made the fight against exclusion one of its stated priorities, affirmed his support for hip-hop culture in the name of the symbolic rehabilitation of youth from immigrant origins (Dubois 2012).

The new public visibility of French rappers had paradoxical effects (Warne 2003, 114). They were even occasionally regarded as the troublemakers that were so often discussed. Aggrandized through their access to national media, rappers were at the same time marginalized by their association with a stigmatized category of the population—an Otherness inside French society.

The form taken by this Otherness influenced the race politics of rap in France in the early 1990s and benefits from some explanation (De Rudder, Poiret, and Voure'h 2000). Rappers were not assigned to a specific ethnic group—their musical genealogy could categorize them as Afro-European, or the place of the Algerian in French racial Otherness could classify them as Franco-Maghrebian (Shepard 2017). They were instead identified by their distance from the ethnic majority group: though never specifically named, whites who came from the Continent. Therefore, the mainstream media considered rap in France less as the music of a preexisting minority group and more as a practice of social actors of minor status whose common ground was "not to be different but to be subordinate, to be constructed as different from the general world as seen in the world and incarnating the norm" (Guillaumin 1995, 17). Thus, journalists and TV hosts differentiated rappers from both the traditional image of the singer associated with artistic legitimacy as well as from the figure of the ordinary citizen, implicitly thought of as a white person having full political legitimacy within the national community.

At the same time, this visibility contributed to the integration of rappers into cultural industries and reinforced public support for hip-hop. Policies recently put in place by the socialist government facilitated the organization of springboard competitions and rap concerts, the creation of amateur rehearsal places, and the institution of subsidies for hip-hop practices, especially in so-called priority neighborhoods (Lafargue de Grangeneuve 2008). In so doing, they redefined the spaces for hip-hop that had previously been present in the more affluent inner-city areas as well as in the working-class areas at the periphery.

Meanwhile, tapping into the commercial potential of this new scene became a high-stakes game for the monopolistic competition that the major record labels were engaged in, each betting on their own rap group with the hopes of winning big. In addition, this designation of rap to the *banlieues*, as well as the wider media stigmatization of social groups associated with the *banlieues*, were becoming popular themes in rap song lyrics.

Taking advantage of this situation, most of the Paris scene of *Deenastyle* made their first albums with major record labels. Their egotrip tracks or humorous sketches rubbed shoulders with critical social chronicles, thematizing in particular the contempt vis-à-vis youth and racism. The entire rap scene then developed a poetic and rhythmic attention to French and willingly engaged in a higher register of language. The musical compositions brought to the forefront the work of the deejays, often members of the groups themselves, interspersing among the rapped couplets scratches and sampled excerpts drawing from the repertoire of African American music in addition to other sources, like Arabic music and *chanson française*. EJM or Ministère AMER, who released their first album, *Pourquoi tant de haine?* (Why So Much Hate?), in 1992, stood out by creating the first songs explicitly criticizing racism as a system, claiming a black identity in France that broke with the French policy of colorblindness (Mazouz 2017). IAM, meanwhile, affirmed their connection to Marseille and deployed a critique of French centralism. This formal and thematic renewal of French rap was influenced equally by the evolution of the American rap genre, a source of inspiration that remained crucial for the majority of artists, and by the French media agenda, which rappers explicitly commented on.

The gamble taken by major record labels led to mixed commercial results. While such artists as MC Solaar could be successful in 1991 with *Qui sème le vent récolte le tempo* (He Who Sows the Wind Reaps the Tempo) and sales might be high for a first album like *Authentik* by Suprême NTM, other artists signed to a major record label, such as Lionel D or Destroy Man, might sell less and face commercial failures. These difficulties in transforming rap songs into profitable cultural products could be partly explained by the refusal of dominant radio stations to cooperate.

Three "youth" music radio stations at the time covered the majority of the French territory and broadcast the most popular songs of the moment, like Top 40 U.S. stations: Fun Radio, Skyrock, and NRJ. Although they were focused on new releases, they were hostile to the dissemination of rap. In search of melodic hits that people could dance to and whose lyrics would appeal to a wide audience, the programmers of these radio stations refused to broadcast music associated with social problems or perceived as the music of Others. The 1994 vote of the Carignon Law, which contained an article imposing quotas of French-speaking songs played on the radio, soon tempered this rejection. The Top 40 radio stations then opened to French rap, but the expectation for festive and widely appealing pieces remained. From 1994 to 1997, the few new rappers signed by major labels often met the following criteria: refrains that were sung instead of rapped; themes that appealed to a wide audience; and danceable rhythms to galvanize their hit singles, such as those from Alliance Ethnik to Mellowman and IAM's single "Je danse le Mia" (I Dance the Mia).

However, the acts selected by major record labels did not represent the majority of the new rap scene. In the wake of early successes and the structuring of rap-related performance companies, a network of hip-hop entrepreneurs had built the means to produce albums for emerging artists. The Sens Unik group pioneered this approach and created the Unik Record label in 1992. The deejay and composer of MC Solaar also created a label, Jimmy Jay Productions, and made compilations called *Les Cool Sessions*, bringing together such new artists as Démocrates D, Ménélik, and Les Sages Poètes de la Rue. Labels were soon born from other groups as well, like La Cliqua (Arsenal) and IAM (Côté Obscur). Meanwhile, DJ Clyde and DJ Cut Killer developed the idea of the mixtape in France. It was not only in aesthetic terms that these hip-hop participants were inspired by the United States; they observed and adapted marketing practices, as well. These initiatives put an end to the major record labels' monopoly on the selection of rap records available in 1990 to 1993.

The number of new rappers was exploding at that time. Many of them came from factions of the working-class male youth whose futures were jeopardized by the economic crisis and the reforms introduced by the right-wing government starting in 1993. Like La Cliqua or Les Sages Poètes de la Rue, they followed the path of a reimagining of the vision of street life in full development in U.S. rap but also inherited the definition of rap as an expression of the *banlieue* in France and the support given by urban policies to hip-hop practices in priority neighborhoods. During this movement, the Zulu Nation lost even more of its influence: Some considered it to be a kind of elitism among Parisians who were fascinated by the United States, which was far from the reality of French working-class neighborhoods. After Ministère AMER, French rap was renewed through the use of slang and foreign terms by Expression Direkt, Mafia K'1 Fry, and Uptown. In their lyrics, the *banlieues* became a central theme in French rap. Instead of the stereotypical and abstract imagery that dominated television reports, these groups described the ordinary life of working-class neighborhoods marked by drug trafficking, unemployment, and tensions with the police. The mainstream press then popularized an opposition between "cool" rap and "hardcore" rap, dramatizing the aesthetic differences between MC Solaar and NTM, while inferring moral superiority for the former. If NTM was considered to be a violent rap group par excellence, it was less because of a radical political agenda and more because of its fast-paced music and taste for provocation (the name of the group itself is the acronym for the insult *Nique ta mère*, or "fuck your mother"). MC Solaar stood out through the frequency of his puns that, combined with his popular success, soon earned him the ambivalent status of being "the poet of rap" in the mainstream media—a label that downgraded the poetic character of the rest of the rap scene. The opposition between "cool" and "hardcore" rap, although initially artificial, soon fed conflicts. At the heart of the debate was the radio hegemony of party rap hits and the commercial successes of the groups that performed them. In opposition to party rap, there was a growing generation of rappers for whom rap must testify to a violent world marked by injustice. The media's assignment of rap to the *banlieues* made rappers spokespersons rather than artists and became a component of the rapper's artistic practice. But these rappers did not oppose art and denunciation. They linked the two in an aesthetic staging of protest that fed notably on the warlike metaphors of the American rap business (Negus 1999, 97) and soon found economic and media relays in France itself, merchandising an "oppositional avant-garde" (Hammou 2016) in the wake of the film *La Haine* (Hate) and the rap compilation of the same name.

THE OTHER SIDE OF A SOLIDIFYING NATIONAL IDENTITY

It was in this dynamic that the significance of rap music in France grew. On the listeners' side, since 1997, rap had become a musical genre listened to by more than a quarter of fifteen- to nineteen-year-olds. On the artists' side, production increased from two or three albums per year in 1990 to 1992 to more than sixty in 1998, mostly produced by independent labels. The economic success of rap music was commensurate with this evolution. A few hundred thousand records sold in the early 1990s became several million in the early 2000s. Accelerating these transformations, the national radio network Skyrock set itself apart from its competitors by opening its programming (beginning in 1997) to independently produced works of the "oppositional avant-garde." In addition, the station entrusted weekly shows to several figures of the rap scene. NTM, IAM, Secteur Ä, and Cut Killer thus reinforced their role as gatekeepers for the careers of new rappers. With artists now in possession of a specialized press disseminating their artistic news, a radio network broadcasting their records, and several independent labels, rap in France was gradually taking the form of a social world integrated into the record industry, which manifested its coherence by the multiplication of *featurings* between its members (Hammou 2014).

French rap, flourishing economically, was also renewed aesthetically. Spurred by the flows of American rappers Boot Camp Clik, Nas, and Mobb Deep, groups like Fonky Family in their first album, *Si Dieu Veut* (If God

Wants); Ärsenik in *Quelques gouttes suffisent . . .* (A Few Drops Suffice . . .); and the Time Bomb crew contributed to the systematization of "the syllabic ellipse" (i.e., the contraction of syllables in the presence of a mute "e") (Pecqueux 2007), which multiplied the rhythmic possibilities of rap in French and reinforced its effect of realism by bringing it closer to ordinary spoken language. The African roots of rap music were also strengthening, notable in the pharyngealization of pronunciations. Artists, such as Freeman and Rohff, who released a very successful album in 2001, *La vie avant la mort* (Life before Death), were inspired in particular by the Arabic language. These roots were also translated by musical collaborations with *Raï* and Afrobeat artists, such as *Racines*, the eponymous album released in 1999 by the Bisso Na Bisso collective, which is a hybrid of rap and Congolese rumba. Having popular success in France as well as in many African countries, the group won several honors at the African Kora Music Awards. These artists paved the way for musical fusions that would give birth in the mid-2000s to the "Raï'n'B" made popular by DJ Kore & Scalp and, ten years later, to "Afro trap," begun by MHD and popularized through his first LP, *MHD*, in 2016.

At the end of 1999, some media outlets announced the end of the "golden age" of rap. The beginning of the 2000s marked the end of the rapid sales growth of French rap records. This slow growth went on to characterize the second half of the 2000s, a phenomenon that fueled a paradoxical feeling of a market in crisis, when it was actually just stable. But in 2003, the French rap industry, like the country's music industry as a whole, was overtaken by the global record crisis.

From 2000 to 2011, annual sales of albums of all musical genres decreased by 65 percent. The major recording labels broke a record number of contracts with their artists, especially rappers. The sales crisis also led to a collapse of the marketing investments of record companies whose specialized rap publications felt the full impact of these consequences. In the late 2000s, most of the magazines that had existed ten years earlier had disappeared. The crisis also hit the myriad independent rap labels that were created from 1994 to 2001. In the late 2000s, two-thirds of these companies filed for bankruptcy, and the amount of business done by independent rap labels was, like that of the entire record industry, cut in half.

As challenging as the record industry crisis had been, French rap continued to sell a significant number of albums. Dominating the market in that landscape, in 2006, the female rapper Diam's released *Dans ma bulle* (In My Bubble), which became the year's best-seller for France. In addition to her writing skills and vocal technique, Diam's brought the performance of her lyrics to a new level, which would go on to inspire many other rappers. For the majority of rappers, however, the crisis in the record industry reduced hopes of commercial success. The release of MC Jean Gab'1's single

"J't'emmerde" (Screw You) in 2003 was a public and artistic statement on the divisions and rivalries that the growth of the rap market had put on hold. The piece criticized the alleged contradictions of prominent rappers, in particular their aesthetic references to the street or their moralistic pretensions, increasingly associated with Islam (Molinero 2011). "J't'emmerde" participated in a multiplication of larger conflicts, taking to task most of the moment's most commercially successful rappers (such as Booba, Sinik, Rohff, and La Fouine).

Rather than a cross-cutting rift in the world of rap, such as the one between cool rap and hardcore rap, there were personal conflicts in which a heterosexist image of the street was invoked by both parties and whose issues engaged prejudicial relationships or commercial rivalries. Another major novelty was that these conflicts were mediatized well beyond the world of rap itself. Since the end of the 1990s, French rap has become part of a star system in which conflicts (called *clashs* in French) between artists fuel both the promotion of their works and the audience of the media who relay them. In addition, the development of the Internet is transforming the flow of information about these conflicts, previously confined to specialized media and fans of the genre. The publicity given to those rivalries culminated on 15 September 2007, during a report broadcast on the program *50' Inside* on the French television channel TF1. Entitled "La guerre du rap" (The Rap War), this report illustrated the close interdependence among the assignment of rap to the *banlieues* as territories of "new barbarians," the media and economic exploitation of this musical genre as an "Othered" cultural good, and the street rhetoric dominating the French rap music world of the 2000s.

These multiple conflicts in the heart of public attention undoubtedly played a role in Skyrock's 2007 management decision to stop broadcasting specialized programs produced by figures from the rap world. But this choice refers more broadly to a transformation of the radio landscape that affected all youth-oriented networks, which are now giving pride of place to a new musical genre called "groove," a style close to the Anglo-Saxon category of contemporary R&B. Another notable phenomenon is that French rap is now challenged domestically by the level of sales of American rap artists, as radio stations increasingly broadcast their hits. During the 1990s in France, with a few exceptions (including the Fugees), American rap music remained much less popular than French rap music. Stemming from the international success of Eminem, new rappers found a large audience in France, representing a third of sales of rap records in France from 2001 to 2010. In the musical and economic wake of rap, French R&B also became popular. In the mid-2000s, almost as many French R&B albums were sold as French rap, and collaborations between rap artists and R&B became more widespread.

In early 2010, hip-hop music (in the broad sense) was more present and diverse than ever. Negligible during the first half of the 1990s, cumulative sales of rap and R&B albums exceeded forty million in the 2000s, or 5 percent of total album sales in France. According to surveys conducted by the French Ministry of Culture, the number of regular rap listeners tripled from 1997 to 2008. R&B had become the favorite genre of women ages fifteen to thirty, and rap was the favorite genre among men in the same age bracket (Hammou and Molinero 2019). France was witnessing a profound transformation of its musical landscape: the end of the musical hegemony of *la variété* in favor of more segmented musical tastes, combining pop and rock with a strong musical component from African American music.

Rap, however, remained closely associated with the public problem of the *banlieues*. In the mid-1990s, police unions denounced the lyrics of some raps and tried to sue the artists—often to no avail. In 1995, an NTM concert in La Seyne-sur-Mer changed the game. On this occasion, it was not the official lyrics that were attacked in court but rather insults that the group had directed at police present during the concert. The following year, NTM's trial became a widely publicized case and an opportunity for public debate on rap violence and the freedom of speech. Government ministers and parliamentarians mostly remained quiet on the subject, though statements in the press revealed differences of opinion within the right-wing government led by Alain Juppé (Silverstein 2002).

Police unions were not the only ones who believed that certain rap songs, or even French rap as a whole, were unacceptable. On the far right of the political spectrum, the popularity of rap among French youth was a cause for worry, especially as it was accompanied more than ever by subversive texts criticizing their nationalist and racist agenda. In the second half of the 1990s, some rappers, like La Rumeur, Fabe, and Yazid, performed a postcolonial memory of the slave trade, colonization, the history of immigration, and the continuities between these past situations and the contemporary state's treatment of racial minorities and the working classes in France (Tevanian 2009). French rap saw itself asserting a critical citizenship. It was now denouncing explicit racism and the extreme right but also the hardening of police repression and the abstract universalism dominating French public life. Collective pieces with explicit political aims were emblematic, such as "11'30 contre les lois racistes" (11:30 against Racist Laws; 1997). This critical citizenship, in more or less insistent forms, was found in the 2000s in growing parts of the rap scene, from Saïan Supa Crew to Casey, and including KDD, Sefyu, and Psy 4 de la Rime.

A fraction of the parliamentary right turning more willingly to the extreme right led to a direct confrontation between the French political class and French rap. Two court cases stood out: the La Rumeur case and the Sniper case. In April 2002, between the two rounds of the presidential election, La Rumeur published a promotional magazine accompanying the release of its first album, *L'Ombre sur la mesure* (Shadow on the Beat). One of the members of the group, Hamé, wrote a satirical article denouncing the rhetoric of fearmongering over crime and zero tolerance, the impoverishment of working-class neighborhoods, and the police violence that their inhabitants are subjected to. The right-wing politician Nicolas Sarkozy, then minister of the interior, filed a complaint for defamation of the national police. He soon became president of the French Republic in 2007. The state appealed the three successive acquittals, which refuted the ministry's claims, before a fourth trial definitively acquitted Hamé in June 2010.

The second case involved the group Sniper. In 2003, Nadine Morano, an elected official of Pour un movement populaire (UMP, the political majority party), took up denunciations of rap purveyed by far-right groups and was indignant at songs that, in her view, "incite[d] hatred and violence and flout[ed] the republican values of France."[1] The Ministry of the Interior filed a complaint for "incitement to injure and kill police and state officials."[2] The group argued during their trial that the offending song, "La France," is "un appel à l'aide" (a call for help) and not "un appel au meurtre" (a call for murder). Their case was dismissed by the court in 2005. During the same year, however, the criminalization of rappers was becoming widespread. The deaths of Bouna Traoré and Zyed Benna, two teenagers fleeing police, caused riots throughout France starting in October. According to the right-wing representative François Grosdidier (UMP), French rap was responsible for the riots and, on 14 March 2006, he submitted a bill denouncing about fifteen rappers and aiming to "strengthen the control of acts of provocation that incite discrimination, hatred, or violence,"[3] supported by nearly a hundred fellow members of the National Assembly.

Throughout President Nicolas Sarkozy's five-year term (2007–2012), members of parliament repeated the same wish. In this increasingly conservative political climate, French rap offered an area of economic and symbolic value not without exoticism to artists who often belonged to racialized minorities. It was also a way for these artists to showcase minority politics and challenge the homogenizing and discriminatory conceptions of belonging to the national community (Sonnette 2015) that were dominating public debate.

CONCLUSION: THE AESTHETIC RENEWAL AND COMMERCIAL SUCCESS OF FRENCH RAP

At the end of the 2000s, French rap showed signs of running out of steam. It seemed to have exhausted the realist vein of the particular conception of "street life" introduced in the mid-1990s. Between the political criminalization of rap and the worsening clashes between rappers, the dominant media visibility of the genre came from miscellaneous news stories, assigning rap early on to the *banlieues*. In increasingly racialized public debate, marked by the growth of Islamophobia, rappers embodied the figure of a new domestic enemy. Emblematic of this period, paparazzi photos of the rapper Diam's wearing a head scarf were published by the press and caused a national controversy at a time when a draft of a law banning Muslim women from wearing a full veil in public places was being debated. Record sales declined: From 2009 to 2012, less than one million French rap albums were sold annually. However, an artistic and economic revival is occurring, driven by a new generation of stage-trained artists, new vocal techniques, and clever promotional use of the Internet.

Starting in the mid-2000s, open-mic events in the form of battles between MCs (Guillard 2014) developed throughout France. The competition "Dégaine ton style" (Whip Out Your Style), inaugurated in 2002 in the Parisian suburb of Les Ulis, was a pioneer in this format. The next occurrence of the competition, driven by the success of the film *8 Mile*, made its mark and propelled its winner, Sinik, to the rank of national star of the rap scene. In the second half of the 2000s, other open-mics were born, like the French version in 2004 of New York City's "End of the Weak" or "Rap Contenders" in 2011. These open-mics exacerbated the valorization of the punch line and the sense of derision, in pornographic registers of insult tactics that already had a long history (Vettorato 2012). The question of street credibility was less important than obscene humor and witty comebacks. Among those who excelled at this were members of the collective L'Entourage, including Nekfeu, who became one of the major figures in the rap scene in 2015 with his album *Feu* (Fire).

In 2009, another competition was born, created by hip-hop festival organizers and concert venue programmers who wanted more stages to be available to rappers. They succeeded in setting up events in Lyon (L'Original festival), Nantes (Hip Opsession festival), and Perpignan (Ida y Vuelta festival) and organized the Buzz Booster competition every year thereafter, with regional qualification contests leading to a final, national event. These events helped prove that rap was not just in Paris and Marseille—two cities that would soon join the festival circuit through the Paris Hip Hop Festival and the Marseille concert auditorium L'Affranchi.

French rap was also renewed through developments in vocal techniques. Popularized by T Pain and then Lil Wayne, the usage of auto-tune was adopted by Booba in his 2009 album *0.9*. Four years later, stylistic innovations from the stages of Atlanta and Chicago were reappropriated in France and led to the success of rapper Kaaris and his first album, *Or Noir* (Black Gold), in 2013. Called "trap" music in France, this rap style was inspired by the drill music of Chief Keef and Lil Reese.

Whether their music emphasized the use of auto-tune (Jul, SCH, Damso, Niska) or featured vocal techniques inspired by drill music (Lacrim, Gradur, Alonzo), whether they harnessed new Reggaeton beats (Shay) and afro trap

(MHD) or offered a technical rap made of punch lines and fast flows (Sofiane), all these new artists had something important in common: They showed a mastery of social networks and image in their promotion. YouTube videos of la Sexion d'Assaut's freestyles made them well known even before the solo successes of its members Black M or Maître Gims (the latter's album, *Subliminal*, was one of France's top sellers in 2013). A productivity hitherto unknown in French rap allowed Jul to release several albums a year beginning with *Dans ma paranoïa* (In My Paranoia) in 2014. PNL struck the imagination by the production of spectacular scripted music videos made using a drone accompanied by an almost complete lack of communication in traditional media. In addition, a growing number of artists emerged, such as Soprano, Lartiste, Chilla, and Marwa Loud, who—with or without autotune—mixed rap and singing.

Hip-hop music has a thematic diversity that makes it a genre with plural musical identities. The classic hip-hop themes of Demi Portion or Bigflo & Oli rub shoulders with the gangsta world of Booba, Lacrim, and Alonzo. PNL, Fianso, and Kalash Criminel reinvent street rap, while Orelsan depicts the misanthropic and misogynistic universe of a failed middle class. Social criticism, meanwhile, is always present, at the heart of the repertoires of Lino, Keny Arkana, Médine, and Casey, or at the turn of a verse or a punch line, as in most of French rap, always favoring a countercultural imagination and provocative catchphrases, as the unclassifiable works of Youssoupha testify. At the end of the 2010s, commercial success was once again present for French rap and, more broadly, the "urban pop" it nourished, as the give-and-take between rap and song had increased. Hip-hop music, in the largest sense, made the most of the development of music streaming and increased its successes in the French music charts, holding from about 3 percent of the record market share in 2011 to nearly 9 percent in 2017.[4]

REFERENCES

Bocquet, José-Louis, and Philippe Pierre-Adolphe. *Rap ta France*. Paris: Flammarion, 1997.
De Rudder, Véronique, Christian Poiret, and François Vourc'h. *L'inégalité raciste: L'universalité républicaine à l'épreuve*. Paris: PUF, 2000.
Dubois, Vincent. *La politique culturelle: Genèse d'une catégorie d'intervention publique*. Paris: Belin, 2000 (2012).
Gilroy, Paul. *The Black Atlantic: Modernity and Double Consciousness*. London: Verso, 1993.
Guillard, Séverin. "'To Be in the Place': Les open mics comme espaces de legitimation artistique pour les scènes rap à Paris et Atlanta." *Belgeo* 3 (2014). doi: 10.4000/belgeo.13025
Guillaumin, Colette. *Racism, Sexism, Power, and Ideology*. London: Routledge, 1995.
Hammou, Karim. *Une histoire du rap en France*. Paris: La Découverte, 2012.
———. "Between Social Worlds and Local Scenes: Patterns of Collaboration in Francophone Rap Music." In *Social Networks and Music Worlds*, edited by Nick Crossley, Siobhan McAndrew, and Paul Widdop, 104–21. London: Routledge, 2014.
———. "Mainstreaming French Rap Music: Commodification and Artistic Legitimation of 'Othered' Cultural Goods." *Poetics* 59 (December 2016): 67–81.

Hammou, Karim, and Stéphanie Molinero. "Plus populaire que jamais? Réception et illégitimation culturelle du rap en France (1997–2008)." In *Les scènes musicales et leurs publics en France (XVIIIe–XXIe siècles)*, edited by Caroline Giron-Panel, Solveig Serre, and Jean-Claude Yon. Paris: Garnier, 2019. https://halshs.archives-ouvertes.fr/halshs-01807237

Lafargue de Grangeneuve, Loïc. *Politique du hip-hop: Action publique et cultures urbaines*. Toulouse, France: Presses Universitaires du Mirail, 2008.

Mazouz, Sarah. *La République et ses autres: Politiques de l'altérité dans la France des années 2000*. Lyon, France: ENS Lyon, 2017.

Molinero, Stéphanie. "The Meanings of the Religious Talk in French Rap Music." In *Popular Music and Religion in Europe: New Expressions of Sacred and Secular Identity*, edited by Thomas Bossius, Andreas Hager, and Keith Kahn-Harris, 105–23. London: I. B. Taurus, 2011.

Negus, Keith. *Music Genres and Corporate Cultures*. London: Routledge, 1999.

Pecqueux, Anthony. *Voix du rap: Essai de sociologie de l'action musicale*. Paris: L'Harmattan, 2007.

Sermet, Vincent. *Les Musiques soul et funk: La France qui groove des années 1960 à nos jours*. Paris: L'Harmattan, 2008.

Shepard, Todd. *Sex, France, and Arab Men, 1962–1979*. Chicago: University of Chicago Press, 2017.

Silverstein, Paul A. "'Why Are We Waiting to Start the Fire?': French Gangsta Rap and the Critique of State Capitalism." In *Black, Blanc, Beur: Rap Music and Hip-Hop Culture in the Francophone World*, edited by Alain-Philippe Durand, 45–67. Lanham, MD: Scarecrow Press, 2002.

Sonnette, Marie. "Des mises en scène du 'nous' contre le 'eux' dans le rap français: De la critique de la domination postcoloniale à une possible critique de la domination de classe." *Sociologie de l'Art-OPuS* 23–24, no. 1 (2015): 153–77.

Tevanian, Pierre. "Entretien avec Mohamed Bourokba, dit Hamé, du groupe La Rumeur." *Mouvements* 57, no. 1 (2009): 120–36.

Tissot, Sylvie. *L'État et les quartiers: Genèse d'une catégorie de l'action publique*. Paris: Seuil, 2007.

Vettorato, Cyril. "'Ça va être un viol': Formes et fonctions de l'obscénité langagière dans les joutes verbales de rap." *Cahiers de littérature orale* 71 (2012): 115–40. doi: 10/4000.clo.1492

Warne, Chris. "Curiosity, Fear, and Control: The Ambiguous Representation of Hip Hop on French Television." In *Group Identities on French and British Television*, edited by Michael Scriven and Emily Roberts, 108–18. Oxford, UK: Berghahn Books, 2003.

DISCOGRAPHY AND FILMOGRAPHY

8 Mile. Dir. Curtis Hanson. Universal, DVD. Originally released in 2002.

Ärsenik. *Quelques gouttes suffisent . . .* Hostile Records, compact disc. Originally released in 1998.

Bisso Na Bisso. *Racines*. BMG, compact disc. Originally released in 1999.

Booba. *0.9*. Universal, compact disc. Originally released in 2009.

Chagrin d'Amour. "Chacun fait (c'qui lui plaît)." Barclay, vinyl. Originally released in 1981.

Dee Nasty. *Paname City Rappin'*. Funkzilla, vinyl. Originally released in 1984.

Diam's. *Dans ma bulle*. EMI, compact disc. Originally released in 2006.

Fonky Family. *Si Dieu Veut*. Small, compact disc. Originally released in 1997.

IAM. "Je danse le Mia." *Ombre est lumière*. Delabel, compact disc. Originally released in 1993.

Jimmy Jay. *Les Cool Sessions*. Jimmy Jay Productions, compact disc. Originally released in 1993.

Jul. *Dans ma paranoïa*. Liga One Industry, compact disc. Originally released in 2014.

Kaaris. *Or Noir*. Therapy Music, compact disc. Originally released in 2013.

La Haine. Dir. Mathieu Kassovitz. Lazennec, DVD. Originally released in 1995.

La Rumeur. *L'ombre sur la mesure*. EMI, compact disc. Originally released in 2002.

Maître Gims. *Subliminal*. Sony Music, compact disc. Originally released in 2013.

MC Jean Gab'1. "J't'emmerde." Dooeen' Damage, compact disc. Originally released in 2003.

MC Solaar. *Qui sème le vent récolte le tempo*. Polydor, compact disc. Originally released in 1991.

MHD. *MHD*. Universal, compact disc. Originally released in 2016.

Ministère AMER. *Pourquoi tant de haine?* Musidisc, compact disc. Originally released in 1992.

Nekfeu. *Feu*. Polydor, compact disc. Originally released in 2015.

Rohff. *La vie avant la mort*. Hostile Records, compact disc. Originally released in 2001.

Sniper. "La France." *Du rire aux larmes*. Desh, compact disc. Originally released in 2001.

Sugar Hill Gang. "Rapper's Delight." Vogue, vinyl. Originally released in 1979.

Suprême NTM. *Authentik*. Epic, compact disc. Originally released in 1991.

Various Artists. *Rappattitudes*. Virgin, compact disc. Originally released in 1989.

———. *11'30 contre les lois racistes*. Cercle Rouge, compact disc. Originally released in 1997.

Chapter Two

Hip-Hop Music and Rap in Cities in Crisis

The Case of Marseille

Jean-Marie Jacono,
Translated by André Pettman

Nearly forty years after its appearance, rap continues to occupy an important place in France's two largest cities, Paris and Marseille.[1] Placed in the category of urban music, this artistic genre often conflated with hip-hop,[2] has a strong following among French youth.[3] It has not been a marginal musical trend for quite some time. Since the phenomenal success of "Je danse le Mia" (I Dance the Mia) by Marseille group IAM in 1993, rap has taken a large portion of the public by storm. Its musical themes and expressions are diversified depending on groups' artistic strategies. The presence of rap is of such importance that in 2018, during the presentation of the Victoires de la Musique—the annual prizes of song and popular music in France—the majority of awarded artists were rappers or were influenced by hip-hop music. Today, this music has become what is called in France *les musiques de variété* (Davet 2018, 16): that is to say, a mainstream trend of the music industry. It has become normalized. Rap has profoundly evolved.

The expression "urban music" connotes the link with the city. A rap group always has connections with the place in which it began. Their city of origin continues to fashion their identity. Now, despite the action of state and local powers, French cities and their suburbs remain marked by social inequalities and important problems. Unemployment, poverty, and delinquency are extremely present, and many inhabitants, mainly originating from North Africa and sub-Saharan Africa, are victims of discrimination and racism. What impact do these situations have on today's rap music? Do famous groups—who must produce concerts, make music videos, and please an audience larger than that of poor neighborhoods—still allude to these issues?

A city emblematic of French rap, Marseille represents a good study site to measure the degree of normalization of this artistic expression. This large port has transformed since the end of the 1990s. Marseille has become a very attractive tourist city. *The New York Times* even designated it in 2013 as the number 2 tourist destination in the world because of its cultural vitality, which has recently opened itself up to forms of hip-hop culture (Cohane 2013).

Marseille, however, is also a city of poverty, drug trafficking, and violence. It is France's dirtiest and most polluted city. Marseille remains a city in crisis, situated as it is on the Mediterranean as the border between the north and the south: that is to say. between Europe and Africa. It remains a city of immigrants and foreigners. Its local identity and multicultural reality remain very strong. On 5 November 2018, the collapse of two old buildings in the downtown Noailles neighborhood killed eight inhabitants. It revealed the appalling living conditions of poor people and the buildings' years of neglect by City Hall services.

How do these dimensions appear in rap? Do they become marginal because of the transformation of the city and rap's evolution into a music of entertainment? Are there specific aspects tied to ethnic minorities or to Islam? Can we really speak of the existence of a *local* music scene?

These questions steer an examination of a regular theme in the study of popular music: the analysis of the relationship between "global" and "local." But it is also about explaining the reasons for rap's success: Has the genre changed much since the early 1990s, or has it remained the same? What role do musical dimensions play today? Even if rap is influenced by other arts, the examination of the relationship between lyrics and music remains very pertinent to grasp its evolution. From this perspective, I explain later why I use the term "rap" rather than "hip-hop" to analyze the role of this music in a city in crisis.

THE EMERGENCE OF RAP IN A DIVIDED CITY

Several images are associated with Marseille. They have taken on the dimension of a myth. First, Marseille brings to mind a picturesque French port and funny inhabitants, speaking with gestures and a theatrical accent. This postcard cliché was developed in films by Marcel Pagnol and Marseille operettas by Vincent Scotto during the 1930s. It never disappeared. From this period, however, another image appears: that of a cosmopolitan city of trafficking and of gangsters, exposed in cinema in *Justin de Marseille* by Maurice Tourneur (1935). It is also perpetuated in other popular works, such as the John

Frankenheimer movie *French Connection II* (1975) and the Netflix television series *Marseille* (2016), which depict the struggles surrounding local politics for control of the city. These two topics, however, do not mention the social and urban economic realities that influence the practice of hip-hop and rap. They obscure a crisis that is foremost social and economic.

Marseille, the principal port of the French colonial empire until 1962, was a city of transit but also an industrial and working-class city in the twentieth century. Thousands of foreigners from notably Italy and Armenia but above all from former French colonies found work there. They settled in Marseille, which had nine hundred thousand inhabitants in 1975. However, after 1960, port activities and local industries (metalworking factories, food-processing industries, oil mills, and soap factories) progressively collapsed due to decolonization, the oil crisis of 1974, and the concentration of businesses (Dell'Umbria 2006, 530). The city's economic crisis began. Workers did not exceed 9.5 percent of the active population in 2010, 32.5 percent less than in 1954 (Peraldi, Duport, and Samson 2015, 10). Marseille's population was in decline, claiming no more than 798,000 inhabitants in 1999. It became an administrative city in which the employed (17 percent) and the retired (24 percent) constituted significant subgroups. Unemployment impacted Marseille more than other cities in France: 17.3 percent in 2010 versus 11 percent in Paris (Peraldi, Duport, and Samson 2015, 10). The unemployment rate in Marseille remains higher today than that of France overall.[4] The most significant figure, however, concerns poverty: 26 percent of the Marseille population was below the poverty line in 2009. This figure has hardly changed. Five of Marseille's sixteen districts are among the poorest in France, according to an official study from 2016 (INSEE 2016). The third district, near the city center, is even considered the most destitute urban area in Europe, with 51.3 percent of the population below the poverty line. The neighborhoods that make up these districts and their large blocks of subsidized apartment buildings represent concentrations of all the social difficulties of these times. Poverty, of course, is not confined to these areas; lack of job security reaches into other parts of the city, and drug dealing remains present everywhere. The film *Chouf* by Karim Dridi (2016), which takes place in the northern district housing projects of the Busserine, shows its devastating effects, much like the polemical book by journalist Philippe Pujol (2016).

Rap and hip-hop have taken root in the disadvantaged neighborhoods of this very expansive city (60,000 acres) where there are no real suburbs. Marseille is traditionally divided into two opposing sectors: a poor area near the port (the northern neighborhoods) and a residential area (the southern neighborhoods). This division of urban space is nevertheless schematic. Despite its significant pockets of poverty in the north, Marseille resembles an urban mosaic in which multiple contrasts appear. The downtown is inhabited by a poor, immigrant population, a unique occurrence in France. Close by, the neighborhood of La Plaine welcomes alternative youth and a sector of musical activities. Poor housing projects also exist in the southern neighborhoods. However, as I explain later, changes are now occurring.[5] That said, Marseille's immigrant and foreign populations in 2010 were vastly smaller than those of Paris (Peraldi, Duport, and Samson 2015, 18).

It is in this city in decline that hip-hop progressively appeared. Dance was the initial (1984) and most important form of local expression (Valnet 2013, 24–27). The first rap group, IAM, gradually formed two years later and emerged in 1989, at the same time as ragamuffin groups (Massilia Sound System, Jo Corbeau) and local rock (the band Quartiers Nord, founded in 1977). The multiethnic origins of the six members of the group IAM are consistent with that of the city: Three of them are white, and three are black. Thus, rap became the dominant form of hip-hop culture in Marseille. It was primarily aimed at the poor or rebellious youth of the northern district projects, like the Panier and Belsunce, or a more central one, such as La Plaine. There is a sense of identity that manifests itself not by postcolonial demands but rather in recognition of the city's special features. IAM labels it the "planet Mars" in their first album (1991). It is about being in opposition to Paris above all but to the rest of France, too, as well as the state and the political system that condemns what occurs in Marseille. There is also this sense of identity in IAM's second album, *Ombre est lumière* (Shadow Is Light, 1993). The songs' lyrics denounce racism and the harshness of life in the projects due to tragic incidents ("L'aimant" [The Magnet], 1993) or drugs ("Sachet blanc" [White Baggie], 1993). This social critique is one of IAM's major themes. I must add the group's assertiveness and the evocation of an imaginary world linked to ancient Egypt, as well as various themes linked to the youth of the neighborhoods or to funny situations (Kosmicki 1999, 96).[6] There is neither a hardcore dimension nor the provocations of gangsta rap. The lyrics are written in everyday French but also use forms of slang and neologisms invented in the neighborhoods. IAM appears as the voice of the dominated stemming from immigration. Opposite the postcard clichés ("Marseille ville du soleil"; Marseille, City of the Sun), IAM claims in their titles the "dark side," inspired by films from the *Star Wars* series. This expression symbolizes the world of the dominated relegated to the sidelines. The album title *Ombre est lumière* is thus significant.

Rap, like ragamuffin and rock, reinvents the popular culture of Marseille. It personifies the reaction of the working class and the youth toward the crisis of the city. Music plays a major role in this artistic expression (Jacono 2002). Rhythm is essential. It creates a separation from the melodies of Vincent Scotto and the French song traditions of the twentieth century. It is the effects of rappers' flow and the sound of the deejay that mold the body and the reactions of the listener in rap. This presence of rhythm is found in percussive sounds but also in the samples chosen by the deejay. Their diversity is in the image of the ethnic mosaic of the population and the variety of neighbor-hoods in the city. Despite the difficulty in characterizing a style of rap (Krims 2000, 72), the use of musical contrasts must be noted in the productions of IAM and its members (Akhenaton, *Métèque et mat* [Wog-mate], 1995; Kheops, *Sad Hill*, 1997). There are these contrasts:

- in the structure of albums, with an irregular alternation of inserts, musical interludes, and long songs;
- in the asymmetrical structure of certain songs, notably in the refusal to sing along with the chorus (such as in the famous "Je danse le Mia" from *Ombre est lumière*);
- in the presence of spoken segments that evoke a verbal exchange within the declamation (such as in "L'aimant");
- in the different flows of the two rappers (Akhenaton and Shurik'n), which follow each other or alternate, depending on the song;
- in the frequent presence of scratches;
- in the choice of samples that originate from a variety of sources (funk, traditional music, soundtrack of a sound-and-light show of the pyramids of Egypt, etc.) and a perfectly mastered sound mix.

Certainly, one or another of these characteristics is present in other groups in France and in the United States. The combination of these elements linked to rhythm is, however, particularly inventive. It is found in different degrees in Marseille groups that emerge around IAM during the same era and who broach themes linked to the city (Soul Swing, Faf Larage, Fonky Family, Le 3ème Œil). Despite less systematic contrasts, in particular the processing of samples, it is the diversity of the rappers' flows that marks the songs of the group Soul Swing (*Le retour de l'âme soul* [The Return of the Soul], 1996). It is the frequent changing of the sample in the middle of a song that charac-terizes the productions of Fonky Family, despite an approach differing from IAM's sound ("Sans rémission" [Without Remission] and "La Résistance" [The Resistance], from *Si Dieu veut* [If God Wants], 1997). These are inserts, varied introductions sometimes drawn from televised serials ("La Boomba") and relays of rappers on a melodic loop that are found with Le 3ème Œil (*Hier aujourd'hui demain* [Yesterday Today Tomorrow], 1999), a group from the Félix-Pyat projects of the northern districts.

These multiple contrasts demonstrate the rappers' identities. Their sonor-ous and musical contradictions, however, are linked with the city. The contrasts affirm diversity. They also help to symbolically break the imprison-ment in the neighborhood or the city, during an era in which rap is considered to be a marginal music form. The mastering of technology is an artistic gesture but also an act of a social and political nature: It allows for the seizing of the sound space. The usage of contrasts also leads to another

tempo that breaks the usually homogeneous tempo of songs. It affirms the
mobility and fluidity of the subject or group. We find ourselves in the presence of a "trans-subjective" subject, which relates to the individual as well as
to a social group.

ARTISTIC EVOLUTION AND GENTRIFICATION

This relationship with the city evolved at the end of the twentieth century,
once rap became a recognized artistic genre in 1994. The artistic evolution of
rappers is the first reason. It brought rap closer to song formats. Moreover,
rap was supported by officials in the political framework of the city as a hip-
hop culture art form. Lastly, Marseille in the 1990s was transforming and
gentrifying. This reaction from political and economic milieus toward the
crisis of the city has an impact today on hip-hop culture.

A real turning point underlined by Karim Hammou (2012) actually occurred starting in 1999. Popular music studios and radio stations disseminat-
ed new groups and new codes to expand their audiences. The influence of the
international music mainstream led to the presence of common elements
shared by French song traditions. The sung refrain developed. What was
once an exception ("Harley Davidson," IAM, 1993) became the norm. Thus,
"Le son des bandits" (The Sound of Bandits), the hit song from the debut
album by the Marseille group Psy 4 de la Rime, *Block Party* (2002), alternated between flow and sung refrain. Instruments were even used in albums or
onstage. The rhythms changed in nature: The dance aspect appeared under
the influence of American R&B. This is a very different type of dance from
the break dance present at the beginning of hip-hop. The regular rhythms of
R&B connote, in essence, entertainment. They are used in a varied manner in
IAM's third album, *L'École du micro d'argent* (The Silver Microphone
School, 1997), considered one of French rap's greatest albums due to its
shocking song titles denouncing poverty and injustices ("Petit frère" [Little
Brother]; "Demain c'est loin" [Tomorrow Is Far]). This record also signaled
a break. It no longer made use of extremely varied samples but employed a
minimalist sound, deeply worked during the mix. The artistic preoccupations
of IAM, which were no longer principally aimed at the Marseille public, now
dominated. The group became autonomous from the city, although Marseille's situation continued to inspire it. Their songs mainly addressed moral
issues rather than intimate dramas (Jacono 2016). While still working on
texts that must resonate with listeners, IAM even used R&B ("Nous" [We],
in *Revoir un printemps* [See Spring Again], 2003). Nevertheless, the link
with the situation of the city cannot be omitted. It was a constant presence in
the solo work of Soprano (rapper from the group Psy 4 de la Rime), from his
first successes ("Halla" [Chaos] and "À la bien" [To the Good], on *Puisqu'il*

faut vivre [Since We Must Live], 2007). "À la bien," which contains a sung chorus, is a hymn to the youth in the neighborhoods of a changing city.

Four major transformations occurred in Marseille during the first two decades of the twenty-first century: a large urban planning operation around the port, significant tourism development due notably to the increase in cruises, the organization of cultural demonstrations of an international scale, and, finally, an institutional transformation with the formation of the Aix-Marseille Provence metropolis (2016). The renovation of Marseille was decided by the French state. In 1995, it created the Euroméditerranée agency, tasked with renovating the neighborhoods in decline near the port and creating a new downtown. The goal was to welcome forty thousand new inhabitants following an extensive construction project intended to establish a business district, large high-rise apartment buildings, commercial spaces, and recreational areas. These architectural innovations symbolize the city's new identity. Beyond the urban renewal and the creation of a Marseille skyline that was previously lacking, Euroméditerranée aims to integrate Marseille into the sphere of globalization. In a globalized economy that brings together existing activities (maritime traffic, shopping centers, cruises) and new ones (companies using digital technologies, important cultural institutions), Marseille places itself as the southern door to western Europe. Euroméditerranée affects all domains of urban and cultural life but is also the starting point of other construction projects seeking to bring downtown neighborhoods back into the fold by installing new inhabitants.[7] The urban renewal paves the way for a gentrification that normalizes Marseille into a bourgeois-bohemian city, attractive and entertaining, where the poor population is pushed to the outskirts. It is a project in the tradition of the destruction of popular downtown neighborhoods during the nineteenth century, which was already denounced in Provençal in the songs of poet Victor Gelu (1806–1885), voice of the common people of Marseille. Today, these renovations will result in a population increase and the development of neo-Marseille residents also attracted by the cultural revival of the city.

Culture indeed plays a key role in this change, much like in other Provence cities.[8] Instrumental to urban regeneration, culture is the foundation of the city's transformation into an attractive metropolis. It transforms Marseille into a cultural object. Thus, it plays a structural role within the urban renewal (Maisetti 2014, 35). New cultural sites established in old industrial buildings have appeared in the Belle-de-Mai neighborhood. Near the port, new institutions, such as the Fonds régional d'art contemporain (FRAC), the Villa Méditerranée, the Regards de Provence museum, and especially le Musée des civilisations de l'Europe et de la Méditerranée (MuCEM, 2013), have seen the light of day, housed in buildings with bold architecture. These institutions extend the work done by the creation of chic shopping centers, business headquarters, luxury residences, and tourist sites. Standardizing culture and commerce, placing cultural institutions at the same level as businesses, and celebrating the modernity of this union are also goals of the Euroméditerranée project. Urban renewal produces a change in the values linked to the culture. It leads to a new social order based on the shift from market consumption to cultural consumption within the same space. One of the most significant symbols is the organization of arty evenings of electronic music hosted by deejays on the rooftop of the shopping center Les Terrasses du port, built along the quays of the renovated industrial port. Thus, festivities prevail in gentrified spaces.

Major events punctuate this cultural boom. They do not improve the lot of the most disadvantaged but make the city attractive. The most spectacular were "Marseille-Provence Capitale européenne de la culture" in 2013, followed today by "Marseille Provence 2018 Quel Amour!" Do these events have any relation to rap and hip-hop culture?

MAKING THE CITY ATTRACTIVE

The year 2013 saw the consecration of the new Marseille. Despite the organization of popular events, the prestigious programming of "MP 2013" implemented by the city, regional officials, business leaders, and the state kept hip-hop and rap at a distance. For that matter, local cultural associations have been unequally included in events (Maisetti 2014, 89–119). This situation led to reactions in the rap world. Since 2012, the "cultural capital of Europe" has been strongly criticized by Keny Arkana, an antiglobalization activist deeply engaged against forms of injustice. In "Capitale de la rupture" (Capital of Rupture), from the album *Tout tourne autour du soleil* (Everything Revolves around the Sun, 2012), this rapper vigorously denounces gentrification; the cultural year activities; and the normalization of the city by the Euroméditerranée agency, city hall, and real estate issues. This protest against the destruction of popular neighborhoods is carried out with a very rhythmic flow, on a fast tempo (120 bpm), like certain songs by Public Enemy. This political rap distinguishes itself from other trends by its rhythmic vigor.

Although rappers rejected their sidelining in 2013, Arkana's resounding protest remains isolated. There is no local rap music scene, except for amateurs who practice it in subsidized venues. Public support for hip-hop does exist. The concert hall L'Affranchi in Saint-Marcel of the eastern districts is dedicated to rap and has been labeled a "Scène de musiques actuelles" (Scene of Contemporary Music) since 1998 by the Ministry of Culture. It receives grants as part of the city's urban-renewal contract.

The attitude of the authorities in relation to hip-hop is thus changing, little by little. It begins with the recognition of street art. Overrunning the boundaries of the alternative neighborhood of La Plaine and the northern districts' flea markets, street artist frescoes decorate the walls of the L2 urban bypass linking the city's north and east sectors since 2017. These immense, inventive paintings modernize the image of the city. They give it a hip look. Along similar lines, hip-hop is now ostensibly represented in "Marseille Provence 2018 Quel amour!" Special programming is visible online (www.hiphopsociety.fr). Implemented by two organizers, the Association for Support of Innovative Music (AMI) and Radio Grenouille, it is scheduled in Marseille and nearby cities. These have been active for a long time in a place where rappers were welcomed since the 1990s, the Friche de la Belle-de-Mai, near the city center. The programming brings together graffiti artists, deejays, and dancers. But hip-hop society is mainly about street art and dance. Rap is practically absent from the program, unlike slam. The most important groups in Marseille are not included. Therefore, political and cultural authorities make a distinction with regard to hip-hop. Dance and street art, arts without lyrics that enhance the cultural appeal of the city and give it an arty appearance while appearing to be marginal, are fully recognized. Rap remains suspicious or kept away because of its possibility of expressing subversive speech. Cultural normalization thus impacts hip-hop culture.

It would be tempting to consider rap as the only rebellious expression in hip-hop capable of expressing the lives of the dominated. Let's not forget, however, that it is influenced by mainstream music. A provocative and commercial rap style appears elsewhere in Marseille with Naps, SCH, and especially Jul, prolific author of nine albums since 2014. The latter is very popular among the youth because of often vulgar lyrics. The repetitive rhythms of his music composed from the Pro Tools audio-digital platform reflect the influence of technology and electronic music. The poetic aspects of rap disappear in favor of sound effects and the repetition of the same rhythmic patterns. It is no longer a question of giving an answer to the victims of the city's crisis but of creating an atmosphere close to that of the nightclubs as in "Gros" (Big) on *Je tourne en rond* (I Turn in Circles, 2015).

We can characterize current rap in Marseille in four trends:

1. Distancing from Local Problems

This is the case of the group IAM, who continues an astonishing artistic career. The themes of their songs deal mainly with political, philosophical, and moral questions. Local realities are mentioned only marginally ("Notre-Dame veille" [Notre Dame Cathedral Keeps Watch] from the album *Arts martiens* [Martian Arts], 2013). Yet the rappers of IAM participated in concerts supporting the Noailles victims, when a major support concert at Espace Julien on 21 December 2018 brought together Marseille's main rappers.

2. Participation in the Process of Urban Restructuring and Gentrification

It manifests itself mainly with Jul's repetitive music and soundscapes, de- rived from the most commercial electronic music, whose globalized rhythms enliven evenings sometimes organized by the municipality. The most com- mercial rap, indifferent to the situation of the city, can be included in this trend.

3. Expression of a Nonconfrontational Identity

And yet, some of these voices are ambivalent. In Jul's song titles and video clips, he also cultivates a link with his neighborhood. He manifests the pres- ence of the dominated, even if his speech is not one of protest. Soprano is also a complex singer. His productions are quite varied. "Ce qu'on laisse à nos mômes" (What We Leave Our Kids) and "On a besoin de toi" (We Need You) fall into song format in an album marked by the declamation and rhythm of rap (2010's *La Colombe* [The Dove] and "Le diable ne s'habille plus en Prada" [The Devil No Longer Wears Prada] on *L'Everest* from 2016). Soprano often refers to the world of the projects, but he evokes them without the least bit of rebellion, as in a song coauthored with Jul, "Marseille c'est . . ." (Marseille Is . . .), on *L'Everest*: the daily life of the youth is presented in a fun way. Soprano also presents his city in "Chez nous" (With Us, 2018), a song written by Jean-Jacques Goldman, heavyweight of the music industry, and co-performed by a singer also from Marseille, Patrick Fiori, on his album *Promesse* (Promise, 2017).

4. Resistance

It is notably embodied by Keny Arkana's productions, in which she speaks to the victims of crisis but especially to politicized youth looking for an alterna- tive. This political rap aims to generate awareness of Marseille's evolution and the revolt.

   More than thirty years after the arrival of rap, Marseille remains a poor city. Urban renewal has led to gentrification and to the arrival of new inhabi- tants in a privileged and normalized area. This project masks the gravity of the situation. The city sinks deeper into crisis. It is "a visible illustration of the defects of the French Republic" (Pujol 2016, 216). Social decomposition, political cronyism, and delinquency play into the hands of the National Front that today controls a section of the northern districts. The development of the Euroméditerranée, urban renewal, and gentrification create new barriers for the working class. Urban space remains a place of confrontation and exclu- sion as demonstrated by the struggle of the inhabitants of La Plaine in au- tumn of 2018 to maintain the most popular market and a convivial space at the Jean-Jaurès square in the center of Marseille.[9] In this situation, hip-hop is no longer a marginal artistic culture linked primarily to the dominated. It has lost a part of its originality. In contributing to the cultural attractiveness of the city, dance and street art play a much more ambiguous role. It is the same for some rappers, even if its tie to their project plays an important role for their identity. Repetitive rhythms and the desire to create atmospheres are, above all, entertainment. They lead neither to rebellion nor to original musical forms. The evolution of hip-hop and of rap thus shows their normalization in French society. The inventiveness of rap is maintained, however, in a context quite different from that of the 1990s.

REFERENCES

Cohane, Ondine. "2. Marseille: On the Mediterranean, Art, and Plenty of It." *The New York Times*, 11 January 2013.

Crane, Sheila. *Mediterranean Crossroads: Marseille and Modern Architecture*. Minneapolis: University of Minnesota Press, 2011.

Davet, Stéphane. "La Pop se pique de hip-hop." *Le Monde*, 10 February 2018, 16–17. https://www.lemonde.fr/culture/article/2018/02/10/la-pop-se-pique-de-hip-hop_5254734_3246.html

Dell'Umbria, Alèssi. *Histoire universelle de Marseille, de l'an mil à l'an deux mille*. Marseille: Agone, 2006.

Donnat, Olivier. *Les Pratiques culturelles des Français à l'ère numérique: Enquête 2008*. Paris: La Découverte/Ministère de la Culture et de la Communication, 2009.

Gasquet-Cyrus, Médéric, and Cyril Trimaille. "Être néo quelque part: La gentrification à Marseille et ses implications sociolinguistiques." *Langage & Société*, no. 162 (2017): 81–105.

Hammou, Karim. *Une Histoire du rap en France*. Paris: La Découverte, 2012.

INSEE. "Provence-Alpes-Côte d'Azur: Plus de 850.000 personnes vivent sous le seuil de la pauvreté." 19 December 2016. https://www.insee.fr/fr/statistiques/2532762

———. "Le taux de chômage augmente de 0.2 point au premier trimestre 2018 après avoir diminué de 0.7 point au trimestre précédent." 23 May 2018. https://www.insee.fr/fr/statistiques/3547180

Jacono, Jean-Marie. "Musical Dimensions and Ways of Expressing Identity in French Rap: The Groups from Marseille." In *Black, Blanc, Beur: Rap Music and Hip-Hop in the Francophone World*, edited by Alain-Philippe Durand, 22–32. Lanham, MD: Scarecrow Press, 2002.

———. "Le rap peut-il aborder la question de l'intimité? Les productions du groupe IAM." In *Chanson: Du collectif à l'intime*, edited by Joël July, 61–77. Aix-en-Provence: Presses Universitaires de Provence, 2016.

Kosmicki, Guillaume. "L'évolution du groupe IAM: Un parcours thématique et musical sensé." In *Paroles et musiques à Marseille*, edited by Médéric Gasquet-Cyrus, Guillaume Kosmicki, and Cécile Van den Avenne, 93–108. Paris: L'Harmattan, 1999.

Krims, Adam. *Rap Music and the Poetics of Identity*. Cambridge: Cambridge University Press, 2000.

Maisetti, Nicolas. *Opération culturelle et pouvoirs urbains: Instrumentalisation économique de la culture et luttes autour de Marseille-Provence Capitale européenne de la culture*. Paris: L'Harmattan, 2014.

Nasiali, Minayo. *Native to the Republic: Empire, Social Citizenship, and Everyday Life in Marseille since 1945*. Ithaca, NY: Cornell University Press, 2016.

Peraldi, Michel, Claire Duport, and Michel Samson. *Sociologie de Marseille*. Paris: La Découverte, 2015.

Pirenne, Christophe. *Histoire musicale du rock*. Paris: Fayard, 2011.

Pujol, Philippe. *La Fabrique du monstre*. Paris: Les Arènes, 2016.

Swedenburg, Ted. "Islamic Hip-Hop versus Islamophobia: Aki Nawaz, Natacha Atlas, Akhenaton." In *Global Noise: Rap and Hip-Hop outside the USA*, edited by Tony Mitchell, 57–85. Middletown, CT: Wesleyan University Press, 2002.

Valnet, Julien. *M.A.R.S. Histoires et légendes du hip-hop marseillais*. Marseille: Wildproject, 2013.

DISCOGRAPHY AND FILMOGRAPHY

Akhenaton. *Métèque et mat*. Delabel, compact disc. Originally released in 1995.

Arkana, Keny. *Tout tourne autour du soleil.* Because Music, compact disc. Originally released in 2012.

Chouf. Dir. Karim Dridi. Tessalit Productions. Originally released in 2016.

Fiori, Patrick. *Promesse*. Sony Music France, compact disc. Originially released in 2017.

Fonky Family. *Si Dieu Veut*. Small, compact disc. Originally released in 1997.

French Connection II. Dir. John Frankenheimer. Twentieth Century Fox. Originally released in 1975.

IAM. *De la planète Mars*. Virgin France, compact disc. Originally released in 1991.

———. "Je danse le Mia." *Ombre est lumière*. Delabel, compact disc. Originally released in 1993.

———. *L' École du micro d'argent*. EMI Music France, compact disc. Originally released in 1997.

———. *Revoir un printemps.* Hostile Records, compact disc. Originally released in 2003.

———. *Arts martiens.* Def Jam France, compact disc. Originally released in 2013.

Jul. *Je tourne en rond*. Liga One Industry, compact disc. Originally released in 2015.

Justin de Marseille. Dir. Maurice Tourneur. Pathé-Nathan. Originally released in 1935.

Kheops. *Sad Hill*. Delabel, compact disc. Originally released in 1997.

Le 3ème Œil. *Hier aujourd'hui demain*. Columbia Records, compact disc. Originally released in 1999.

Marseille. Creator Dan Franck. Federation Entertainment, Netflix. Originally released in 2016.

Psy 4 de la Rime. *Block Party*. 361 Records, compact disc. Originally released in 2002.

Soprano. *Puisqu'il faut vivre*. Fairp Music, compact disc. Originally released in 2007.

———. *La Colombe*. EMI Music France, compact disc. Originally released in 2010.

———. *L'Everest*. Warner Music France, compact disc. Originally released in 2016.

Soul Swing. *Le retour de l'âme soul*. Night & Day, compact disc. Originally released in 1996.

Chapter Three

"Fear of a Black Planet"

*The Transnational Racial Politics of
Hip-Hop in France, 1990–1991*

Samir Meghelli

When the seminal American hip-hop group Public Enemy arrived in Paris several days after the April 1990 release of their *Fear of a Black Planet* album to perform at the Zénith concert hall, they were met by police in riot gear preparing for a potential race war. Although hip-hop was widely seen as a fun, harmless American import when it first arrived in France in the early 1980s, by the end of the decade it aroused tremendous fear among much of the French public and political class for its perceived growing influence on their country's racial politics. In ways that have gone largely overlooked, the late 1980s and early 1990s were a critical moment when the transnational circulation of ideas about race deeply shaped how hip-hop would become rooted along the racial and spatial fault lines in French society. Both postcolonial youth and the French government sought to appropriate hip-hop's perceived blackness and Americanness, although to different ends. While the government very publicly supported French youth's embrace of hip-hop in order to quell social unrest, it also worked to distance itself from what it criticized as the harsh realities of a presumed American "multiculturalism." Meanwhile, postcolonial youth were empowered by the idea of a cultural form that could help articulate their racialized experiences in an otherwise emphatically (and purportedly) color-blind national context.

Although Public Enemy had performed in Paris before—at the Mutualité in 1987 and at Le Globo in 1988—it was their April 1990 concert that garnered unprecedented attention. The political climate in both the United States and France fueled the heightened scrutiny to which the event was subjected. And that historical moment at the turn of the 1990s offers a useful window into how the American group's arrival was part of a watershed for both French hip-hop and French racial politics. Less than a year before the Paris concert, Public Enemy's song "Fight the Power" appeared as the anthem in Spike Lee's 1989 film, *Do the Right Thing*, which explored volatile racial tensions in a Brooklyn neighborhood. The film was inspired by the 1986 death of Michael Griffith, who—along with two others—was attacked by white residents in the Howard Beach neighborhood of Queens, New York City. Spike Lee explained, "As far as I'm concerned, racism is the most pressing problem in the United States; and I wanted the film to bring the issue into the forefront where it belongs" (Kaufman 1989). In the closing credits, Lee dedicates the film to the families of six victims of anti-black violence (primarily perpetrated by police officers) in New York City from the late 1970s through the 1980s. In the lead-up to the film's release, white journalists used sensationalist language to warn of its potential for inciting riots. Film critic David Denby wrote that Spike Lee is "playing with dynamite in an urban playground" and that "the response to the movie could get away from him" (Denby 1989). Political columnist Joe Klein warned that "if Lee does hook large black audiences . . . they [might] react violently—which can't be ruled out" (Klein 1989). Featured in the main title sequence as well as in various scenes where it is playing on character Radio Raheem's boombox, Public Enemy's "Fight the Power" powerfully spoke out against the status quo of race relations in the United States, with Chuck D.'s booming voice that demanded, "Give us what we want [and] what we need," proclaiming that "our freedom of speech is freedom or death" and, most famously, "we got to fight the powers that be!"

As part of their international tour for the release of their third studio album, *Fear of a Black Planet*, Public Enemy was set to perform in April 1990 at the prestigious Zénith concert hall in Paris. The album could not have been more aptly titled, if only because the music and ideas of Public Enemy struck utter fear in much of the French public. More than anything, it was the frank, incisive talk about race and racial inequality that jarred French sensibilities. The French republican political tradition of race-blindness that traditionally precludes the acknowledgment of "race" also often deems discussion of it as "anti-French" (Constant 2009; Keaton 2010). Public Enemy, on the other hand, advocated a stark view of racism and argued for the necessity of addressing it head-on. And yet, few in France could deny that there were already rumblings of social and racial unrest in their country, as an increasing number of incidents of police brutality and anti-immigrant violence had occurred in the preceding months and years (Bachmann and Le Guennec 1996). But seeing postcolonial youth embrace the music of Public Enemy came as a shock to much of the rest of France and became a source of paranoia over the possibility of the infiltration of American racial ideologies into the neighborhoods of the working-class *banlieues* (the disproportionately immigrant outer cities—frequently translated into English simply as "suburbs"—that became increasingly stigmatized over the course of the 1980s and 1990s in ways similar to the American so-called "inner city").[1]

In the days leading up to the Zénith concert, the French National Police feared the possibility of—and sought to prevent—racial unrest. They even met with the concert organizers, a group of young hip-hoppers from Saint-Ouen and other Paris-area suburbs who had formed a promotions company called IZB, to gather intelligence about the upcoming event and devise a robust security plan. The two main founders of IZB, brothers Angelo and Jean-Marie Gopée, claimed that "the police headquarters wanted to prohibit the concert because of all the hype by the media" (Dufresne 1991, 41; my translation).[2] This was not uncommon since, as journalist Olivier Cachin noted, early coverage of French rap often conflated the music with violence and the *banlieues*:

> In the first years that there were pieces in the French press about rap, it was exclusively linked to the suburbs, and further than that, to the riots in the suburbs. You know, if there's a trashcan burning or cars being turned over or young guys throwing stones, [it was like,] "Hey, rap music!" There were ludicrous pieces, even in good [news]papers like, for example, *Le Canard Enchaîné*. . . . That was one of the big frustrations of the artists and of me at the time: that it was never seen as a music, it was like a sociological move-ment. . . . It was always like, "Oh, the suburbs are burning? Let's talk about hip hop!" (Cachin 2008)

For the April 1990 Public Enemy concert, the story was no different. The news media played a central role in further promoting the already prevailing sense of fear. The many French hip-hop fans that attended the concert recall with disbelief and disgust—even many years later—the surrounding media coverage.

Two important figures of the French hip-hop scene, DJ Fab and his long-time collaborator Awer, have vivid memories of the experience. Awer ex-plained, "I remember the first time Public Enemy came to the Zénith. Man, the coverage on the TV news was like that of the beginning of the [Gulf War]. All the TV channels were like, 'Tonight, there will be a big war here'" (DJ Fab and Awer 2008). DJ Fab added, "I remember, me and [the rapper I deejayed for] EJM appeared on a TV show. They followed us for 24 hours leading up to the concert, came to my [house], everywhere. . . . They fol-lowed us with a camera, like 'We're going to a Public Enemy show with EJM and his crew, to find out what this is all about.' It was like France was under attack!" (DJ Fab and Awer 2008). Awer interjected, "It was crazy, man. One p.m., opening of the news: 'Tonight, at the Zénith: Public Enemy, this group of, almost like, terrorists,' you know? 'All of the kids from the *banlieues* will be coming.' . . . People were scared. You could see the cops were everywhere. It was crazy. It was like we were at war" (DJ Fab and Awer 2008). Stéphane Begoc, a graffiti writer and journalist best known by the moniker SEAR—also a member of the IZB collective that organized the concert and who later that same year launched the influential French hip-hop zine *Get Busy*—recalled the hysteria:

> There were nonstop debates on the radio, on TV, with rumors circulating that whites weren't going to be allowed into the concert, those kinds of things. It was total craziness. The *peak* of the stupidity was Guillaume Durand on channel 5. This guy was in the stands at the Zénith acting as if he was a war zone reporter and every ten minutes was providing updates for the news about what was happening, if a white person had been killed, if a pigeon had been run over by a black car. [Laughter] . . . It was really crazy, there were blockades of CRS national police in front of the Zénith and even guys on the roof of the venue to be able to surveil everything. (Batista 2016)[3]

The archival television footage reveals the remarkable accuracy of these recollections. The day after the concert, the midday news of Antenne 2 opened its broadcast by announcing, "Public Enemy in concert at the Zénith in Paris: an event much awaited and feared" (INA, Antenne 2, 1990). The news anchor continued, "With Public Enemy, the message is clear and the symbols powerful."[4] They cut to footage of a group of young Afro-French fans waiting outside the concert venue, pumping their fists and throwing peace signs in the air. The news narrator noted, "It is for them that [Public Enemy] came to perform, but one hour before the concert it was to the journalists that [Public Enemy] addressed themselves" (INA, Antenne 2, 1990).[5] Then came footage of Public Enemy's preconcert press conference, with rapper Chuck D. proclaiming, "We play music, but at the same time, in our music we have a message. And our message is: 'Rebuild and uplift our people.' In the Western world, we've been discriminated against, we've been enslaved. And today it's a different type of mental slavery that's taking place. So, all we wanna do is play our music and fight for what we stand for" (INA, Antenne 2, 1990). In a blatant, willfully inflammatory (mis)translation of the second and third sentences of Chuck D.'s comments, Antenne 2 over-dubbed with the following: "Nous voulons rendre à la race noire sa dignité. Par la faute des blancs, nous avons été victimes de la discrimination, de l'esclavage" (We want to return to the black race its dignity. At the hands of whites, we have been victims of discrimination, of slavery). Rather than use the common French word *l'Occident* (meaning "the West") for Chuck D.'s use of "the Western world," Antenne 2 made the conscious choice to use the much less commonly used and far more shocking term (to French sensibilities) *blanc* (meaning "white"). And where Chuck referred to "our people," Antenne 2 employed the phrase "black race" (*race noire*). The television channel's use of racially antagonistic language was symptomatic of a broader pattern in the news media's treatment of working-class, postcolonial youth (Boyer 1998; Hargreaves 1996; Sedel 2009).

On the evening news of FR3, an anchor opened by saying, "We feared the very worst last night in Paris, but the worst did not come to be." The other anchor added, "No, Paris was not at all burning last night" (INA, FR3, 1990).[6] Continuing with the incendiary language, a reporter narrrated,

> "Not a single white person allowed in the concert hall." That crazy rumor had been circulating all day long. It must be said though that Public Enemy has a bad reputation. In the United States, this group is number one in rap, a music born in the ghettos and which chants its cry of revolt against misery and hopelessness. On stage, Public Enemy only increases their provocations as they advocate the defense of the black race against whites. They're "racist, hateful, and anti-semitic," charge their critics. . . . Yesterday, the concert ended the rumor: a young audience, a lot of blacks, but also some whites. A relaxed ambience. Not the slightest of incidents. (INA, FR3, 1990)[7]

The most widely watched broadcast of nightly news, on channel TF1, covered the concert in much the same way, highlighting the racial dimensions of hip-hop and then gauging the significance of Public Enemy's performance. The anchor began, "Rap is arriving in Europe. This black American musical movement, born several years ago in the poor neighborhoods of New York, has spread across the largest cities in the United States and now it is spreading here. Rap asserts itself firmly against the white *establishment*, and at times, it can go very far in that direction. . . . Public Enemy [performed] yesterday at the Zénith in Paris, and [reporter] Bernard Gely was there to measure the impact" (INA, TF1, 1990).[8] Bernard Gely offered his take: "A good sense for marketing and opinions that cause concern in the United States. Leaders of rap, Public Enemy moves our countrymen more with the force of their music than with their words, which are delivered in English. But overall, the message resonates."[9] They cut to footage of young Afro-French fans at the concert, pumping their fists in the air. Gely continued, "What Public Enemy demands is recognition of a 'black' identity and a world without inequality" (INA, TF1, 1990).[10]

Although the concert happened without incident, the heightened awareness of racial tensions and the increasing popularity of hip-hop both left their mark on the country's collective imagination. SEAR recalled the significance of that moment: "Public Enemy was a foundational group. When they came, we were already deep into rap, but it was like they had definitively proven something: with Public Enemy, no one could any longer deny that hip-hop was the most important musical and cultural movement since rock 'n' roll. They embodied and symbolized that. There are few groups who had as important an impact as them" (Batista 2016). Daniel Fourneuf—an early dancer and deejay in the Paris hip-hop scene who went on to manage the first hip-hop clothing and music store in France and all of Europe, Ticaret—reflected on Public Enemy's role in fostering pride among Afro-French youth: "Public Enemy was a group that was deeply 'black power,' that revived the Black Panther mentality, and recounted that whole history. . . . Young people in Paris were proudly wearing their Africa medallions. . . . We felt represented by their music, which resonated with us" (Anonymous 2019).[11] And Fred Bendongué, a pioneering hip-hop dancer in France, spoke to the broader importance of the cultural movement for postcolonial, *banlieue* youth:

> The hip-hop movement empowered us to recognize our marginalization here in France. We identified with the social conditions, the life, and the struggles of Black people in the ghettos of America. We discovered that we were living the same thing here: racism, exclusion, drugs, crime, etc. In reality, we became a part of the movement because it spoke to us, because even if we were 6,000 kilometers away, it brought us closer together. (Bendongué 2014)

THE RISE AND RACIAL POLITICS OF FRENCH RAP

When hip-hop first received widespread, extended exposure in France in 1984 with the world's first regularly, nationally broadcast hip-hop television show—*H.I.P. H.O.P.* on channel TF1—it was largely treated as a fad and perceived as innocuous entertainment. The reemergence in 1990 of hip-hop in French public consciousness came with deeply controversial news coverage and growing government interest in the movement. Both the French mass media and political discourse witnessed a proliferation of references to the fear and possibility of the "Americanization of French ghettos," the "Americanization of the French race problem," the "Americanization of French gangs," and, of course, the "Americanization of French culture" (Crowley 1992; Wacquant 1999; Body-Gendrot 2000). Increasingly understood as tied to issues of racial and spatial injustice in France, hip-hop became a key prism through which these fears were refracted. For French hip-hoppers, these same discursive tropes were used to bring attention to their own plight. Rather than adopt American rap wholesale, these artists drew on particular aspects of the iconography, style, and lyrical subject matter of their fellow hip-hoppers on the other side of the Atlantic, all the while recontextualizing them in ways that spoke to their unique French experience. Only when this began to occur—in the late 1980s—was there a flourishing of the French rap scene.

From the beginning of hip-hop's arrival in France, aspiring rappers sought to imitate their American counterparts. The earliest French rappers, dating to at least 1982, largely attempted to rap in English. This was inevitably a doomed pursuit, since few youth could speak English fluently and a mere copying of American raps left little room for creativity or innovation. One of the first widely heard French rappers was DJ Dee Nasty, who could be heard on a range of pirate radio stations in the early 1980s. He described the process by which he and his rapping partners first adopted the style and attempted to mold it to fit the French language:

> Everyone was rapping in English. But we said, "No, the only way for this art to progress is to rap in French." So, at the beginning, what we said was, "What we're gonna do is take the newest American rap songs and do adaptations of them in French." The most memorable—or, really, the easiest example to give—is with Melle Mel's [song], "New York, New York/Big city of dreams/ But everything in New York ain't always what it seems." We turned it into, *"Paname, Paname/Grande ville des rêves/Mais tout à Paris n'est pas ce qu'il paraît"* [Paris, Paris/Big city of dreams/But everything in Paris ain't always what it seems]. (Bigeault 2005)

Although this entailed a mere translation of American lyrics into French, Dee Nasty and others were able to perfect aspects of the practice of rapping as they performed these verses, such as flow, cadence, rhythm, speed, and intonation. In time, and at the urging of American hip-hop figures like Afrika Bambaataa, French youth began writing their everyday experiences into their lyrics and inflecting their rhymes with their own linguistic particularisms.[12] The French vernacular known as *verlan*, in which syllables of words are reversed, was a widespread feature of not only the language of many *banlieue* youth but also eventually of French rap lyrics.[13]

In October 1988, DJ Dee Nasty was hired by Radio Nova, and he opened the airwaves to French rappers from around Paris, inviting them to come perform on his show, *Deenastyle*.[14] Each outer-city and Paris neighborhood had crews of rappers, and the radio show became home to many of their first public performances. Every major French rap group from the region that later became famous—such as NTM from Saint Denis, Ministère AMER from Garges-Sarcelles, Les Little MCs from Vitry, Assassin from Paris and its suburbs, and MC Solaar from Maisons-Alfort and Villeneuve-Saint-Georges—appeared on Dee Nasty's show. For the first time, a consistent French rap scene had emerged. Rapping styles became more complex and nimble, and the content of rap lyrics often broached pressing social issues. Even as French rappers continued to be inspired by American artists, they were capturing dimensions of uniquely French postcolonial youth life that were nowhere else present in their society's public sphere.

In one example, Stomy Bugsy, a young rapper of Cape Verdean descent from the northern Paris suburb of Sarcelles who cofounded the group Ministère AMER, improvised a rap on the *Deenastyle* show that related his quotidian experience of confronting the skinhead gangs that controlled particular sections of Paris, just as he commented on the media representation of

him and his crew as a so-called gang.[15] His rap—done in French—was
punctuated with an English refrain that he borrowed from the recently released American rap song "Black Is Back" (1989) by New Jersey artist
Lakim Shabazz that sampled Malcolm X's voice and echoed the teachings
and philosophy of the Nation of Gods and Earths.[16] Bugsy exclaimed repeatedly in English in his otherwise French-language freestyle, "So, I say, 'Black
is Back'/So, I say, 'Black is Back'!" Many observers feared and criticized
French rap for importing racially charged and allegedly uniquely American
issues that had no place in the French context. But Bugsy and rappers like
him were drawing on tropes from the American hip-hop scene—where black
nationalist lyrics, iconography, and styles predominated in the late 1980s—
and recontextualizing them in their own local worlds where they faced real
targeting by skinheads and discrimination of all kinds (Brinbaum and Cebolla Boado 2007; Heath, Rothon, and Kilpi 2008; Silberman and Fournier
2007; Simon 2003; and Vallet and Caille 1999). Through the African
American idiom of rap, French artists were articulating racialized and spa-
tialized realities that were not otherwise easily expressed in a society that
insisted on a color-blind discourse (Keaton 2010). When countercultural
guru and founder of *Actuel* magazine Jean-François Bizot questioned Stomy
Bugsy's friend and rap group manager Kenzy about whether this "afrocen-
trist style" was going to catch on, he replied, evidently irritated, "Like some
trend, you mean? . . . With what we experience here [in France], we're seen
as niggers by the cops who follow us everywhere. And we'll never just forget
that" (Bizot 2005, 25).[17] And when Bizot asked why they chose "Knowledge
Is a Weapon" as their group slogan, Kenzy explained, "Because we realized
how important it is for us in the suburbs . . . to know our history. In school,
they didn't teach us anything about African history. Nothing. . . . We were
angered when we learned that even in Africa they also teach so little of our
history" (Bizot 2005, 24–25).[18] Even as Stomy Bugsy and his group,
Ministère AMER, drew on American influences, they made clear that they
were not claiming some superficial Americanness but rather embraced their
African heritage. Mocking an imaginary *traître* (traitor) who does just the
opposite, Stomy Bugsy rapped on the group's first EP record, "You claim
America/Your origins are in Africa/Your mom calls you Mamadou/But you
took the name Andrew" (Ministère AMER 1991).[19]

    This impulse to seek out and claim one's history and heritage was com-
mon among the French hip-hop community, which was disproportionately
comprised of postcolonial youth. The French context made this a controversial stance, since to take such vocal pride in any other identity aside from the
immediately national one was considered un-French (or even anti-French).
But hip-hop became a conduit for many to question this rigid, singular formulation of Frenchness. Graffiti artist Mag 3, whose real name is Juan Massenya and who is of Martinican descent, was interviewed by a television

crew about this very issue while still a student at the University of Paris–VIII in Saint Denis. He asserted, "Growing up, everyone's talking about the Gauls, the Gauls, the Gauls—showing a photo of a blond-haired, blue-eyed Gaul. After a while, you say to yourself, 'I don't look anything like a Gaul.' You have to find out about your own history, your own people. And, in a way, that's what this [hip-hop] movement is about" (Génération Zulus 1991). These were the artists—and the spirit—that inspired the first compilation of French rap music, *Rapattitude*.[20] Released in June 1990, only two months after Public Enemy's concert at the Zénith, the album featured ten artists from around the Paris region, including many who had appeared on DJ Dee Nasty's *Deenastyle* Radio Nova show, such as Assassin, NTM, EJM, and New Generation MCs. *Rapattitude* brought mainstream attention to the indigenous French rap scene for the first time and inspired major record labels to begin signing French rappers, ultimately leading to the flourishing of the genre that occurred during the 1990s.

NEW YORK AND THE SPECTER OF THE "AMERICAN SYNDROME"

By the summer of 1990, not long after Public Enemy's Zénith show and the release of *Rapattitude*, hip-hop carried radically divergent meanings for its French adherents and critics. For French hip-hoppers, New York was the birthplace and breeding ground of the cultural movement with which they deeply identified, a site of exceptional creativity and style, a rich source of their cultural imaginary (particularly through film, television, and music), and a symbolic site of Afro-diasporic cultural and political empowerment. On the other hand, for many public officials and much of French society at large, New York—and, by extension, the United States—was the embodiment of failed urban policy, neoliberal capitalism, and entrenched racism, as well as proof of the failure of a presumed "American" model of multiculturalism (Body-Gendrot 2000; Crowley 1992; Fassin 1999; Green 1999; and Wacquant 1999). As the French faced what they considered a continuing "crisis" (manufactured as it may have been) of a lack of assimilation/integration by its postcolonial populations, they feared that the infiltration of American racial ideologies into the French context would further destabilize an already fragile social/racial landscape. References to "New York" and "America" proliferated in the mass media as policy makers, intellectuals, and the general public pondered whether the many (partly accurate, partly exaggerated) problems of American cities would soon take root in France. And since "hip-hop" was understood by many French to be a quintessentially American "ghetto" phenomenon, the fact of its adoption by postcolonial youth stirred fear that it would act as a vector for the transmission of American social ills.

This recurring comparison reached a crescendo at the turn of the 1990s. In one striking example (among many others), Philippe Broussard of *Le Monde* was documenting the "proliferation of gangs in the Paris suburbs" and anxiously asked, "Will Paris imitate New York, where gangs fight over streets and drug markets with gunshots from .357 Magnums?" (Broussard 1990).[21] He continued, "The risk exists because these kids are growing in number and live on a foreign planet somewhere between Manhattan, Dakar, and Argenteuil. They pretend to be the warriors of Harlem while in Cergy-Pontoise, and pretend that there are Central Parks in Evry" (Broussard 1990).[22] Further extending the stereotypes, Broussard wrote, "Often forced to grow up on their own in dislocated families (notably the Guadeloupeans), these crossbred sons of Africa and the Bronx, who wear shiny chains, backward hats, and baggy jeans, imagine themselves being as charming as Eddie Murphy and stronger than Myke [*sic*] Tyson" (Broussard 1990).[23] Similarly exaggerated fears appeared in local newspapers across the Paris region. In *93 Hebdo*, the weekly newspaper of the Seine-Saint-Denis *département*, photos of the graffiti-scrawled suburban train system appeared with the subtitle, "The halls are beginning to resemble the New York subway," noting that the B Line was experiencing "on average, a mugging every two days" (Anonymous 1990).[24]

Sociologist Loïc Wacquant described the context in which these kinds of comparisons were being drawn, explaining that France was witnessing "the rise of urban inequalities, xenophobia, and protest movements of youth from the working or lower class '*banlieues*'" (Wacquant 1999, 130). This prompted a "new type of discourse on 'ghettoization' that suggested an abrupt convergence between the dispossessed neighborhoods of the French and the American city" (ibid.). Wacquant observed that:

> In only a few years, a moral panic has spread according to which the deteriorating *cités* (public housing projects) of the urban periphery are on the verge of being transformed—indeed have already been remade—into so many "ghettos," repositories where all the ills afflicting the lower reaches of French society accumulate and brew. Arising out of nowhere and appearing everywhere at the same time, fed by stereotypes imported from across the Atlantic (Chicago, the Bronx, Harlem . . .), this trope has imposed itself as one of the clichés of contemporary public debate on the city. (Wacquant 1999, 130)

Historian Nancy Green argued that this tendency to use America as a foil for France came to pervade even scholarly work on French immigration, which "refer time and again to the United States" (Green 1999, 1199). Green noted that "America is . . . used rhetorically and politically to interpret France," and that "decoding the United States is most often a way of encoding France: that France is a melting pot/country of immigration just like the United States;

that the United States has renounced its literal melting pot to follow a dangerous path of diversity, which France should in no way copy; or that an American model of warring communities is not nearly as grim as some pundits like to point out and is therefore usable" (Green 1999, 1199).

The predominant mode of New York/Paris comparison in the late 1980s and early 1990s was clearly one in which media and public figures were "obsessively invoking the specter of the 'American syndrome' [of failed multiculturalism and widespread ghettoization] at every turn" (Wacquant 1999, 131). This was confirmed when left-wing, Socialist Prime Minister Michel Rocard proclaimed in *Le Monde* on 7 December 1989 that France "cannot be 'a juxtaposition of communities.' It is a society in which 'the adherence to a set of common values is primordial.' France does not have to follow the Anglo-Saxon models, which allow ethnic groups to barricade themselves within geographic and cultural ghettos, resulting in 'a soft form of apartheid'" (Green 1999, 1198). These public figures, as Wacquant noted, served as "prophets of doom and gloom" who were "playing up sensationalistic and exotic images 'made in the USA' (as striking as they [were] fuzzy)" (Wacquant 1999, 131).

"JACK LE RAPPEUR" AND TRANSATLANTIC HIP-HOP RELATIONS

When François Mitterrand became president in May 1981, he named Jack Lang his minister of culture. In a historic move, the ministry's budget was nearly immediately doubled, providing unprecedented funding for cultural initiatives (Poirrier 2004). Each year thereafter, the budget continued to grow until it surpassed 1 percent of the French government's total budget in 1993, just as Jack Lang's tenure ended (Lang and Helvig 2009, 142). Within months of the election of Mitterrand and nomination of Lang, clashes occurred between police and immigrant youth in the Minguettes housing projects in the Lyon suburbs (Dikeç 2007, 42–43). This placed immediate pressure on the new administration to address the issue of poor social conditions in public housing complexes and to resolve the ongoing violent conflicts between youth and police in these neighborhoods.

In the months and years that followed, Jack Lang oversaw a cultural policy that was carried out in tandem with a new urban policy. In both cases, a primary concern was the "integration" of postcolonial youth. Since hip-hop increasingly became a central force in their everyday lives, the Ministry of Culture sought to target this newly arriving and influential cultural movement. As Loïc Lafargue de Grangeneuve explained, "the public administrations put in place a group of programs intended for hip-hop for the reason that the majority of its practitioners—youth living in the suburbs, often of immigrant descent (notably African and Maghrebi)—embody sociological characteristics that define them as a 'problem populations,' and therefore a potential target for public policy" (Lafargue de Grangeneuve 2008, 9).[25] As Lang served as minister of culture from 1981 to 1992 (except 1986–1988), he became the figurehead of the ministry's engagement with hip-hop. Critics on the right often sardonically referred to him as "Jack le Rappeur." This image was solidified when, several months after the infamous Public Enemy concert, he appeared in a two-page photograph spread with a group of hip-hoppers—including those who had organized the concert—in *VSD* magazine and publicly promised to commit two million francs to support hip-hop initiatives (Lang 1990). In that cover story, he famously proclaimed (referring to hip-hop), "Cette culture, moi j'y crois" (This culture, I believe in it; Lang 1990). The front cover included the headline "Generation Rap: Music, Graffiti, Style, the Rage of Rap Has Conquered Our High Schools and Our Suburbs [*Banlieues*]: Investigation about This Phenomenon That Came from the Sidewalks of New York" (Lang 1990).[26]

At the very moment that questions of "integration" came to the fore in the mass media and in national political debate in the late 1980s and early 1990s, the Ministry of Culture (along with other government organizations, such as the Fonds d'Action sociale pour les Travailleurs immigrés et leurs Familles, or Social Action Fund for Immigrant Workers and Their Families) sponsored a transatlantic conference on hip-hop that brought a large group of French hip-hop artists, social workers, police officials, and elected officials to the Apollo Theater in Harlem to dialogue with their American peers. This conference, which occurred in November 1991, represented an attempt by the French state to gain a better understanding of this (African) American cultural movement that, by this period (and as they saw it), had invaded France's most troubled neighborhoods and overtaken the youth. The inclusion of law enforcement, social workers, and government officials in the French delegation was evidence of the degree of utter fear and misunderstanding that accompanied hip-hop in France.

Longtime music industry businessman and political insider Jean-François Michel launched a nonprofit organization called World Culture that was the main coordinating body for the conference. According to Michel, World Culture was created with the idea that "at a time when the North–South gap is growing deeper, . . . culture is an essential means of dialogue" (Loupias 1991, 128).[27] He continued, explaining that the organization "initiates encounters between the two 'camps'; but also between countries and cities that share the same problem, like urban violence, for example. New York, the city of rap, the most open-minded city in the world, but which is also full of ghettos, seemed a fitting candidate" (Loupias 1991, 128).[28] The goals of this Paris-to-Harlem trip were two-fold: raise awareness, create dialogue between different social actors (artists, social workers, elected officials, etc.), and then implement it in the long-term. One example: After this trip, there will be a program with police officers (an eight-month training program), with the F.A.S. [Social Action Fund for Immigrant Workers and Their Families], the Inter-Ministerial Delegation on Cities, and the Ministry of Culture. Institutions have difficulty working transversally, and we're here to help them. (Loupias 1991, 128)[29]

The French delegation included approximately fifty members representing more than ten different cities, including Paris, Saint-Denis, Clichy La Garenne, Creil, Bondy, Méru, Lille, Toulouse, Angoulême, Nantes, Saint-Quentin, Marseille, and Montpellier. In addition to more than a dozen hip-hoppers, the delegation included journalists, local government officials (including at least one mayor), social workers, and law enforcement officials, who were "particularly motivated by the issue of delinquency in problem districts" (Anonymous 1991). The kinds of professions represented in the delegation made clear that this transatlantic conference was organized as a kind of fact-finding mission through which various representatives of the French state were hoping to learn what this cultural movement was all about and how they could expect it to develop in their country in the future. Over the course of three days, all the delegates would participate in panel discussions with their American counterparts, including a range of artists, intellectuals, and journalists, such as hip-hop pioneer Afrika Bambaataa, rapper Harmony, City College professors Leonard Jeffries and James Small, journalists James G. Spady and Joan Morgan, and radio DJ Gary Byrd. The French delegates were also going to be taking part in a trip to Newark Arts High School to meet with students, paying a visit to a Harlem police precinct to talk with law enforcement officials, and then going on a tour of the neighborhood.

Christophe Lacroix, graffiti writer and cofounder of the influential French hip-hop zine *Get Busy*, offered his perspective on the organizers' intentions: "They wanted to understand the cultural phenomenon and the bridges between our worlds, like why the same things [exist—such as hip-hop—] in the Bronx and in Harlem and in Saint-Denis, and Sarcelles, and Orly, you know" (Lacroix 2008). Journalist and French delegate Olivier Cachin added, "It was very [naive]. It was like, 'So, the hip-hop stars from America welcome their equivalent from France. And we're going to have a discussion and talk and exchange ideas.' . . . That was the idea" (Cachin 2008). But as William Grimes of *The New York Times* noted, "The rude awakening came early. American rap, and the rhetoric surrounding it, turned out not to be as the French had expected. Many participants said they had come unprepared for the anger and stark racial division they encountered. . . . Suddenly, they found themselves face to face with American racial politics" (Grimes 1991, C11). Grimes characterized the conference as "a weekend rich in mutual incomprehension despite the simultaneous translations" (Grimes 1991, C11).

The French journalists agreed. Olivier Cachin said, "It was very weird because it was two worlds that couldn't speak to each other" (Cachin 2008). *Le Monde*'s Thomas Sotinel wrote that "a good portion of the time was spent overcoming misunderstandings" (Sotinel 1991). It was "three days [of] cultural electroshocks," ultimately revealing "the divisions in the French microcosm transplanted in New York. Elected officials and educators leaped out of their chairs when a member of the [French rap] group Assassin declared, 'France is a racist society'" (Sotinel 1991).

The three-day symposium ended on a characteristically shocking note—shocking, at least, to the French officials and educators. One of the few women hip-hop artists to present on a panel, Harmony, posed a final question to the audience: "How many people here want peace?" (Grimes 1991, C12). Everyone's hand went up in unison. She paused, then concluded her remarks, "Don't you know that there has to be war before there can be peace?" At that moment, "there was a sharp intake of breath among the French delegation" (Grimes 1991, C12). Sotinel noted that, at the very end of the trip, just as the delegation was going to be taking off for France, a French "educator discreetly but firmly cursed 'the myth held by the Ministry of Culture that the [French] housing projects are reservoirs of creativity,'" a myth he felt resulted in "holding onto illusions and wasting money" (Sotinel 1991).

The airplane ride back to Paris was a lively one. Journalist Olivier Cachin described the sentiments shared by many of the attendees: "We thought, 'What a trip!' We were very happy to have been there, but it's not exactly what we or [the organizers] expected. It was like, 'There's still a long way to go to extend the French-American friendship as far as hip-hop music was concerned.' I think the most surprised were the people who organized it. They didn't expect that at all. . . . It didn't turn out the way it was supposed to turn out" (Cachin 2008). Graffiti artist Christophe Lacroix at first hesitated but then agreed to speak with one of the traveling journalists who wrote for the conservative *Le Point* magazine:

> I remember having an argument with people on the plane, especially with a guy from *Le Point*. I talked to that guy for almost three hours on the way back on the plane. I tried to explain [hip-hop] and all that. . . . I was giving [answers] from my heart, but that guy already knew what he wanted to write. When the article came out, I [saw] he was completely taking my words out of context. . . . I was trying to explain why [hip-hop] is something important, why it is a movement and a culture, and not just a trend. Whereas he was like, "This is those funny young black and Arab guys dressing crazy, talking on some bullshit music, and dancing with crazy moves." (Lacroix 2008)

Even if, as some journalists suggested, the symposium did not turn out as the organizers had hoped, it still revealed a great deal about the state of the transnational hip-hop cultural movement. On the one hand, the government officials, law enforcement, and educators in the French delegation demonstrated how woefully ignorant they remained of the deep-seated racism in the United States and in their own country. That they were continually shocked to hear denouncements of racism and, especially from the hip-hoppers in their own delegation, suggested their fundamental blindness—as is symptomatic of French republicanism—to the racial dimensions of the social order. On the other hand, for the French hip-hoppers who traveled to New York, it was like a pilgrimage to the mecca of the cultural movement, its birthplace and breeding ground. They showed solidarity with their American counterparts who spoke out forcefully against racism, since they, too, knew what it was like to be profiled by the police, to be relegated to living in under-resourced neighborhoods, and more generally to be faced with discrimination (Spady 2009). On an artistic and personal level, they were also able to build connections with their American counterparts that would last for many years to come.[30]

REFERENCES

Anonymous. "Peur sur la Ligne B." *93 Hebdo*, 12 January 1990, 30.
———. "Hexa . . . Rap." Official *World Culture* Conference Documentation. New York City, 1991.
———. "Dan de Ticaret, un pionnier au cœur de Paris." *Sneakers Culture*, accessed 19 April 2019. https://www.sneakers-culture.com/dan-de-ticaret-un-pionnier-au-coeur-de-paris/
Bachmann, Christian, and Nicole Le Guennec. *Violences Urbaines: Ascension et chute des classes moyennes à travers cinquante ans de politique de la ville*. Paris: Albin Michel, 1996.
Batista, Lelo Jimmy. "1990: Quand Public Enemy faisait trembler la France." *Noisey*, accessed 1 July 2016. https://noisey.vice.com/fr/article/64wdwg/1990-quand-public-enemy-faisait-trembler-la-france-ina
Bendongué, Fred. Email interview with the author. 23 October 2014.
Bigeault, Daniel (DJ Dee Nasty). Interview with the author. 28 June 2005. Paris, France.
Bizot, Jean-François. *Vaudou & compagnies: Histoires noires de Abidjan à Zombies*. Paris: Actuel/Éditions de Panama, 2005.
Bocquet, José-Louis, and Philippe Pierre-Adolphe. *Rap ta France: Témoignages.* Paris: La Sirène, 1996.
Body-Gendrot, Sophie. "Des Ghettos Américains aux Banlieues Françaises." In *Faut-il s'accommoder de la violence?* edited by Thomas Ferenczi, 139–62. Brussels: Éditions Complexe, 2000.
Boyer, Henri. *Scènes de télévision en banlieues: 1950–1994*. Paris: L'Harmattan, 1998.
Brinbaum, Yaël, and Hector Cebolla Boado. "The School Careers of Ethnic Minority Youth in France: Success or Disillusion?" *Ethnicities* 7, no. 3 (2007): 445–76.
Broussard, Philippe. "L'été zoulou: Les bandes de jeunes noirs sont de plus en plus nombreuses en région parisienne." *Le Monde*, 11 August 1990.
Cachin, Olivier. Interview with the author. 4 December 2008. Paris, France.
———. *Rapattitude*. Paris: FNAC, 2012.
Constant, Fred. "Talking Race in Color-Blind France: Equality Denied, 'Blackness' Reclaimed." In *Black Europe and the African Diaspora*, edited by Darlene Clark Hine, Trica Danielle Keaton, and Stephen Small, 145–60. Urbana: University of Illinois Press, 2009.
Crowley, John. "Minorités ethniques et ghettos aux États-Unis: Modèle ou anti-modèle pour la France?" *Esprit* 182 (June 1992): 78–94.
Denby, David. "He's Gotta Have It." *New York Magazine*, 26 June 1989, 53–54.

Desse (Desdémone Bardin), and SBG (Sébastian Bardin-Greenberg). *Freestyle*. Paris: Massot & Millet, 1993.

Dikeç, Mustapha. *Badlands of the Republic: Space, Politics, and Urban Policy*. Malden, MA: Blackwell, 2007.

DJ Fab, and Awer. Interview with the author. 1 December 2008. Paris, France.

Doran, Meredith Christine. "A Sociolinguistic Study of Youth Language in the Parisian Suburbs: *Verlan* and Minority Identity in Contemporary France." Ph.D. dissertation, Cornell University, 2002.

Dufresne, David. *Yo! Révolution Rap: L'Histoire, Les Groupes, Le Mouvement*. Paris: Éditions Ramsay, 1991.

Fagyal, Zsuzsanna. "Syncope: De l'irrégularité rythmique dans la musique rap au dévoisement des voyelles dans la parole des adolescents dits 'des banlieues.'" *Nottingham French Studies* 46, no. 2 (2007): 119–34.

———. *Accents de banlieue: Aspects prosodiques du français populaire en contact avec les langues de l'immigration*. Paris: L'Harmattan, 2010.

Fassin, Eric. "'Good to Think': The American Reference in French Discourses of Immigration and Ethnicity." In *Multicultural Questions*, edited by Christian Joppke and Steven Lukes, 224–41. New York: Oxford University Press, 1999.

Génération Zulus. Interview with Mag 3 (Juan Massenya). Channel 5, 1991.

Green, Nancy. "*Le Melting-Pot*: Made in America, Produced in France." *Journal of American History* 86, no. 3 (1999): 1197–1213.

Grimes, William. "Traveling from France to Harlem to Study Rap Culture at Its Root." *The New York Times*, 18 November 1991, C11–C12.

Hargreaves, Alec. "A Deviant Construction: The French Media and the 'Banlieues.'" *New Community: Journal of the European Research Centre on Migration and Ethnic Relations* 22, no. 4 (1996): 607–18.

Heath, Anthony F., Catherine Rothon, and Elina Kilpi. "The Second Generation in Western Europe: Education, Unemployment, and Occupational Attainment." *Annual Review of Sociology* 34, no. 1 (2008): 211–35.

INA (Institut National de l'Audiovisuel). Midday News (1 p.m.), Antenne 2, 12 April 1990. Paris, France.

———. Evening News (7:30 p.m.), FR3, 12 April 1990. Paris, France.

———. Evening News (8 p.m.), TF1, 12 April 1990. Paris, France.

Kaufman, Michael T. "In a New Film, Spike Lee Tries to Do the Right Thing." *The New York Times*, 25 June 1989, H1.

Keaton, Trica Danielle. "The Politics of Race-Blindness: (Anti)Blackness and Category-Blindness in Contemporary France." *DuBois Review* 7, no. 1 (Spring 2010): 103–31.

Klein, Joe. "Spiked? Dinkins and *Do the Right Thing*." *New York Magazine*, 26 June 1989, 14.

Knight, Michael Muhammad. *The Five Percenters: Islam, Hip Hop, and the Gods of New York*. Oxford, UK: Oneworld, 2007.

Lacroix, Christophe ("TEXACO"). Interview with the author. 26 June 2008. Paris, France.

Lafargue de Grangeneuve, Loïc. *Politique du hip-hop: Action publique et cultures urbaines*. Toulouse: Presses Universitaires du Mirail, 2008.

Lang, Jack. "Jack Lang: Je crois à la culture rap." *VSD* 687, 31 October 1990, 41.

Lang, Jack, and Jean-Michel Helvig. *Demain comme hier: Conversations avec Jean-Michel Helvig*. Paris: Fayard, 2009.

Louis, Patrick, and Laurent Prinaz. *Skinheads, Taggers, Zulus & Co*. Paris: La Table Ronde, 1990.

Loupias, Bernard. "World Culture: Le dialogue à tout prix." *Le Nouvel Observateur*, 19 December 1991, 128.

Miyakawa, Felicia M. *Five Percenter Rap: God Hop's Music, Message, and Black Muslim Mission*. Bloomington: Indiana University Press, 2005.

Nuruddin, Yusuf. "The Five Percenters: A Teenage Nation of Gods and Earths." In *Muslim Communities in North America*, edited by Yvonne Yazbeck Haddad and Jane Idleman Smith, 109–32. Albany: State University of New York Press, 1994.

O'Connor, Kathleen Malone. "Alternative to 'Religion' in an African American Islamic Community: The Five Percent Nation of Gods and Earths." In *Introduction to New and Alternative Religions in America, Volume 5: African Diaspora Traditions and Other American Innovations*, edited by Eugene V. Gallagher and W. Michael Ashcraft, 23–58. Westport, CT: Greenwood Press, 2006.

Poirrier, Philippe. "French Cultural Policy in Question, 1981–2003." In *After the Deluge: New Perspectives on the Intellectual and Cultural History of Postwar France*, edited by Julian Bourg, 301–23. Lanham, MD: Lexington Books, 2004.

Sedel, Julie. *Les médias et la banlieue*. Paris: Le Bord de l'Eau, 2009.

Silberman, Roxane, and Irene Fournier. "Is French Society Truly Assimilative? Immigrant Parents and Offspring on the French Labour Market." In *Unequal Chances: Ethnic Minorities in Western Labour Markets*, edited by Anthony F. Heath and Sin Yi Cheung, 221–69. London: Oxford University Press, 2007.

Simon, Patrick. "France and the Unknown Second Generation: Preliminary Results on Social Mobility." *International Migration Review* 37, no. 4 (2003): 1091–1119.

Sotinel, Thomas. "Des Français en plein cœur de Harlem." *Le Monde*, 19 December 1991.

Spady, James G. Interview with the author. 14 August 2009. Philadelphia, PA.

Stovall, Tyler. "From Red Belt to Black Belt: Race, Class, and Urban Marginality in Twentieth-Century Paris." In *The Color of Liberty: Histories of Race in France*, edited by Sue Peabody and Tyler Stovall, 351–70. Durham, NC: Duke University Press, 2003.

Tissot, Sylvie. *L'État et les quartiers: Genèse d'une catégorie d'action publique*. Paris: Seuil, 2007.

———. "'French Suburbs': A New Problem or a New Approach to Social Exclusion?" *Center for European Studies Working Papers Series* 160 (2008).

Vallet, Louis-André, and Jean-Paul Caille. "Niveau en français et en mathématiques des élèves étrangers ou issus de l'immigration." *Économie et statistique* 293 (1999): 137–53.

Wacquant, Loïc J. D. "America as Social Dystopia: The Politics of Urban Disintegration, or the French Uses of the 'American Model.'" In *The Weight of the World: Social Suffering in Contemporary Society*, edited by Pierre Bourdieu et al., 130–39. Stanford, CA: Stanford University Press, 1999.

———. "French Working-Class *Banlieue* and Black American Ghetto: From Conflation to Comparison." *Qui Parle* 16, no. 2 (2007): 1–23.

DISCOGRAPHY AND FILMOGRAPHY

Do the Right Thing. Dir. Spike Lee. Universal Pictures. Originally released in 1989.

Grandmaster Flash and the Furious 5. "New York, New York." Sugar Hill Records, vinyl. Originally released in 1983.

Ministère AMER. *Traîtres*. Musidisc, compact disc. Originally released in 1991.

Public Enemy. "Fight the Power." *(Music From) Do the Right Thing*. Motown, vinyl. Originally released in 1989.

———. *Fear of a Black Planet*. Def Jam, compact disc. Originally released in 1990.

Shabazz, Lakim. *Black Is Back*. Tuff City Records, vinyl. Originally released in 1989.

Various Artists. *Rapattitude*. Labelle Noire/Virgin Music, compact disc. Originally released in 1990.

Chapter Four

Ghetto Patrimony

Rap and Racialization in France

Paul A. Silverstein

On 24 November 2005, French Minister of Justice Pascal Clément opened an investigation into seven rap groups accused of promoting "l'incivilité, ou pire le terrorisme" (incivility or, worse, terrorism) among France's "jeunes déracinés, deculturés" (uprooted, decultured youth). Clément's action responded to a petition, initiated by Gaullist deputy François Grosdidier and signed by nearly a quarter of the French Parliament, which came in the immediate aftermath of three weeks of violent confrontations between young residents of peri-urban *cités* or *quartiers populaires* (housing projects) and the French police, during which ten thousand cars were burned and some 4,800 young men arrested in 280 municipalities across the country.[1] The rappers cited in the petition were a motley collection of multiracial, hardcore artists, whose offending lyrics Grosdidier had unsystematically collected from the Internet with the help of his son. They included some artists (113 and Monsieur R) who were popular stars, others (Smala and Salif) who were less well known, and several (Fabe, Lunatic, and Ministère AMER) who had not performed in as many as ten years. What united them, according to Grosdidier, was their endorsement of "racisme anti-blanc" (anti-white racism) and "haine de la France" (hatred for France) (Kessous 2005).

While the petition was clearly an effort to identify scapegoats for the recent outer-city (*banlieue*) violence—with African immigrant polygamy also cited as to blame—the prosecution of French rap artists was not particularly new. Indeed, Ministère AMER had already in 1997 been found guilty of "provocation to murder" for their song "Sacrifice de poulets" (Chicken Sacrifice).[2] Monsieur R (Richard Makela) was at the time of the petition preparing for a civil case of pornography initiated by Gaullist deputy Daniel Mach

47

against the song "FranSSe"—which includes a rape fantasy in which France is presented as a *salope* (slut) whom one should not forget to "baiser jusqu'à l'épuiser" (screw to exhaustion) and whose music video includes images of sex acts performed with the French flag by two naked white women called "les Gauloises."[3] Earlier criminal cases had been brought in 1996 against the pioneer hardcore duo Suprême NTM,[4] in 2002 against Hamé (Mohamed Bourokba) of the group La Rumeur,[5] and in 2004 against the megapopular trio Sniper,[6] all for some version of public abuse, defamation, or incitement to violence against the national police. Their recordings have further been subject to periodic bans from the national airwaves, and in a number of instances, scheduled concerts had been canceled by conservative mayors.

What is particularly interesting about Grosdidier's petition, then, is not the threatened prosecution of the groups in question nor even the implication that their verbal violence abetted physical violence. Rather, it is its explicit racialization of the conflict in the accusation of "antiwhite racism" leveled at the rap artists. In so doing, the petition ironically deployed a language and ethic of antiracism to fight against rappers whose very political project is self-consciously antiracist: namely, to articulate the racial discrimination and institutional exclusion experienced by *cité* youth. This occupation of a racialized moral high ground dovetailed with the larger law-and-order attitude of then–Interior Minister Nicolas Sarkozy, who in 2003 threatened to prosecute Sniper on similar grounds, declaring their lyrics to be racist and anti-Semitic.[7] Sarkozy subsequently appointed Grosdidier his party's national secretary for integration, praising the latter for his work in breaking the taboo around the antiwhite racism of certain rappers (Kessous 2006).[8]

The appropriation of antiracist discourse by the French political right represents a significant shift in the ideological landscape in which race and space have become the contested grounds of the French nation. On the one hand, the move parallels an earlier tactic by xenophobic National Front leader Jean-Marie Le Pen, who in the 1980s redeployed the tentative multiculturalist vision of a "droit à la différence" (right to difference) within a "France plurielle" (pluralist France), as put forth by the Socialist Party and its client antiracist organization SOS-Racisme, to argue against integration and assimilation policies as injurious to immigrant (not to mention French) sacrosanct identity and thus morally repugnant.[9] The resulting reversion of antiracist organizations to a universalist discourse of a "droit à la ressemblance" (right to resemblance) within a putatively raceless France of individual citizens created the ideological trap sprung by Sarkozy and Grosdidier, according to which any discussion of discrimination qua racial discrimination is understood as reifying racial difference and thus potentially abetting sectarian *communautarisme* (communalism), if not racial hatred. Arguably, this tactic of ideological appropriation, alongside the growing security discourse and blame-the-victim orientation of recent French debates around immigration, urban exclusion, and Islamic practice, represents another example of the growing acceptance of National Front ideals by the French political main-stream—what is generally referred to in France as "la lépenisation des es-prits" (the LePenization of minds; Le Goaziou and Mucchielli 2006, 155).

On the other hand, the very use of a racialized language of whiteness in the petition follows Sarkozy's larger policy shift to an American model of neoliberal governmentality that combines elements of affirmative action (called in French *discrimination positive*), the privatization of state functions, and enhanced measures of domestic security—all of which have only in-creased in the wake of the 2008 financial crisis and the 2015 Paris attacks. In particular, Sarkozy, in his various political roles, has actively created official ethnic and religious interlocutors and sought to intervene in religious affairs, establishing an elected Conseil Français du Culte Musulman (CFCM, French Council of the Muslim Faith) in 2003, appointing a "Muslim prefect" in 2004, and in 2018 calling on theological authorities to convene an Islamic equivalent of Vatican II to render obsolete those verses of the Qur'an "call-ing for the punishment of Jews, Christians, and unbelievers."[10] These meas-ures indicate a partial shift from the treatment of the French polity as an undifferentiated group of commensurable citizens to its management and surveillance as a set of incommensurable, or even conflicting, communities. The denunciation of rappers (implicitly of color) as engaged in "antiwhite racism" reimagines the French nation along a racialized schema, with those of color required to continually prove their loyalty to France—a political imaginary previously decried as "Anglo-Saxon" and considered anathema to the French republican model of citizenship and *laïcité* (state secularism).

In what follows, I explore how French hardcore (or "gangsta") rap artists negotiate this shifting political and ideological landscape of race.[11] Drawing on a "ghettocentric" imaginary of local *cité* belonging via images largely appropriated from African American popular culture, these artists project both a microlocal identity and a transnational solidarity across "ghetto" spaces that simultaneously racialize *banlieue* space and spatialize French racial otherness for their multiracial and multiethnic listening publics who cannot be easily reduced to a bipolarity of blackness and whiteness.[12] From this ghettocentric subject position, rap artists engage in a vehement denuncia-tion of the lived conditions of social and economic exclusion in the *banlieue* housing projects, deploying lyrical, often sexualized violence as political critique. In the context of a history of violent confrontations with the police and the progressive securitization of the *quartiers populaires*, and in a situa-tion of ongoing marginalization from the formal political realm, the violence of words and deeds must be understood as an effort of direct political en-gagement (Kherfi and Le Goaziou 2006). The *caillera*[13]—the "social bandit" operating outside of the law (Hobsbawm 1959)—thus emerges as a recurrent proto-political figure that hardcore rappers ambivalently avow and disavow, often identifying with it allegorically (if not autobiographically) while be-moaning it as ultimately ineffective in promoting lasting social change. In the end, it is precisely this racialized, sexualized, and violently independent sub-ject—literally, the *racaille* (scum) whom Sarkozy claimed that he was going to "power wash" from the streets of France during the early days of the 2005 confrontations—who constitutes the abject figure of French republican fanta-sies of docile integration and raceless citizenship, as the constitutive outside for a postcolonial France.

THE POLITICAL ECONOMY OF FRENCH RAP

Recent criminal prosecutions and *affaires* appear at first blush to indicate a prolonged standoff between rap artists and the French state, a perpetual struggle between the voice and the sword. However, the history of French hip-hop points to as much collusion as conflict between professional rappers and state institutions. Indeed, the French state has consistently encouraged music, like sports, as part of its larger civilizing-cum-integrating mission to produce compliant immigrant and lower-class subjects, as a means to defuse the resistant politics of labor unionism or, in recent years, religious revival-ism.[14] Athletes and musicians are consistently promoted by state officials and the national media as idealized role models of "integration" into French bourgeois society and are severely chastised when their words and deeds do not match this preassigned role.[15] Their financial success and fame are de-ployed as the goals to which the *banlieue* youth should aspire, as the fulfill-ment of larger consumerist desires that, in the normative narrative, are achieved meritocratically through education, hard labor, and bodily training.

Since rap's explosion onto the French musical mainstream in the early 1990s, hip-hop artists have indeed become the heroes for many young *cité* residents, though as much for their performative rejection of the French "system" as for their material success, for their consistent refusal to play by the rules and their expected roles. Introduced to French audiences by a series of traveling New York shows from 1982 to 1984, the French hip-hop move-ment remained largely underground for the better part of the 1980s, relegated to either pirate radio stations or weekly shows of mainstream stations like the diminutive Radio Nova.[16] However, the genre quickly found fertile ground, both in the *banlieues*, where listening youth experienced firsthand parallels to the stories of the "street" and the "hood" told by African American rap-pers, as well as among a larger voyeuristic public attracted to the expressive artistic styles and the sensationalist visions of "ghetto" culture. If French break-dancers, graffiti artists, and deejays quickly improvised on themes imported from the United States, it was not until after 1991 that French MCs were able to break through the infrastructural and financial constraints of

musical production and cut the first albums where their rapping took precedence over the deejay's mixing and scratching. In the wake of the platinum
sales of MC Solaar's 1992 debut album, major multinational record companies like Sony, BMG, EMI, Barclay, and Warner recognized the commercial
viability of French rap and began to seek out new artists across the *banlieue*
landscape.

French state policies of neoliberal urban renewal largely encouraged this
corporate penetration of the postindustrial *banlieues* (Silverstein 2006,
292–95), and state protectionism of the French music market (with the 1994
Carignon Law setting radio air-play quotas of 40 percent for French musicians) ironically abetted the corporate colonization of *banlieue* space and the
commodification—and hence the increased visibility and profitability—of
lyrical "hate" (*haine*) directed against the state and its representatives.[17]
Since the mid-1990s, nearly every French hip-hop album, regardless of exact
musical style or degree of political consciousness of the performers, includes
at least one song that explicitly tackles questions of urban exclusion, discrimination, or police violence. In spite of the existence of parallel "cool" and
Sufi sub-genres, the general hardcore orientation has imposed certain musical limits on French hip-hop, with heavy beats and aggressive vocal flows
generally overpowering melodic progressions. Background samples and musical citations are largely taken either from other rap artists' tracks or from
other African diaspora musical genres, like jazz, funk, soul, R&B, and reggae.

The commercial pressures on French rap artists place them in a precarious
position whereby their successful commodification of symbolic violence,
resistance, and *caillera* life risks being taken as evidence of them having
"sold out." Many hardcore acts have entered complex sponsorship arrangements with sportswear and telecommunications companies to market, alongside the musical singles and albums, T-shirts and baseball caps emblazoned
with the groups' logos; DVDs of music videos, concert footage, or mini-
documentaries based on the musicians' lives; or cellular phone ring-tones
featuring excerpts from hit tracks. Advertisements for these cross-marketed
goods are featured in CD booklets, fanzines, and websites, the latter of which
generally provide portals for online shopping. Even the most politically conscious groups like NTM, Assassin, and La Rumeur—whose critiques of neo-
liberalism and money's general tendency to, in the words of NTM, rot people
("pourri[r] les gens")—have participated in similar merchandizing ventures
of self-commodification.[18]

However, these groups have not simply become clients of the large multinational corporations with whom they are contracted. Increasingly they have
engaged in what I have elsewhere termed "guerrilla capitalism" (Silverstein
2002, 52–54; 2006), in attempts to gain control of the production and marketing ends of the business through the establishment of their own localized

record labels, production cooperatives, and street-marketing companies. While these independent organizations are often affiliated with or distributed through major record companies, they nonetheless provide more lucrative profit-sharing opportunities for the artists in question, as well as for the ability to promote younger rappers' careers. Such ventures seal such younger rappers' positions within networks of patronage that go beyond legal obligations and bypass formal commercial arrangements, providing the means for flexible accumulation outside of organized corporate capitalism.

GHETTOCENTRICITY

Beyond the obvious financial gains, guerrilla capitalist ventures secure rapper authenticity and partially insulate them from accusations of having "sold out" insofar as they ally successful artists with recurrent figures of street lore: pimps, drug dealers, and other economic opportunists operating on the margins of legality. In general, the *caillera* persona has come to dominate the self-presentation of many male (and even some female) rappers, in terms of their autobiographical boasts; their dress; their gang-style poses and gestures; and the images and sounds of violence in their songs, videos, and cover art. The group 113, for instance, has serially represented itself in song as "marginal" figures "hors la loi" (outside the law) and "insoumis" (insubordinate and unbowed).[19] In general, rappers-cum-*cailleras* come to represent latter-day incarnations of the "social bandits" or "primitive rebels" whose genealogy Eric Hobsbawm has traced to moments of social breakdown.[20]

The figure par excellence in the rappers' rebellious self-fashioning is Jacques Mesrine, the iconic "public enemy number 1" of the 1960s and 1970s from the Parisian suburb of Clichy who perpetrated a series of spectacular bank robberies, kidnappings, and jailbreaks, before being killed by the police in questionable circumstances.[21] Mesrine has since become the object of a veritable cult in the *banlieues* and a frequent reference in song lyrics. Monsieur R even released a 2006 track ("Ennemi public #1") that features voice samples from prison interviews with Mesrine, thus creating a dialogue between rapper and bank robber as equally rebellious personae.[22]

Nonetheless, in spite of such repeated references, the *caillera* remains an ambivalent figure for French rappers. For instance, the Fonky Family's citation of Mesrine in their track "La furie et la foi" (Fury and Faith) occurs as part of a larger jeremiad against life in the *cités*, bemoaning the youth's hagiography of Mesrine as a role model (Fonky Family 1997). More generally, rappers since NTM have warned against the dangers of life on the streets, with even 113 explicitly rejecting thug life as a long-term project in "L'âge de meurtre" (The Age of Murder) on *Les Princes de la ville* (Princes of the City) from 2000. And yet, the need to embrace a bandit persona persists, particularly in light of the continued commercialization of hardcore rap. Indeed, rappers publicly deploy their censorship and court cases to further their polemical critique of the French state and to resolidify their own identity as musical rebels. Their comeback albums meticulously replay the history of their legal prosecution, including mock news reports from the trials or scripted interviews with journalists in which they relate their own versions of the cases.[23] Throughout, rappers accuse France of hypocritically disregarding its explicit liberal values of equal citizenship, for disproportionately policing and jailing French men and women of color. Moreover, they cite the prosecution and censorship to which they have been subject as further proof of their authenticity and legitimacy. They boast that they have come through the cases stronger than ever and unrepentant in their critique.

This situational—if ambivalent—alliance with the "street" and its boastful claims of guerrilla capitalist rapacity is supplemented by rap artists' ghettocentric orientation in their self-organization and symbolic economy and by their emphasis on local identification and action that transcends intervening diacritics of race, ethnicity, or religion. As with other hip-hop genres and urban art forms that have flourished in the French *quartiers populaires*—such as grafitti artistry and parkour freerunning—rappers have creatively appropriated the urban spaces in which they live and re-deployed them for athletic or aesthetic purposes.[24] They have engaged in what Michel de Certeau has termed "spatializing practices" (de Certeau 1984, 96), constructing alternate social totalities and subjectivities on the embers of built and dilapidated (sub)urban forms, endowing them with frameworks of value and hierarchy not necessarily isomorphic with those projected by the integration projects of the French nation-state. For de Certeau, such forms of appropriation amount to contemporary equivalents of "poaching," with rap artists making a living through the reinvention and reaestheticization of everyday *cité* life—living, as de Certeau would have it, "on the property of others" (de Certeau 1984, xii).

Elsewhere, I have discussed this reaestheticization of everyday *cité* life in terms of the organization of posses; graffiti tags; and the use of local imagery and identifiable figures in song lyrics, shout-outs, and album cover art (Silverstein 2002). What I am interested in here is the rappers' invocation of a common *cité* culture or "patrimoine du ghetto" (ghetto heritage) that takes immediate precedence over their sense of belonging to the French nation—a sense of belonging challenged on a quotidian basis by heavy-handed and discriminatory urban policing.[25] This identification is largely expressed through a gendered kinship idiom in which their age-mates are addressed as classificatory "brothers" and "sisters," and the larger *cité* community as their "family" or "clan."[26] The fraternity they invoke through this idiom is explicitly contrasted with the *fraternité* of the French national triptych that they depict as racist and hypocritical.[27]

Rappers repeatedly express solidarity with their "brothers" killed by police violence as well as with others who decide to take to the streets in (sometimes violent) protest. They promise to remember the struggles of their parents—"les années sanglantes" (the bloody years) of colonial violence, debilitating factory work, and wartime anti-immigrant violence—and vow to repay the blows that their parents received.[28] Finally, rappers hope for a future of "urban peace" and desire their children to grow up with greater life chances than those of their parents.[29]

In these ways, the invocation of familial belonging and community solidarity proposes local patriotism in the place of national identity. 113 refers to Vitry-sur-Seine as "ma patrie" (my country),[30] much as Assassin had claimed in the early 1990s about the 18th *arrondissement* of Paris.[31] And, yet, such hyperlocal infranationalism risks devolving into sectarian conflicts pitting individual families, gangs (*bandes*), and *cités* against their neighbors in battles over scarce resources, territorial control, local influence, or musical superiority. Aware of this potential, rap artists seek to transcend particularist identifications of race or space and envision a mode of ghettocentricity in which different urban experiences in the *cités* or *quartiers populaires* are treated as commensurable and the basis for a unity of struggle. They denounce the intra- and inter-*cité* violence that results from a hypertrophied localism. Monsieur R, for instance, evoked the ways in which xenophobia emerges from an overemphasis on consanguinity as the basis of society, as a preference for one's children over cousins and cousins over neighbors.[32] Fonky Family similarly condemned how protecting one's classificatory family can devolve into protracted violence.[33]

In response, rappers call for a recognition of the fundamental equivalence of the *cité* condition, often in performed collaborations between artists from different regions in which they shout out to their different constituencies and implicitly call for a transcendence of their differences. They evoke a commonality of socioeconomic condition, a singular class position that unites residents across the peri-urban landscape, regardless of particular neighborhood, religion, or ethno-racial background. Ultimately, they call for solidarity in the broader combat against the state.[34]

Furthermore, "le patrimoine du ghetto" is understood to transcend the spatial boundaries of France. Not surprisingly, the United States is particularly "good to think" (to use anthropologist Claude Lévi-Strauss's famous expression; 1963, 89) for French rappers attempting to find a vocabulary and musical style to express the conditions of life in the *quartiers populaires*, seeing in the history of African American struggle an important precedent for their own politics of resistance. Even rap prosody exhibits an American influence, with French iambs often replaced by English-style trochees in many rappers' staccato flows. Frequent collaborations between French and American artists invoke an "underground connection" that has endured since at least the 1920s, as Tyler Stovall, Samir Meghelli, and Hisham Aidi, among others, have chronicled.[35] African American writers, like James Baldwin, Ralph Ellison, Audre Lorde, and Richard Wright, have long served as explicit models for French men and women of color who began to pen their own quasi-autobiographical novels of social recognition during the early 1980s (Hargreaves 1991). Indeed, the history of the French civil rights movement— from the 1983 March for Equality and against Racism (colloquially known as the *Marche des Beurs*) through to the founding of the Indigènes de la République movement and political party in the wake of the 2005 urban uprisings—has been premised on 1960s black activism, with the former particularly drawing on the legacy of Martin Luther King Jr., and the latter, on Malcolm X and the Black Power militants.[36] Images of African American musical, political, and sporting figures are recurrent in filmic and musical self-representations of the *cités*, even as French rap artists simultaneously distance themselves from depictions of gang violence and racial nationalism associated with the American "ghetto."

The deployment of American imagery and invocation of a transatlantic hip-hop underground connection extends the spheres of fraternity in rap artists' pan-ghetto imaginary. In contrast, references to "Africa" are embedded in a discourse of *maternity*. If explicit Afrocentrism is rare, many artists do revalorize Africa through positive references to a "motherland" (*terre-mère*) that encompasses those of North African, West African, and Caribbean background.[37] More generally, French rappers borrow the language, symbolics, and stylistics of Rastafarianism, allegorizing France as "Babylon" and singing of the enduring effects of African colonial racism and violence.[38] Such invocations of a metaphorical Africa point to a larger racialized discourse of blackness that, while drawing on the intellectual heritage of *négritude*, does not reduce race to a singular black-white polarity.[39] Islamic motifs, in particular, supplement the African imagery of many rap groups, particularly those with Franco-Maghrebi members. The trials and tribulations of the artists are represented as a *hejira* (exodus), their destination as "Paradise," and the state officers who stand in their way as *Shaitan* (Satan).[40] The Islam invoked is directly consonant with Rastafari ideology, and indeed the two semio-religious systems are often found represented on the same tracks in almost seamless fashion.

In the end, the "Africa" in French rap denotes a flexible category of identity and orientation that resignifies blackness in terms of local spatial belonging and global "ghetto patrimony." Multiracial and multiethnic rap groups consistently mark their multiple belongings as being both white and black or black and Arab.[41] Kery James, a Franco-Antillean convert to Islam, while invoking his own black pride throughout his œuvre, explicitly imagines a form of racial unity beyond skin color.[42] The rap collective, Mafia K'1 Fry—whose name signifies "African Mafia" in *verlan* and whose logo is an outline of the African continent—includes artists of sub-Saharan African, North African, Caribbean, and European backgrounds and produces songs that invoke these different genealogical connections. What unites the various artists as members of the African Mafia, then, is not their origins but rather their unity of vision; their class position; and, above all, their residence in the southern suburbs of Paris. In other words, while French rappers clearly draw on and reproduce a black Atlantic, which Paul Gilroy has provocatively described as a "counterculture of modernity," the "double-consciousness" that they experience and express derives less from any notion of race as a naturalized set of somatic qualities than from their common *cité* upbringing and their cultural markers as *cailleras* (Gilroy 1993, 1–5). If Africa and African America are "good to think" for French hardcore rap groups, it is because they stand in for an imagined solidarity of racialized marginality.

CONCLUSION: POLITICS OF LOVE, POLITICS OF HATE

The inclusiveness of French hip-hop racial discourse goes largely unrecognized by French officials who find themselves the frequent object of rap artists' critique and who tend to respond by accusing the rappers themselves of inciting violence and "antiwhite racism." Nonetheless, insofar as hardcore rappers' ability to market racialized urban tensions has solidified their role as high-profile organic public intellectuals in the *quartiers populaires*, they have become de facto political actors. Increasingly, the rap artists' commodified dissent and calls for a transnational ghetto uprising to "burn Babylon" have been tempered by their self-positioning within a national frame, as French citizens of color, as the new *indigènes* (natives) of the republic, envisioned as a new generation of *sans-culottes* ready to storm the Bastille— imagery found in many rap albums since the 2005 "insurrection."[43]

In the end, this transformation of the racialized *caillera* into the modern *sans-culotte* delimits a hip-hop space of expressive politics in which an avowal of blackness or autochthony outlines a counterfraternity of those marginalized from the structures of racist nationalism and global (neo-)imperialism. In so doing, rap artists transform ideologies of racial particularity (whether Afrocentrism, Rastafarianism, or *négritude*) into symbolism of universal difference premised less on particular somatic features or cultural diacritics than on spatial and class positioning. By deploying these formulations through a masculinized rhetoric of allegorical violence against a racist state, they maintain authenticity and legitimacy both within their home neighborhoods and across the global hip-hop nation—all the while enjoying sustained commercial success.

In this respect, the accusations of "antiwhite hatred" leveled by Grosdidier and Sarkozy against hardcore rap artists need to be understood simultaneously as a concerted effort to displace blame for the failure of state civilizing/ integrating projects onto marginalized French men and women of color and their public intellectuals and as a purposive misrecognition of affective evocations of translocal solidarity ("love") as racial divisiveness ("hate").[44] Such accusations indicate a novel formulation of a racial counterrhetoric—what Sadri Khiari (2009) calls a "colonial counter-revolution"—that, while appropriating the language of universalism and antiracism, projects racialized peri-urban residents as a threat to national unity. In the end, such a mutual projection of the *caillera* as the abject subject of the French nation—as a new, postcolonial martial race—risks only perpetuating the securitization and criminalization of life in the *quartiers populaires*, on the one hand, and violent resistance to the "system," on the other. As Monsieur R warned in his 2000 hit "Quoi ma gueule" (What's the Problem with My Face), if the French police continue to treat French men and women of color as hoodlums, they will eventually put on their collective "cagoule" (hood).[45]

REFERENCES

Aïchoune, Farid, ed. *La Beur generation*. Paris: Sans Frontières/Éditions Arcantère, 1985.

Aidi, Hisham D. *Rebel Music: Race, Empire, and the New Muslim Youth Culture*. New York: Random House, 2014.

Balibar, Étienne. "Is There a 'Neo-Racism'?" In *Race, Nation, Class: Ambiguous Identities*, edited by Étienne Balibar and Immanuel Wallerstein, 17–28. New York: Verso, 1991.

Bancel, Nicolas, and Jean-Marc Gayman. *Du guerrier à l'athlète: Eléments d'histoire des pratiques corporelles*. Paris: PUF, 2002.

Bazin, Hugues. *La culture hip-hop*. Paris: Desclée de Brouwer, 1995.

Bloom, Peter J. "The State of French Cultural Exceptionalism: The 2005 Uprisings and the Politics of Visibility." In *Frenchness and the African Diaspora: Identity and Uprising in Contemporary France*, edited by Charles Tshimanga, Didier Gondola, and Peter J. Bloom, 227–47. Bloomington: Indiana University Press, 2009.

Bouamama, Saïd, Hadjila Sad-Saoud, and Mokhtar Djerdoubi. *Contribution à la mémoire des banlieues*. Paris: Éditions du Volga, 1994.

Boubeker, Ahmed, and Mogniss H. Abdallah. *Douce France: La saga du mouvement Beur*. Paris: Im'media, 1993.

Bouteldja, Houria, and Sadri Khiari. *Nous sommes les Indigènes de la République*. Paris: Éditions Amsterdam, 2012.

Cachin, Olivier. *L'offensive rap*. Paris: Gallimard/Découvertes, 1996.

Cannon, Steve. "Paname City Rapping: B-Boys in the *Banlieues* and Beyond." In *Post-Colonial Cultures in France*, edited by Alec G. Hargreaves and Mark McKinney, 150–66. London: Routledge, 1997.

Caussé, Bruno. "Zinedine Zidane, la légende ternie." *Le Monde*, 11 July 2006.

Certeau, Michel de. *The Practice of Everyday Life*. Translated by Steven Rendall. Berkeley: University of California Press, 1984.

Darby, Paul. *Africa, Football, and FIFA: Politics, Colonialism, and Resistance*. London: Frank Cass, 2002.

Dély, Renaud, and Gilles Renault. "NTM: 'La France, c'est flippant.' Musique, banlieue: les rappeurs parlent, une semaine après leur condamnation." *Libération*, 22 November 1996.

Derderian, Richard L. *North Africans in Contemporary France: Becoming Visible*. New York: Palgrave Macmillan, 2004.

Désir, Harlem. *Touche pas à mon pote*. Paris: Grasset, 1985.

Deville-Danthu, Bernadette. *Le Sport en noir et blanc: Du sport colonial au sport africain dans les anciens territoires français d'Afrique occidentale (1920–1965)*. Paris: L'Harmattan, 1997.

Dubois, Laurent. *Soccer Empire: The World Cup and the Future of France*. Berkeley: University of California Press, 2010.

Fassin, Didier. *Enforcing Order: An Ethnography of Urban Policing*. Cambridge, UK: Polity Press, 2013.

Gallissot, René. *Misère de l'antiracisme. Racisme et identité nationale: le défi de l'immigration*. Paris: Éditions Arcantère, 1985.

Gilroy, Paul. *The Black Atlantic: Modernity and Double Consciousness*. Cambridge, MA: Harvard University Press, 1993.

Gross, Joan, David McMurray, and Ted Swedenburg. "Arab Noise and Ramadan Nights: Raï, Rap, and Franco-Maghrebi Identity." *Diaspora* 3, no. 1 (Spring 1994): 3–39.

Guénif-Souilamas, Nacira. "Zidane: Portrait of the Artist as Political Avatar." In *Frenchness and the African Diaspora: Identity and Uprising in Contemporary France*, edited by Charles Tshimanga, Didier Gondola, and Peter J. Bloom, 205–26. Bloomington: Indiana University Press, 2009.

Hajjat, Abdellali. *La Marche pour l'égalité et contre le racisme*. Paris: Éditions Amsterdam, 2013.

Hargreaves, Alec G. *Voices from the North African Immigrant Community in France: Immigration and Identity in Beur Fiction*. New York: Berg, 1991.

———. *Immigration, "Race," and Ethnicity in Contemporary France*. London: Routledge, 1995.

Hélénon, Véronique. "Police: Rap Music in France and the Prosecution of Supreme NTM." *Black Renaissance/Renaissance Noire* 1, no. 3 (1998): 233–40.

Hobsbawm, Eric. *Primitive Rebels: Studies in Archaic Forms of Social Movement in the 19th and 20th Centuries*. New York: Praeger, 1959.

———. *Bandits*. New York: World Publishing Company, 1969.

Jobard, Fabien, and René Lévy. *Police et minorités visibles: Les contrôles d'identité à Paris*. New York: Open Society Institute, 2009.

Kelley, Robin D. G. "Kickin' Reality, Kickin' Ballistics: Gangsta Rap and Postindustrial Los Angeles." In *Droppin' Science: Critical Essays on Rap Music and Hip Hop Culture*, edited by William Eric Perkins, 117–58. Philadelphia: Temple University Press, 1996.

Kessous, Mustapha. "Des parlementaires réclament des poursuites contre des rappeurs." *Le Monde*, 24 November 2005.

———. "Les poursuites contre le rappeur Monsieur R. jugées irrecevables." *Le Monde*, 27 June 2006.

Kherfi, Yazid, and Véronique Le Goaziou. "Les émeutiers: entre violence et résignation." In *Quand les banlieues brûlent . . . Retour sur les émeutes de novembre 2005*, edited by Véronique Le Goaziou and Laurent Mucchielli, 87–97. Paris: La Découverte, 2006.

Khiari, Sadri. *La Contre-révolution coloniale en France: De de Gaulle à Sarkozy*. Paris: La Fabrique, 2009.

Krims, Adam. *Rap Music and the Poetics of Identity*. Cambridge, UK: Cambridge University Press, 2000.

Lapeyronnie, Didier. "Primitive Rebellion in the French *Banlieues*: On the Fall 2005 Riots." In *Frenchness and the African Diaspora: Identity and Uprising in Contemporary France*, edited by Charles Tshimanga, Didier Gondola, and Peter J. Bloom, 21–46. Bloomington: Indiana University Press, 2009.

Le Goaziou, Véronique, and Laurent Mucchielli, eds. *Quand les banlieues brûlent . . . Retour sur les émeutes de novembre 2005*. Paris: La Découverte, 2006.

Lévi-Strauss, Claude. *Totemism*. Translated by Rodney Needham. Boston: Beacon Press, 1963.

Mbembe, Achille. "The Republic and Its Beast: On the Riots in the French *Banlieues*." In *Frenchness and the African Diaspora: Identity and Uprising in Contemporary France*, edited by Charles Tshimanga, Didier Gondola, and Peter J. Bloom, 47–54. Bloomington: Indiana University Press, 2009.

Meghelli, Samir. "Returning to *The Source*, En Diaspora: Hip Hop in France." *ProudFlesh: A New Afrikan Journal of Culture, Politics, and Consciousness* 3 (2004): n.p.

Mesrine, Jacques. *L'instinct de mort*. Paris: JC Lattès, 1977.

Mucchielli, Laurent. "Le rap, tentative d'expression politique et de mobilisation collective des jeunes des quartiers relégués." *Mouvements: Sociétés, Politique, Culture* 3 (March–April 1999): 60–66.

Parti Socialiste. *La France au pluriel*. Paris: Éditions Entente, 1981.

Prévos, André J. M. "Hip-Hop, Rap, and Repression in France and the United States." *Popular Music and Society* 22, no. 2 (1998): 67–95.

———. "Postcolonial Popular Music in France: Rap Music and Hip-Hop Culture in the 1980s and 1990s." In *Global Noise: Rap and Hip-Hop outside the USA*, edited by Tony Mitchell, 39–56. Middletown, CT: Wesleyan University Press, 2001.

———. "Two Decades of Rap in France: Emergence, Developments, Prospects." In *Black, Blanc, Beur: Rap Music and Hip-Hop Culture in the Francophone World*, edited by Alain-Philippe Durand, 1–21. Lanham, MD: Scarecrow Press, 2002.

Silverstein, Paul A. "Sporting Faith: Islam, Soccer, and the French Nation-State." *Social Text* 18, no. 4 (2000): 25–53.

———. "'Why Are We Waiting to Start the Fire?': French Gangsta Rap and the Critique of State Capitalism." In *Black, Blanc, Beur: Rap Music and Hip-Hop Culture in the Francophone World*, edited by Alain-Philippe Durand, 45–67. Lanham, MD: Scarecrow Press, 2002.

———. *Algeria in France: Transpolitics, Race, and Nation*. Bloomington: Indiana University Press, 2004.

———. "Guerrilla Capitalism and Ghettocentric Cosmopolitanism on the French Urban Periphery." In *Frontiers of Capital: Ethnographic Reflections on the New Economy*, edited by Melissa S. Fisher and Gregory Downey, 282–304. Durham, NC: Duke University Press, 2006.

———. "Kabyle Immigrant Politics and Racialized Citizenship in France." In *Citizenship, Political Engagement, and Belonging: Immigrants in Europe and the United States*, edited by Deborah Reed-Danahay and Caroline B. Brettell, 23–42. New Brunswick, NJ: Rutgers University Press, 2008.

———. *Postcolonial France: Race, Islam, and the Future of the Republic*. London: Pluto Press, 2018.

———, "Sounds of Love and Hate: Sufi Rap, Ghetto Patrimony, and the Concrete Politics of the French Urban Periphery." In *Music, Sound, and Architecture in Islam*, edited by Michael Frishkopf and Federico Spinetti, 255–79. Austin: University of Texas Press, 2018.

Silverstein, Paul and Chantal Tetreault. "Urban Violence in France." *Middle East Report Online*, 15 November 2005. https://merip.org/2005/11/urban-violence-in-france/

Stovall, Tyler. *Paris Noir: African Americans in the City of Lights*. New York: Houghton Mifflin, 1996.

Swedenburg, Ted. "Homies in the 'Hood': Rap's Commodification of Insubordination." *New Formations* 18 (1992): 53–66.

Taguieff, Pierre-André. *Face au racisme*. Paris: La Découverte, 1991.

Tshimanga, Charles. "Let the Music Play: The African Diaspora, Popular Culture, and National Identity in Contemporary France." In *Frenchness and the African Diaspora: Identity and Uprising in Contemporary France*, edited by Charles Tshimanga, Didier Gondola, and Peter J. Bloom, 248–76. Bloomington: Indiana University Press, 2009.

Wacquant, Löic J. D. "Pour en finir avec le mythe des 'cités-ghettos': Les différences entre la France et les Etats-Unis." *Les Annales de la Recherche urbaine* 54 (1992): 21–30.

———. *Urban Outcasts: A Comparative Sociology of Advanced Marginality*. Cambridge, UK: Polity Press, 2008.

DISCOGRAPHY AND FILMOGRAPHY

113. *Ni barreaux, ni barrières, ni frontières.* Invasion Records, compact disc. Originally released in 1998.

———. *Les Princes de la ville.* Alariana/Double H/Sony, compact disc. Originally released in 1999.

Assassin. *Le Futur que nous réserve-t-il?* Delabel, compact disc. Originally released in 1992.

———. *L'Homocide volontaire.* Delabel, compact disc. Originally released in 1995.

Fonky Family. *Si Dieu veut . . .* Sony, compact disc. Originally released in 1998.

James, Kery. *Si c'était à refaire.* Warner, compact disc. Originally released in 2001.

James, Kery, and Mac Tyer. *Patrimoine du ghetto.* Xplosif/Musicast, compact disc. Originally released in 2005.

La Haine. Dir. Mathieu Kassovitz. Lazennec. Originally released in 1995.

La Rumeur. *Volet 2: Le Franc-tireur.* FUAS Music, compact disc. Originally released in 1998.

———. *L'Ombre sur la mesure.* La Rumeur/EMI, compact disc. Originally released in 2002.

Lunatic. *Mauvais œil.* Warner, compact disc. Originally released in 2000.

Ma 6-T va crack-er. Dir. Jean-François Richet. Actes Prolétariens. Originally released in 1997.

Mac Kregor, and Hematom Concept. *Insurrection.* Hematom Concept, compact disc. Originally released in 2006.

Mafia K'1 Fry. *La Cerise sur le ghetto.* Sony/EMI, compact disc. Originally released in 2003.

Malik, Abd Al. *Dante.* Polydor/Universal, compact disc. Originally released in 2008.

Mesrine: L'instinct de mort. Dir. Jean-François Richet. La Petite Reine. Originally released in 2008.

Mesrine: L'ennemi public N°1. Dir. Jean-François Richet. La Petite Reine. Originally released in 2008.

Ministère AMER. *95200.* Hostile/Delabel, compact disc. Originally released in 1994.

Monsieur R. *ANTICONstitutionnellement.* XIII BIS Records, compact disc. Originally released in 2000.

———. *Politikment incorrekt.* Diamond, compact disc. Originally released in 2005.

———. *Black Album.* Diamond/Nocturne, compact disc. Originally released in 2006.

Rockin' Squat and Supernatural. *Le Flow: The Definitive French Hip Hop Compilation.* Delabel, compact disc. Originally released in 1998.

Sinik. *Sang froid.* Six-O-Nine/Warner, compact disc. Originally released in 2006.

Sniper. *Du rire aux larmes.* Desh/Warner, compact disc. Originally released in 2001.

———. *Gravé dans la roche.* Desh/Warner, compact disc. Originally released in 2003.

———. *Trait pour trait.* Desh/Warner, compact disc. Originally released in 2006.

Suprême NTM. *Authentik.* Sony/Epic, compact disc. Originally released in 1991.

———. *J'appuie sur la gachette.* Sony/Epic, compact disc. Originally released in 1993.

———. *Paris sous les bombes.* Sony/Epic, compact disc. Originally released in 1995.

Trust. *Répression.* Epic/CBS Disques, vinyl. Originally released in 1980.

Various Artists, *Insurrection.* Hematom Concept, compact disc. Originally released in 2006.

———. *La Haine: Musiques inspirées du film.* Delabel, compact disc. Originally released in 1995.

———. *Le Flow: The French Hip Hop Avant-Garde.* Delabel, compact disc. Originally released in 1998.

———. *Urban Peace.* Barclay. Originally released in 2002.

———. *Patrimoine du ghetto.* Xplosif Music/Musicast, compact disc. Originally released in 2005.

———. *Sachons Dire Non.* Untouchable/EMI, compact disc. Originally released in 1998.

———. *Sachons Dire Non 2.* EMI, compact disc. Originally released in 2001.

Youssoupha. *NGRTD.* Bomayé Music, compact disc. Originally released in 2015.

An earlier version of this essay was published in French in James Cohen, Andrew J. Diamond, and Philippe Vervaecke (eds.), L'Atlantique multiracial: Discours, politiques, dénis *(Paris: Karthala, 2012), and parts were subsequently reproduced in Paul A. Silverstein,* Postcolonial France: Race, Islam, and the Future of the Republic *(London: Pluto, 2018). I am grateful to the publishers for permission to draw from this earlier work. Thanks to Hisham D. Aidi, Alain-Philippe Durand, and Olivier Esteves for helpful comments and suggestions on various versions.*

Chapter Five

Rap Music in Guadeloupe, an Overseas French Department in the Caribbean

1980s to the Early 2000s

Steve Gadet,
Translated by Richard J. Gray II

Within popular culture, rap and hip-hop are often confused. The terms represent two different realities, but they are frequently used interchangeably. For a better understanding of the issues that I discuss, it is good to recall that hip-hop culture is a mix of cultural elements, including rap; the visual arts, like graffiti and tag; the art of "deejaying," which consists of organizing and producing sounds with two or three vinyl turntables; and, lastly, the dance that is called breakdancing. Rap is an element of the mix. When I use these terms, it is to make reference to the two distinct realities, notably rap for music and hip-hop for the four cultural elements.

No current publications exist that properly address the presence of hip-hop culture in the West Indies, Guadeloupe in particular. It must be said at the outset that it is impossible for me to situate all the groups that have performed or that are operating in Guadeloupe in the limited space given to me here. I endeavor mainly to trace the arrival and principal components of rap in Guadeloupe between the 1980s and the beginning of the 2000s. There are many video and audio materials, as well as witnesses of its history but little writing on the subject. Between 2008 and 2011, I conducted a series of interviews with participants of the hip-hop culture of the West Indies. These interviews were held in Guadeloupe, Martinique, and metropolitan France. This chapter has also been supplemented by my experience as a rapper and producer since 1998. My understanding of the inner workings allowed me to approach other participants in an atmosphere of trust. I was thus able to obtain information firsthand. I could also identify what the uninitiated would not see and interpret it through the use of sociological tools.

Guadeloupe is located between the Dominica Island and the islands of Antigua and Barbuda in the north of the Lesser Antilles. Guadeloupe became a possession of France in 1635. In 1946, it was established as a French overseas department (DOM) at the same time as Martinique, La Réunion, and Guyana. These islands have, however, periodically and to this day, been rocked by independence, anticolonial, and autonomous movements.

HOW DID HIP-HOP CULTURE ARRIVE IN GUADELOUPE?

Many witnesses of the arrival of hip-hop in Guadeloupe have cited several consistent sources. The first is the program *H.I.P. H.O.P.*, broadcast in 1984 on French television channel TF1, presented by Sidney, the first black deejay of the French media landscape. This program was very popular and exposed France and the West Indies to hip-hop culture. It only lasted a year, but it made an impact, especially on young Guadeloupeans, who could pick up the cultural expressions contained in the program. It aired on Sundays at 2 p.m. A dancer and rapper himself, Sidney hosted the entire show via a rap flow. The guests featured on the show came from France and the United States. Dance steps were also taught to the television viewers, who, once the program had ended, scurried to try them with their friends. The seeds of the program fell on fertile soil in Guadeloupe: the imagination of young Guadeloupeans. These hip-hoppers began to experiment with rap and used dance moves to build their identities and their rapport with the world around them.

The first exchanges took place between friends, then, in a second period, within the popular locations of their places of residence. In Guadeloupe's largest city, Pointe-à-Pitre, Sécid Tower quickly became a primary gathering place, as did Champ d'Arbaud in Basse-Terre. The first official rap group to emerge in Guadeloupe was called The New Force, also known as TNF. Their MC and leader is Walker MC, Linaker is their "beat boxer," and DJ Spag presides at the turntables. In 1990, they self-produced *Hugo*, the first rap mixtape in Guadeloupe, evoking, among other themes, Hurricane Hugo that struck the island the preceding year.[1] Fans could obtain records in Pointe-à-Pitre at the Discorama store or in Basse-Terre at the shop of Henri Béville, who specialized in international music. Others had relatives who traveled worldwide and brought back records from their stopovers.

The first deejay in the history of Guadeloupean rap is DJ Kandia. He arrived on the music scene at the beginning of the 1980s. He is essential in the evolution of rap music and hip-hop culture in Guadeloupe for several reasons. He was one of the first to host a radio program dedicated to rap music. Hailing from Pointe-à-Pitre, he copresented a very famous, popular program on Kadans FM radio along with Eben, a young rapper who would later become a French rap figure. They broadcast rap music and welcomed artists in the studio. Another reason DJ Kandia is essential is because he was the first to set up musical activities in Pointe-à-Pitre at Sécid Tower, a legendary place for urban cultures in Guadeloupe.[2]

Other groundbreaking radio stations that started reserving special times for urban music are Radio Gayak and Bazin FM. With regard to the latter, Didier Tabor and Trafyk Jam are representative of the hosts. Beginning in 1989, Éclair FM provided a space of expression to rap music for Basse-Terre listeners. The program *Rap Éclair* was presented by Eben and Baby Bronx, a young Basse-Terrian hip-hopper. At times, Eben was at the turntables, and Bronx rapped. They broadcast music and received guests. Eben arrived from continental France with a particular interest in the media and the objective of using hip-hop to animate street and private parties. Young Guadeloupeans also fed their passion by listening to Radio Bis programs from Martinique. On Saturday evenings, the top program dedicated to rap, *Sunshine Mix*, was presented by Shakima and DJ Patpo. It was the most popular rap music broadcast in Martinique in the 1990s. Several local performers acknowledged during our interviews that they discovered rap music via this program. Furthermore, cassette recordings of Radio Nova, a Parisian radio station, fed the growth of rap in the West Indies. Some vacationers from continental France would bring new rap songs with them. Moreover, radio stations were not the only media that played a part in importing hip-hop culture and increasing its popularity in the French Caribbean. For instance, in Pointe-à-Pitre, American films that were shown at Cinéma Rex, such as *Beat Street* (1984), retraced rap's development and became a gateway into hip-hop culture for some. Those that happened to catch English-speaking television from Montserrat, a British island in the Caribbean, fed off of American clips, as well.

The first followers of hip-hop culture in Guadeloupe influenced nearly all modes of expression, namely rap, the visual arts, deejaying, and dance. As hip-hop culture started to broaden, an increasing number of street rivalries, foreign to the hip-hop community, began to break out. Thefts and holdups became common, intensifying tensions among individuals. In order to end this vicious circle, the so-called Big Brothers of the period, such as Groover, DJ Kandia, and Beef, organized a meeting against violence at the Sécid Tower. Resolutions were made, and free speech was encouraged. Since this now-famous gathering, the period of Carnival has become an annual date during which performers from the various urban cultures (rap, dance hall, graffiti, deejaying) meet and express themselves.

Thus, hip-hop culture spread out and took root in Guadeloupe. It continued to transform itself through gatherings in front of and within schools on the island. Friendships between participants consolidated new groups and fed competition. Some encounters were put together by the Office Municipal de la Culture et du Sport (OMCS, the Municipal Office of Culture and Sports) and similar organizations; others were spontaneous. What happened during these meetings? One of Guadeloupe's first hip-hoppers, Bronx MC, recalled in our interview that, at the beginning, there were many challenges between the dancers in the public space or at parties. The atmosphere was very competitive. As for the rappers, they willingly participated in singing competitions during community gatherings to try to be heard or to collect some tip money. Young hip-hoppers used to meet up at the old Raizet Airport or in the parking lot of the area supermarkets. Hip-hop became a true group phenomenon, and it spread in this way from person to person.

The 1990s marked a new turning point with an increase in media coverage of rap music, notably by way of leading radio program *Freestyle* on Radyo Tambou (105 FM). It quickly became the launching pad of other phases of rap in Guadeloupe.

THE RADYO TAMBOU ERA: *FREESTYLE* 105 FM

Between 1995 and 1997, Radyo Tambou became an inescapable reference for rap music in Guadeloupe. It is a radio station that, even if it clearly displays nationalist positions, does not consider young fans of hip-hop culture as simple imitators of American culture. The radio station management regarded these artists as young Guadeloupeans articulating the reality of the land in all its linguistic, social, and historical complexities. We owe this vision to the group Nèg Avan Tou, also known as NAT, who were entrusted with running and animating the program. Their philosophy and their motivation no doubt convinced the Radyo Tambou management to give them a space to express themselves. Several rappers and groups emerged via Radyo Tambou: Karukéra Crew (alias KC), N'O Clan (N'O), Lacroix City (LCC), Neg Zayann, De Tout Fason (DTF), Punany Clan, Le Tchò, Fanatyk (FNTK), and Khyla, to name only the most prominent.

According to several participants, the ambiance of the radio studio was very intense, even intimidating for those on the show for the first time. Some were not invited to return, as they did not have the needed assurance and composure to handle these live appearances. The group N'O Clan was the first to introduce battling on the show, what would become known as "clash culture" in French media and would strongly influence many young Guadeloupeans. N'O Clan was indeed one of the first groups to bring to the microphone the kind of street life and its brutality as they knew it, having grown up themselves in this kind of environment. Other groups, like KC, have inherited the more peaceful tradition of Zulu Nation, which saw in hip-hop an opportunity to promote love, peace, and fun.[3] Why? Quite simply to remain faithful to themselves, since the members of KC did not have the same upbringing as N'O Clan. For these young Guadeloupeans, hip-hop culture was, before all else, a way for rappers to write and recount their own lives. Radyo Tambou was the mandatory rite of passage for MCs. Consequently, nearly all those who ended up releasing albums went through Tambou, such as Karukéra Crew, Malkhéma, La Horde Noire (associated with Karukéra Crew), and NAT (which became Gwada Nostra).

If Riko Debs, the first producer and manager of a label devoted to rap in Guadeloupe, is indispensable for the development of this musical genre, the group NAT is crucial as well for its hosting of *Freestyle* 105 FM. For three years, their charisma, endurance, and organizational skills allowed them to successfully produce this radio program. Every Friday evening from seven to eleven, up to fifteen MCs would express themselves on a single microphone and two turntables. This included managing the animosity and misunderstandings that often occurred among those who direct or push forward new trends. The team was composed of four deejays (Malik, Budah, Roy, and Grego) and two deejays/rappers (Warner and Erka). The latter two acknowledged the influence of the first radio programs dedicated to urban music in Guadeloupe mentioned previously. The group NAT was formed in 1995 with its performers and another MC in the person of Toon. They took another deejay, Moody Mike, under their wing, who, in turn, would become a leading figure of hip-hop culture in Guadeloupe. Their message, "Neg Avan Tou" (Negro First and Foremost), clearly matched the editorial line of the radio station. Black people, the "negro," had to carry a message for their compatriots. As rappers, their message had to appear in the lyrics. But, as Guadeloupeans, their message also had to show in their actions. NAT drew from such revolutionary African American groups as Public Enemy. The question of identity was very important from the start. These young people were determined to assert themselves as blacks. They had the full support of the radio station management.

The radio program's hosts wanted to create a movement, not a trend. Graffiti artists, dancers, rappers, and deejays became associated with NAT. They were not just a rap group; they were hip-hop, representing all elements of the culture. Before thinking about a musical or artistic career, the rappers of the group were committed to denouncing certain injustices and to evoking the atmosphere and problems of the Pointe-à-Pitre neighborhoods they came from. The Tambou experience ended for several reasons, however, which led to artistic and logistic upheaval. With some leaving to pursue their studies while new members arrived from other groups, NAT was reborn as Gwada Nostra.[4] The loss of a rapper named Plucky also had an impact on the forming of a new group.

At the beginning of the 1990s, television station Canal 10 became the gateway for new rap developments, featuring recent clips and American programming. Another radio program emerged during the 1996–1997 season on La Une Radio, and lasted until 1999. It was called *Hip Hop Sessions*.

THE RECORD ERA

As early as 1996, an album lit the fuse of Creole rap and inspired certain creators in Guadeloupe: *Kimmannyèoupédimwenanbagaykonsapéfèt?!* (Howwasitpossibleforthistohappen?!), released by Rodolphe Richefal, also known as Nèg Lyrical, of Martinique.[5] For example, Fuckly, who enjoyed the first sales success of the Guadeloupean era of recorded rap, credits this album and a song by the group in which Richefal had first performed ("Pli ta pli tris" [Having the Last Laugh] by Lé Nèg ki pa ka fè la fèt) with greatly reassuring him in his use of the Creole language. Richefal and Lé Nèg ki pas ka fè la fèt were the first in the West Indies to do this and to disseminate it on the radio or through their albums.

Many other recordings soon followed. It is nearly impossible to mention them all here, but I can report on the creation dynamics of the initial projects, particularly those that opened doors for the rest. To do this, I now turn to the first structures that were founded to focus only on commercializing urban music. Without forgetting the 1990 TNF album that I mentioned earlier, the first record produced during this era to meet popular success outside of insider circles is *Mi La Sa Ka Bay* (Here's Where It's Happening), performed by La Horde Noire and produced by Riko Debs. The group's members— Daly, Tysmé, Darkman, Edinyo, and Sherkann—came from Abymes and Pointe-à-Pitre. The song that made them famous was the single that gave the album its title, "Mi La Sa Ka Bay." This rather festive song addresses a moment of relaxation that young Guadeloupeans are familiar with during the holiday season. This period is suitable for celebrations and outings with friends because it also signals the end of the school year and final exam results. After achieving hit status in the summer of 1998, in December it became the first Guadeloupean rap song to enter the video age, with a clip commissioned by the label Riko Rekords and produced by Jean-Luc Stanislas.[6] La Horde Noire's album became instantly popular and reached many Guadeloupean homes due to its audiovisual format. It was to be the first of a long series, the first rap clip of any origin that many in Guadeloupe had ever seen. The album consists of six songs and two interludes hosted by DJ Moody Mike. Previously, there had only been reggae or dance-hall albums, with no rap albums written from A to Z by Guadeloupeans. Sales were not considerable, but the critical success was great. The imagination of young Guadeloupeans deepened and broadened.

When La Horde Noire broke up for a variety of reasons, another artist took up revolutionizing rap music in Guadeloupe: Joseph Régis, also known as Fuckly. Unlike his predecessors, he was not a student and therefore had more time on his hands and became very talented. Riko Debs invested in the production of his album. Although he was initially part of a group, Fuckly quickly realized that a solo career would make the developing of a sound business operation more efficient for him. His first album, *Fuckly Is GGDN*, came out in June 1999.[7] Skud (alias Frédéric Caracas), a colleague of Fuckly's, and DJ Parrain of Black Label wrote the album. The recording and production took place in the famous Henry Debs studios in Pointe-à-Pitre, done by the master himself. Prior to the album's release, Debs alternated between doubt and boldness, confidence and fear, as to the kind of reception this work would get. While the album was a great success with young listeners, its sexist lyrics were strongly criticized by older generations. That said, the media went along with the release, and Fuckly's career took off from Pointe-à-Pitre to Paris and Marseille, with the album selling close to eighteen thousand copies. Fuckly's next album, *L'indiscipliné* (The Undisciplined), was equally successful and sold just under nineteen thousand copies. Several of its singles—"La bande à GG" (GG's Gang), "Batmania," and "An ni marre" (Fed Up), for example—have marked the history of Guadeloupean rap. To this day, they remain the best-selling rap albums of the West Indies. Fuckly was one of the most original and dynamic creators of his time. He gave another direction and stature to Guadeloupean rap by making it popular in spite of his subversive and untenable side. It is, in fact, this part of his personality that permitted him to put himself behind a microphone and on-stage.

The production of mixtapes and local albums exploded. After Gwada Nostra's first album, *Pur Hip-Hop Gwada* (Pure Guade Hip-Hop) in 2001, N'O Clan's *N'Othérapie* (N'Otherapy) and Karukéra Crew's *Wòch goumé a vié nèg* (Throwing Rocks, the Art of Combat for Old Negroes) came out in 2002. Darkman followed with the album *Darky le jour, Darkman la nuit* (Darky by Day, Darkman by Night) in 2003 and many more.

At that juncture, however, the arrival of CD burners on the market intervened, cutting record sales in half. Selling compact discs became more difficult, especially when the target public was young and did not have sizable purchasing power. During these initial record experiments, Riko benefitted from the moral and logistic support of his now-deceased father, Henri. Riko, though, always handled the artistic and marketing choices on his own. Artist tours from the label took place on the islands of Guadeloupe, Martinique, and Saint-Martin and in metropolitan France. Urban media outlets welcomed these hip-hop artists, but musically speaking, the general public had a tendency to perceive Guadeloupe as being primarily the land of zouk and reggae/dance hall. As if the industry problems caused by CD-burner technology were not enough, the advent of the Internet gave urban music sales another major setback, as young French citizens with little disposable income were now able to freely and illegaly download and enjoy their favorite tracks.

None of the official productions extinguished or tempered the self-pro-duced output. Rap is known for its creativity, and its artists are known for their great ability to produce new songs and new concepts. It is a music that responds to the spirit of the times, to the social climate. Thus, it is often a step ahead of the game. Deejays like Moody Mike, Gunshot, or Parrain are important because they energized the local Guadeloupean rap scene by mak-ing mixtapes, producing themselves on the radio, and organizing rap venues. Some artists, like the group N'O Clan, before being affiliated with the Debs label, already had what one calls in hip-hop jargon "underground produc-tions," and that continued even after they were contracted. Some artists—Gwada Nostra and Karukéra Crew, for instance—set up their own structures.

État de siège (State of Siege, 1999) was the first compilation of Guade-loupean rap, gathering Guadeloupean authors from different parts of the island. Among others, it uncovered a second generation of rappers who had remained in the shadows of the first generation's success and were inspired by them. Rudy Séverin, the son of the local cultural figure Max Séverin and a good friend of Henri Debs, established his label, Touloulou Records, with which he went on to produce such rap artists as Khyla. The rap generation from Basse-Terre renewed itself during the second half of the 1990s around such leading groups as Da Fann Tchou, consisting of several rappers and a deejay in the person of DJ Gunshot.

After the radio and record eras came the age of video clips and the Internet. They increased in number at the dawn of 2000 and were produced and used as promotional support. Radio stations lost their leading role in introducing and creating new hip-hop trends. Nevertheless, radio remained an important medium for transmitting songs. During this era of Guadelou-pean rap, three radio programs, all hosted by Brother Jimmy, were key in making the productions of Guadeloupean rappers known but also in introduc-ing American rap into Guadeloupean homes. *Big Up* began in 1996 on Canal 10 and lasted approximately two years. *Réyèl Attitude* (Real Attitude) and *Réyèl an mouv'man* (The Movement of the Real) became popular platforms for young rappers and Guadeloupean deejays on RFO between 1998 and 2000. From the end of the 1990s, an increase in popularity of the reggae/dance-hall movement downgraded rap to secondary importance, despite the fact that some of the leading reggae/dance-hall artists had first expressed themselves through rap music. This period also marked the emergence of artists like Admiral T and the group Karukéra Sound System (KSS).

RAP AND LOCAL CULTURE

Globalization does not prevent any culture from being geographically unique or socially identified. In the construction of cultural identities around products of popular culture manufactured and sold by European American cultural industries, an interaction exists between local and global forces. In my interviews with Guadeloupean rappers, songwriters, and deejays, many of them told me of their desire to participate in the rise of a Guadeloupean rap, a form open to the world but rooted in local cultural specificities. Since the beginning of the 1990s, members of the Karukéra Crew have expressed interest in making a "return to themselves." They wanted Guadeloupean rap "to sound" Guadeloupean so that it would not simply be like rap from Paris or the Bronx. Others did it spontaneously in several ways: by using the Creole language; by describing their reality in Creole or in French; and, finally, by drawing from their local musical heritage to create rap compositions. This last dynamic gave birth to a movement henceforth recognized here and elsewhere as *Kako mizik* (Kako music). It was founded by Christophe Sophy (a.k.a., Exxòs) and sustained by other artist/producers including DJ Phonie or such singers as Tysmé and Dominik Coco or even G'Ny. This musical dynamic is part of an ideological wave theorized through the concept of "global culture" that recognizes the importance of two cultural forces: the local and the global. Numerous record and stage collaborations also took place between artists from the rap scene and those coming from dance halls, zouk stages, or even *Gwo-Ka* of Guadeloupean folk traditions. Projects, such as Dub n'ka, united *Gwo-Ka* musicians and rap artists. Performers, such as Kassav's founder, Pierre Décimus, or even pillars of the *Gwo-Ka* state like Eric Cosaque, Joby Bourguignon, and Michel Halley, worked within this perspective, as well. Some Guadeloupean rap artists, such as Fuckly, perhaps because of his origins, have naturally been influenced by and have composed from Haitian compas (or Kompa) songs.[8] These experiences multiplied and are still in progress as I write these lines. Dynamics like these are the ways for Guadeloupean rap to distinguish itself from other urban music in the world, particularly that of France and the United States.

Guadeloupean rap managed to be exported in several ways. Some Guadeloupean artists, such as Fuckly, Darkman, Sista Flo, or DJ Gunshot, had the chance to tour off the island, in France, Africa, the United States, Canada, or on neighboring Caribbean islands.

Another way to promote Guadeloupean rap was through the great creativity of Paris-based artists of West Indian origin. Like in the American rap scene (e.g., Kool Herc), many artists coming from the West Indies were among the most remarkable innovators of rap music in France. Here, I am thinking of Kery James, Doc Gynéco, Eben of 2bal 2neg', Joey Starr of NTM, or even Casey. Since the early 1960s, a great number of young West

Indians were pushed toward metropolitan France. Emigration became the only solution to secure a better tomorrow and flee endemic unemployment on the islands. From this emigration, generations of West Indian children were born or arrived very young in continental France. Other Guadeloupean artists, by their Caribbean heritage, left for the United States and settled into the Anglophone and Creolophone scenes. Artists, such as Sista Flo in Florida or even Fugitif Shemshey in New York, managed to make their music known and shared within these regions. They rap in Creole and/or in English and act as ambassadors for their regions. For Sista Flo, a natural bridge was established between her and the Haitian and Creolophone rap scene. A last example is the initiative led by a Guadeloupean rapper and activist named Duspee, who opened another window to Guadeloupean rap via the website hip-hopcarib1.com, which launched at the beginning of the 2000s and provided links to the participants of rap in Antilles-Guyana, Cuba, and Haiti.[9]

THEMES AND GROUPS

The themes that one finds in Guadeloupean rap are as varied as the facets of Guadeloupean society, with its different ethnic communities; social, political, and economic realities; cultural heritage; pathways; and identity struggles, as well as problems with its youth. Themes range from male-female relations to the ability to flaunt one's dexterity to the social realities of the island. The beginning of the 2000s also witnessed the emergence in Guadeloupe of religious rap, performed live and anchored in protestant Christian faith, as exemplified by the group Benaja. Café and Fola, two young rappers from Morne-à-l'Eau, found a place to put forward societal Christian music. After 2005, the crunk wave from Atlanta had Guadeloupean representatives in Dawa and Shaolin Jutsu. During that time, as topics pertaining to the preoccupations of young people living in the street gained attention, the images used to communicate these themes affected the sensibility of a large part of the population, on the one hand, and stirred up unease in the rap community, on the other. The trap music wave with its parade of materialism, sexism, and glorification of robbery and cocaine deals left no one indifferent. Groups such as Section Kriminel, Chienlari, or Dogside, have repeatedly, and for a variety of reasons, made the news. They show a frightening face of Guadeloupe that one cannot ignore if the hope is to eventually fix the societal problems and violence they are denouncing.

Another activity specific to rap is known as *clash* in Guadeloupe (and the rest of France) and *battle* in the United States. It is a verbal confrontation that opposes two rappers or groups of rappers. Rap is an art in which the ego plays a primordial role. The ability to present oneself, to promote oneself, and to defend oneself is crucial. The history of Guadeloupean rap is obviously interspersed with these competitions, but what marked the memory of young Guadeloupean hip-hoppers was the one at the end of the 1990s that saw the group Underground Family pitted against the N'O Clan.[10] Guadeloupean women rappers brought very specific topics with respect to the lives of West Indian women. Artists like Flo and Khyla evoke their femininity, artistic qualities, and attachment to the homeland, as well as motherhood and what they hope to bring with their art. The beginning of the 2000s saw the appearance of a third and fourth generation of rap artists in Guadeloupe. These performers extensively worked their relationship with the public and their exposure on the Internet, social media, and original video clips. Young Chang MC, Miky Débrouya, NDX, Nerka Carter, or even Kid MC stand out among the many new faces during this period.

RAP AND GENDER

For several years after the launching of hip-hop in Guadeloupe, no female rappers were known. It was not until the arrival of Amélie Tintin (a.k.a., Khyla) in the 1990s that a female voice was heard for the first time. Khyla's distinctive feature is that she had to struggle for a long time to express her femininity on the microphone because the male-centric environment of hip-hop did not allow these two universes to go together. She was born in Créteil, in the Paris suburbs, and arrived in Guadeloupe with her father at the age of nine. As a young girl, she was exposed to very difficult life situations, which only pushed her more toward writing and rap. While in high school, she rubbed elbows with local rappers who invited her to the famous sessions of Radyo Tambou. Having made several key connections, she was soon able to share her art with more and more people onstage and on the radio and eventually to produce an album and singles. Her first appearance on Radyo Tambou's *Freestyle* was the symbol of a female stepping onto the turf of a macho universe. The rare women found in the studio were usually friends of rappers. When they found out that Khyla had come to rap, some of the rappers present in the studio immediately attacked her on the microphone. Far from being intimidated, with her rapper reflexes well established, Khyla immediately responded in brutal fashion. From then on, she earned her reputation for excellence and respect on the Guadeloupean rap scene. Moreover, she paved the way for other female rappers, such as Sista Flo. Her first recording took place in 1999 with the album entitled *Féminin au Mic . . .* (Female on the Mic . . .). By her own account, she worked for several years to strike the right balance between her femininity and the toughness that rap sometimes requires.

Sista Flo has a different personality. She began in 1996, then left the island to study in continental France, before moving to the United States. She settled first in Orlando, Florida, in 2001, followed by a move to Miami in 2004. She raps in Creole and is involved with the region's Creolophone Haitian scene. In 2007, being surrounded by Anglophones, she felt the need to rap in English in order to reach her audience but did not reject any of the eclectic themes that came to her mind (social problems, Caribbean culture, meditations, festive topics, and the state of Africa today). Her rationale with representing Africa was to claim her own *créolité* within her dialect, her clothing, and as an unofficial cultural ambassador. Since 2001, she has produced several projects that have been distributed in the United States, France, and the West Indies. There are still very few women in Guadeloupean rap, but they are more numerous among breakers, managers, and members of hip-hop associations.

RAP AND ECONOMICS

During the 1980s, rap artists earned money in singing competitions on the occasion of holiday celebrations. At the end of the 1990s, thanks to Riko Debs's record label, the rap music economy in Guadeloupe became more structured. However, due to the impact of the Internet, economic yields dropped considerably for artists, all the more so as popular rap successes were less numerous. The means for generating revenue were limited to live concerts and other performances; SACEM rights; and, to a lesser extent, album sales.[11] Few artists succeeded in making a living from their art, with the exception of Fuckly, who seems to have been the only one to have played his cards right.

CONCLUSION

As this chapter demonstrates, rap is henceforth part of the Guadeloupean musical heritage; it is not a genre that systematically destroys local culture. It created forms influenced by local traditions thanks to creators who understood one essential thing: It is by creating with our uniqueness and our originality that we enrich the world. As I write these lines, the community spirit of rap and of hip-hop culture in general have become almost nonexistent. This music is lived mainly on the Internet and is becoming rare in public spaces. Those who want to know what the Guadeloupean youth think as well as the great upheavals that the island is experiencing can find answers by listening to local rap. This music provides a summary of societal health. It rejects no temperature; it measures the highest and the lowest. It shows the beautiful and the ugly, the constructive and the destructive.

It played and continues to play a role in the construction of Guadeloupean society and identity. Its future is in the hands of creators and institutions.

Festivals took place in the 2000s to gather its participants. More and more specialized educators use Hip-Hop Based Education because it can play a socio-professional insertion role. It is also in the Creolophone zones of the Americas, as well as in the Francophone areas of the world. Between tradition and modernity, between the global and the local, between the street and the school, Guadeloupean rap still has fine days ahead of it.[12]

DISCOGRAPHY AND FILMOGRAPHY

Admiral T. *Mozaik Kreyol*. Universal Music, compact disc. Originally released in 2003.

———. *Toucher l'horizon*. Universal Music, compact disc. Originally released in 2006.

Beat Street. Dir. Stan Lathan. MGM. Originally released in 1984.

Chienlari. *CLR for Life*. Chienlari Prod. Originally released in 2009.

Darkman. *Darky le jour, Darkman la nuit.* Riko Rekords, compact disc. Originally released in 2003.

Dogside. *Fuckin Dogside*. Dogside Music Group, mixtape. Originally released in 2015.

Dominik Coco. *Lakou Zaboka Project*. Koumbeat Production, compact disc. Originally released in 2003.

FLO. *Aflowdiziak*. X of TDP, compact disc. Originally released in 2001.

———. *The Lost Flows*. Gwadayouth Entertainment, mixtape. Originally released in 2005.

———. *A Long Time Coming*. Flomedia LLC, streaming. Originally released in 2018.

Fuckly. *Fuckly Is GGDN*. Riko Rekords, compact disc. Originally released in 1999.

———. *L'indiscipliné*. Riko Rekords, compact disc. Originally released in 2001.

G'Ny. *Libèté*. Lusafrica, compact disc. Originally released in 2015.

Gwada Nostra. *Pur Hip-Hop Gwada*. Caraïbe Musik Productions, compact disc. Originally released in 2001.

———. *Gwada Nostra*. Nostrategy, compact disc. Originally released in 2003.

Karukéra Sound System. *Rapide*. Groove Magazine France, compact disc. Originally released in 1998.

Kassav. *An ba chenn'la*. GD Productions, vinyl. Originally released in 1985.

———. *Vini Pou*. CBS, compact disc. Originally released in 1987.

———. *Majestik Zouk*. Columbia, compact disc. Originally released in 1989.

Khyla. *Féminin au Mic . . .* Alizés Records, compact disc. Originally released in 1999.

La Horde Noire. *Mi La Sa Ka Bay*. No Test Corporation, compact disc. Originally released in 1998.

Lé Nèg ki pa ka fè la fèt. "Pli ta pli tris." Dancehall Party: Rap & Ragga. Hibiscus Records, compact disc. Originally released in 1994.

Miky Débrouya. *Debrouya I Pop*. Miky Débrouya, streaming. Originally released in 2010.

NDX. *Paperboy*. Julien Canourgues, streaming. Originally released in 2013.

Nèg Lyrical. *Kimmannyèoupédimwenanbagay Konsapéfèt*. Déclic Communication, compact disc. Originally released in 1996.

Neg Zayann. *Révélation*. FM Mizik, compact disc. Originally released in 2007.

Nerka Carter. *Ipop4life*. OD2H-Prod, streaming. Originally released in 2011.

N'O Clan. *Lori6 zoo*. Riko Rekords, compact disc. Originally released in 2000.

Star Jee and Exxòs (Karukéra Crew). *Wòch goumé a vié nèg*. F.W.I. Sons Productions, compact disc. Originally released in 2002.

Young Chang. *100 Zanmi*. Genesiz, compact disc. Originally released in 2006.

Chapter Six

French Rapper-Writers and Activism

Global Black Solidarity and (In)Visibility

Stève Puig

The 1990s are often seen as the golden age for hip-hop in the United States but also in France, where groups like NTM, IAM, and Ministère AMER became references for an entire generation of rap aficionados.[1] Since the beginning of the twenty-first century, the decline of the music industry as well as the rise of new media have pushed artists to diversify and to use different platforms to reach a broader (and perhaps different) audience. Considering the literary tradition in France and the fact that rap music is largely based on rhymes and plays on words, it is not entirely surprising that some rappers have ventured into the publishing industry. Whether these books are autobiographies, traditional novels, or poetic texts that have also been released as songs, they often tend to express the artists' points of view on contemporary politics and seek to change the perception of the French *banlieues* that have become more and more of a cultural nexus since the 1980s.[2] Many of these rapper-writers include references to African American leaders like Malcolm X, Martin Luther King Jr., or other civil rights champions in their work—whether written or spoken—and strive to keep the memory of these leaders alive in various ways. The presence of these leaders in urban French culture is also a sign of growing discontent over the treatment of the Afro-Caribbean community, particularly regarding their lack of representation in politics and in the media.

In his song about French colonialism and national history entitled "Des problèmes de mémoire" (Memory Problems), French Algerian rapper Rocé sings that France has memory problems; that French people know who Malcolm X is but not the FLN; and that they know more about African American culture than Afro-French culture, which indicates that the fascination for

African American icons potentially makes the presence of Francophone African or French Caribbean artists or thinkers even more impalpable in French culture. Basing my reflection on the idea developed by Rocé about French people "knowing about Malcolm X but not Frantz Fanon," I analyze in this chapter the significance of these two African American leaders— Malcolm X and Martin Luther King Jr.—as a source of inspiration for many French rapper-writers, as well as more generally speak about the growing solidarity in France for the injustices that African Americans face today in the United States.[3] Indeed, the popularity of movements like Black Lives Matter in France seems to reinforce the idea of a global black solidarity (arguably initiated by exchanges between French Afro-Caribbean writers during the Harlem Renaissance and beyond), but one can wonder if the numerous allusions to African American leaders like Martin Luther King Jr. or Malcolm X by such rapper-writers as Disiz, Abd Al Malik, or Axiom do not contribute to make the fight by and for Afro-Caribbeans in France even more invisible.

MARTIN LUTHER KING JR. AND MALCOLM X IN FRANCE

Martin Luther King Jr. (1929–1968) and Malcolm X (1925–1965) remain two of the most iconic leaders of civil rights in the United States, the latter often being perceived as generally more radical than the former. Both leaders were a source of inspiration for African and Caribbean communities in France during the civil rights movement of the 1960s and remain icons in the fight for equality in contemporary France as well as in the French-speaking world.

Both went to France to deliver speeches encouraging racial equality and solidarity within the Afro-Caribbean community, their visits sometimes perceived by French officials as a threat. On February 9, 1965, French authorities prevented Malcolm X from entering the French territory where he was supposed to talk to the Afro-Caribbean community. As he was arriving at Orly Airport from London, Malcolm X was told his presence was deemed "undesirable," and later on, a Ministry of the Interior spokesman declared that his conference could "provoke demonstrations that would trouble the public order" (Anonymous 2015). In his talk, Malcolm X intended to evoke the possibility of a black international movement that would include African Americans as well as French people of African or Caribbean descent in France. In one of his last speeches, the leader evoked the problems faced by black communities in England and in France, stating, "France, quietly as it is kept, has a very serious color problem developing because of the migration to France of our people from the French West Indies. . . . The only difference over there and over here being that no one of black skin in France has ever tried to unite the dark-skinned people together" (Malcolm X 2019). Malcolm X was well aware that black leadership was comparatively lacking in Europe and that he could potentially provide some inspiration for black communities in France. French authorities' fear was also tangible in the case of Martin Luther King Jr., under scrutiny as well during his trip to France (Bordenave 2018). In March 1966, for instance, he visited the town of Lyon, where he talked about discrimination in the United States and solidified his status as a champion of racial equality for the French. In 2009, on the anniversary of King's assassination, Lyon's mayor dedicated a wooded space to King in Parc de la Tête d'Or, and in 2011, the city inaugurated a bust in Place Eugène Varlin, a square where he spoke in the 1960s (Anonymous 2011). To commemorate the fiftieth anniversary of King's assassination, Lyon's public library has organized an exhibit called "Martin Luther King, the Broken Dream?" ("Martin Luther King, le rêve brisé?" Bibliothèque Municipale de Lyon, 2018) that explores civil rights history, King's life and work, and his visit to the city. The exhibit features concerts and discussions on contemporary American civil rights activists, and yet one wonders if this kind of celebration could ever be possible for France's own African or French Caribbean activists. When Barack Obama was elected president of the United States in 2008, many wondered if France could potentially vote for a black president (Anonymous 2008), and in 2015, a radio show asked the following question: Does France need a Martin Luther King Jr.? (Elzas 2015).

It has been argued that rap became the vehicle for black activism after the deaths of Malcolm X and Martin Luther King Jr. (Newkirk 2018) and that this new musical genre emerging from New York was a platform to discuss the struggles of the African American community. Some rappers were more inspired by Malcolm X's spiritual stage and his pilgrimage to Mecca, while others were more interested in his political activism. In truth, it is safe to say that Malcolm X represented all these things and that his assassination, at the age of thirty-nine, created a void that continues to lend itself to many different interpretations of the black leader's legacy. Indeed, Malcolm X has been the subject of several biographies—some of them very controversial, like Manning Marable's *Malcolm X: A Life of Reinvention*—and many songs, mostly in hip-hop, which contributed to the creation of a quasi-mythical figure. In a sense, it is hip-hop and movies that have made Malcolm X an icon in urban culture, and for many French rappers, the movie adaptation of *The Autobiography of Malcolm X* by Spike Lee or songs by Public Enemy were the first occasion to learn about Malcolm X.[4]

MARTIN LUTHER KING JR. AND
MALCOLM X IN URBAN LITERATURE

Urban culture in France can be defined as a culture emerging mostly in and around Paris and a mix of elements from the United States—especially African American culture—and from the postcolonial world. Urban music, for instance, often mixes elements of American hip-hop, *raï* or Caribbean, as well as traditional French music. In their volume *Post-Migratory Cultures in Postcolonial France*, Kathryn Kleppinger and Laura Reeck consider urban culture in France as a postmigratory culture that has become a field of study that "falls between French and Francophone studies" (2018, 10). Urban literature is largely the product of the children (or grandchildren) of immigrants who live in the outskirts of Paris and who have been influenced by the hip-hop movement that first had an impact in France in the mid-1980s. Owing to the importance of literature in French culture, there is a strong connection between the world of letters and rap in France, as many rappers can be seen as modern poets or "chansonniers," like Georges Brassens, whose iconic song "Le gorille" (The Gorilla) was covered by rapper Joey Starr on his album *Gare au jaguarr* (Beware of the Jaguar). As Bettina Ghio shows in her work *Sans fautes de frappe* (2016), the connections between literature and rap in France are many, and the French classics are often a source of inspiration for rappers. I have shown elsewhere (Puig 2018) the importance of rapper-writers like Abd Al Malik or Disiz, who have both published books in addition to their musical production. Other rappers, like Akhenaton from IAM, Passi from Ministère AMER, ROST, Oxmo Puccino, Joey Starr, Soprano, and many more, have published books that mostly fall into four categories: the autobiographical book or memoirs, like La Rumeur's *Il y a toujours un lendemain* (There Is Always a Tomorrow) or ROST's *Enfant des lieux bannis* (Child of Banished Places); political fiction, like Abd Al Malik's *L'Islam au secours de la République* (Islam to the Rescue of the Republic) or Disiz's *René*; essays like Axiom's *J'ai un rêve* (I Have a Dream; a clear reference to Martin Luther King Jr.'s famous speech); or volumes that include both poetry and lyrics of published or unpublished songs, like Oxmo Puccino's *Mines de cristal* (Crystal Mines) or Abd Al Malik's *Le Dernier Français* (The Last French Person), for whom American rapper Tupac's *The Rose That Grew from Concrete* might have been an influence.

In the case of what I would call "urban autobiographies," that is, autobiographies of urban artists, many of them describe a rags-to-riches story, including the ups and downs of the life of an entertainer as well as descriptions of life in the *banlieues*, and, for many, an insight into some of the inspiration behind these artists' most popular hits. A majority of these autobiographies mention Malcolm X or Martin Luther King Jr. (sometimes both) as role models for minorities in France. Indeed, in many memoirs, rappers clearly indicate the lack of representation and therefore of role models for the Afro-Caribbean community in France. Such is the case for Passi, mostly known for his solo debut *Les Tentations* (Temptations) and who, in his 2013 book *Explication de textes* (Textual Analysis), mentions the scarcity of Afro-Caribbeans in French cultural or political life:

> What was shown in the media was not our references or our role models. Luckily, elsewhere, there were Blacks who were emerging as examples to follow. I am talking of course about Nelson Mandela,. . .Steve Biko, Kwame Nkrumah, Aimé Césaire, or Frantz Fanon in the French Caribbean. . . . Malcolm X, Martin Luther King, Muhammad Ali proudly showed that the Black man was not less capable than others. (32)[5]

Interestingly enough, Passi mentions Césaire and Fanon but describes these two figures as being from "elsewhere" (i.e., the French Caribbean) and suggests that they cannot exactly speak to and for the French youth growing up in the outskirts of Paris, even though a good portion of these youths have French Caribbean origins. According to this member of Ministère AMER, it is mostly the absence of French blacks in the media that was problematic. In the 1980s and 1990s, the only black characters on television were often found in African American shows like *Martin* or *The Cosby Show*, which had a huge impact on the Afro-Caribbean community in France, and even today, black characters are more likely to be featured in American shows (see Malonga 2005).

For Gaël Faye, also a rapper-writer, one who simultaneously released a best-selling book and album (Grey 2018), the history of African and Caribbean populations in France has never been included in the national narrative, which forced Afro-Caribbean youths to look elsewhere for role models:

> *In your work, are you inspired by American civil rights?*
> It influences me a lot because as a teenager, I went through an identity crisis because I felt like I was Black. So I was able to identify better with the struggles of African-Americans than those of Blacks in France. I find that their history here is muted. We do not know the history of French Caribbean or African migration in France, or the history of Black philosophers, writers, or musicians. Americans have the ability to create myths right away. Angela Davis, Malcolm X, Martin Luther King made me dream so I was inspired by their history. (Laroche 2017)[6]

Many other rapper-writers have mentioned Martin Luther King Jr. or Malcolm X as influential political figures for them, including Joey Starr from the famous group NTM. Starr cites Malcolm X as the main inspiration behind his involvement in Devoirs de mémoires (Duties to Memories)—an association that encourages urban youth to vote: "The starting point was Malcolm X. What interests us is his trajectory. His story can still exist today" (Starr and

Manœuvre 2006, 299).[7] Malcolm X's name recurs many times also in *Il y a toujours un lendemain*, written by Hamé and Ekoué from the group La Rumeur, although this is more the case for Ekoué than for Hamé, the latter being more inspired by Fanon, who gave him the tools to write rap songs (La Rumeur 2017, 140–41). According to rapper-writer Axiom, Martin Luther King Jr.'s message is still a source of inspiration for French urban youth. In his essay *J'ai un rêve*, the rapper-writer urges the inhabitants of the projects to take charge of their futures and to vote during elections. After a few trips to New York and Cincinnati, Axiom (whose real name is Hicham Kochman) imagined that Martin Luther King Jr.'s "dream" of an integrated society could be applicable in France and that several African American leaders, including Barack Obama, could be role models for minorities in France: "My role models in politics are Martin Luther King and Malcolm X" (2012, 15).[8] Axiom does not totally exclude French activists, but when he does evoke some form of activism, it is usually to denounce its inefficiency: "Barack Obama got it right away: it is our turn to get organized, and to make our own leaders come forward. Yes, there are some attempts here and there like the March for Equality [Marche des Beurs] in 1983. . . . None of these initiatives were in vain, that's for sure. Unfortunately, they remain too timid and practically harmless" (8–9).[9] For other rapper-writers, it is the spiritual side of these leaders that has made more of an impression, especially considering the rise of Islamophobia since the 1990s.

It is safe to say that *The Autobiography of Malcolm X* has also inspired in a very meaningful way rapper-writer Abd Al Malik. Indeed, in his first autobiographic book, *Qu'Allah bénisse la France* (May Allah Bless France; published in English as *Abd Al Malik Sufi Rapper*), the author cites a number of influences, including Albert Camus, Aimé Césaire, and Frantz Fanon. But none of these writers have had the impact on him of Malcolm X: "My new playmates were named Seneca, Camus, Epictetus, Orwell, Césaire, Thucydides, Fanon, Saint Augustine, Barjavel, Huxley, or Cheikh Anta Diop. I was particularly affected by anything that dealt with the history and culture of Black people in general. . . . But it was Malcolm X, the Black American Muslim leader, who was a pacifist but who challenged nonviolence, who made the deepest impression on me" (Malik 2009, 35).

More specifically, it is the letter that Malcolm X wrote to his family while he was in Saudi Arabia for a pilgrimage that inspired Abd Al Malik the most, to the point that, in his autobiography, Malik inserts a two-page excerpt from it in which Malcolm X explains that Islam can solve the racial tensions in the United States. Abd Al Malik's fascination for the African American leader actually prompted him to change his name from Régis Fayette-Mikano to Abd Al Malik as he converted to sufism just as Malcolm Little became El Hadj Malik el-Shabazz when he embraced Islam. "My heart had thrilled to the call of Malcolm X and now needed something different," says the slammer in his autobiography (Malik 2009, 37). Like Malcolm X, Abd Al Malik has an idea of a global brotherhood, which would become possible thanks to a spiritual awakening and new forms of *fraternité* (a part of the French Republican motto). In *La guerre des banlieues n'aura pas lieu* (The War of the Suburbs Will Not Take Place), he writes, "I am not talking only about my neighborhood, I am talking about the future of my country. And I could have talked the same way about the projects in the United States, the favelas in Brazil, or the townships in South Africa" (Malik 2011, 22).[10]

The religious or spiritual side of Malcolm X is definitely what has inspired Abd Al Malik the most in his quest for a new identity that would reconcile republican ideals and Islam. Such is also the case for Médine, a rapper-writer from Le Havre who, in a dialogue with historian Pascal Boniface, acknowledges the influence of African American activists on his work (the cover of his album *Arabian Panther* is a tribute to the Black Panthers). Médine also wrote the preface to a recent book on Malcolm X written by Jonathan Demay (2017), in which the artist insists on the religious side of Malcolm X and its influence on youths in the French *banlieues*. Malcolm X is also at the core of fellow rapper-writer Disiz's work. In a recent interview, he suggests that, if some of the youths living in the *banlieues* had read *The Autobiography of Malcolm X*, they would be less tempted by radical Islam (Disiz, *France Inter*, 2015). This is partly why Disiz la Peste (as he was formerly known) tried to have the influential American's book translated again and republished in 2017. Indeed, *The Autobiography of Malcolm X* was last published in France by Grasset in 1993 and since then has been almost impossible to find. This desire led to a benefit concert in 2015, allowing Disiz and a plethora of rappers to raise money and awareness around the idea of a new translation in French of the Alex Haley–penned autobiography.

MARTIN LUTHER KING JR. AND MALCOLM X IN FRENCH RAP

In French rap, many songs mention Martin Luther King Jr. and/or Malcolm X. In 1998, a song dedicated to MLK entitled "30 ans après Martin Luther King" (30 Years after Martin Luther King) featured artists like Fabe, La Brigade, and K-Reen. The fifteen-minute song, which samples the "I Have a Dream" speech, insists on the dream of integration of the Atlanta-born leader and his nonviolent activism (Collectif rap français 1998). Integration being part of the official French discourse, it is no wonder that urban youths would be more receptive to Malcolm X's approach. The tribute to Malcolm X organized by Disiz was a way to prove that his legacy is still vibrant in France and that there is a need to rediscover his work in translation. Disiz hoped that the success of the show would impress Malcolm X's estate so that they would grant him the rights to publish *The Autobiography of Malcolm X* in a new French translation (Disiz, *France Inter*, 2015). The musical homage, entitled "Who Is Malcolm X?" gathered a who's who of contemporary rap, including Médine, Youssoupha, Tiers Monde, Kery James, Casey, Lino, and Disiz himself on 19 May 2015 (Tellah L 2015).

The fascination for Martin Luther King Jr. and Malcolm X found in French rap can partly be explained by the lack of role models in the political world in France. Most of the non-white political figures that were given positions in the French government failed to gain the support of minorities, partly because they were often chosen by right-wing governments (one thinks of Rama Yade, Rachida Dati, or Fadela Amara, for instance, who were hand-picked by then–Minister of the Interior Nicolas Sarkozy). In Juan Gélas and Pascal Blanchard's documentary *Noirs de France* (French Blacks), historian Elikia M'Bokolo noted that there were actually more people of African descent in French politics in times past, citing, for example, Gaston Monnerville from French Guyana, who was president of the French Senate (Gélas and Blanchard 2011, 38'35). The unfair treatment of recent Minister of Justice Christiane Taubira seems a clear indication that France might not be ready for a black president (Stille 2013).

The names of French or Francophone leaders do not always come to mind when one thinks in France of black leaders. Recently, the daughters of Malcolm X and Frantz Fanon, as well as the son of Steve Biko, walked together in a Lyon *banlieue* protest march, and even though some spectators knew the names of Fanon or Biko, it was the name of Malcolm X that spoke to them the most. Some did not know who the French Martinican thinker or the African antiapartheid activists were: "Malcolm X is a reference; Biko and Fanon, don't know them" (Burlet 2012).[11] Many songs that mention Malcolm X or Martin Luther King Jr. (or both) rarely mention any French or Francophone counterparts. Such is the case with Soprano's song "Hiro," a reference to a character who has the gift of time travel in the hit show *Heroes* and which names Martin Luther King Jr., Malcolm X, Nelson Mandela, and even Barack Obama as figures he would like to visit thanks to his magical power. In the song, he says he would have gone to see Martin Luther King Jr. after his speech, to show him the picture of Barack Obama, and that he would have gone to the temple of Harlem to save Malcolm X from the stage before the bullet reached him. The song also lists pop and R&B icons as well as other heroes of the civil rights era, like Rosa Parks, but there is no mention of any Francophone political leaders or activists. Later on, Soprano raps that he could have gone back in time to save Zyed and Bouna, the two young victims of the Clichy-sous-Bois police whose deaths sparked the riots of fall 2005, but even though these two teenagers have become symbols of the struggle against racism in the *banlieues*, they are victims, not leaders.

For many rappers, the key to a black global consciousness is getting acquainted with the work of African American leaders. In many interviews,

Disiz suggests that too many members of the French Afro-Caribbean community do not know who Malcolm X is, nor are they familiar with his work. In his song simply entitled "Malcolm X," he asks multiple times, "Do you really know who Malcolm is?" before pointing out the ambiguities of his personality and wondering if he was a man full of hate or someone who simply cared too much for his own people.

The tribute to Malcolm X is also entitled "Who Is Malcolm X?" which clearly indicates the explanatory nature of the event. As is the case for Abd Al Malik, the most interesting aspect of Malcolm X's life for Disiz is his spiritual side. After being disappointed by the behavior and extremism of the Nation of Islam's Elijah Muhammad, Malcolm X turned to a less radical form of Islam as he traveled to Egypt and Saudi Arabia. It is no secret that Islam is still today a contentious question for the French, who invoke the republican idea of *laïcité* (secularism) to forbid any ostentatious religious signs in the public sphere. For Médine, the concept of *laïcité* and the law against religious signs in public are mostly a way to exclude religious minorities from the public sphere. Recent controversy around the burka also shows that the uproar against religious signs is only an issue for religions other than Catholicism. On the question of Islam, Hishaam D. Aidi writes that there is clearly a sense of debt from the Muslim population in France to African Americans:

> Most French-born Arabs have never been to Harlem but "claim kinship" with African-Americans as they draw inspiration from the black freedom struggle. Numerous French-Arabs (*Beur*) intellectuals and activists have noted their indebtedness to African-American liberation thought, and the secular pro-integration movement of the early 1980s organized campaigns and marches modeled on the US civil rights struggle. (Aidi 2009, 126)

In "Du Panshir à Harlem" (Panjshir in Harlem), Médine names another African American hero, which clearly states what kind of experience he is writing from: "Mes couplets sont nés dans le même bus que Rosa Parks" (My lines were born on the same bus as Rosa Parks). Another rapper, Lino, who was also part of the Malcolm X French tribute, makes it evident that his role model is Malcolm X (whom he calls "Malcolm le rouquin," Malcolm the Redhead). In an interview, he reveals that he considers Malcolm X a "prophet" and explains how his own work has been influenced by American rappers like Tupac (Lino 2018). In the song "Étoile d'un jour" (Star for a Day) from his 2005 album *Les derniers seront les premiers* (The Last Will Be First), rapper l'Algérino pays tribute to Malcolm X. With the help of rapper-writer Soprano, he insists on the sacrifices made by Malcom X, who died because he was fighting racism in the United States; l'Algérino calls him a free man drunk on equality and fraternity.[12] In a song simply entitled "Malcolm" and featuring rapper Mattéo Falkone, Abd Al Malik sings about Neuhof, his old neighborhood near Strasbourg, and mentions Harlem as facing similar issues. He also mentions Malcolm X as a role model, suggesting that following in his footsteps would make him a better man: "From the top of my hip hop, I only see with my heart. . . . My brother, do like Malcolm to be better."[13] There are many other tracks in French rap that mention Malcolm X, Martin Luther King, or other African American leaders, including a song by Ol' Kainry and Dany Dan, featuring Sefyu, Nubi, and Alibi Montana, who, in "Crie mon nom (Remix)" (Yell My Name [remix]), sing, "Call me Malcolm with a bullet-proof jacket."[14] In the song, the four rappers want to be called by other names, mostly those of heroes, fictitious or real, belonging to American culture. Another song by the group KDD entitled "Une princesse est morte" (A Princess Is Dead) is a tribute to first wives and other women who live in their husbands' shadows. The song featured on their 1998 album *Resurrection* was released a few months after Princess Diana's death in 1997, but the lyrics focus mostly on Betty Shabazz, Malcolm X's wife, who died in 1997 a couple months prior, with much less media frenzy.

In French rap and urban literature, the names of Rosa Parks, Martin Luther King, and Malcolm X have been mentioned abundantly in the last three decades, and the tradition of relying on African American leaders or movements in order to foster black pride in the Afro-Caribbean community is still going strong in contemporary France. These leaders have been progressively replaced by more collective movements like Black Lives Matter, which now has a counterpart in Paris. The first major rally of the French version of Black Lives Matter occurred with about six hundred protesters four days after Adama Traoré's tragic death following a police stop in 2016; commentators wondered how the Black Lives Matter movement will (or can) translate into the French context (McAuley 2016).

LGBTQ minorities also look to the United States for ways to organize, as Black Gay Pride has become a Parisian tradition since 2016. According to their official Twitter account, the Black Pride Paris collective's goal is to celebrate "the diversity of the Black LGBTQ community in France."[15] In the world of music, *Afropunk*, the annual Brooklyn-based show celebrating African American music, now has a concert every year in Paris. The media is also part of the "African Americanization" of black France. For instance, since its creation in 2015, BET is now one of the favorite television channels for the "Afro-descendants" (a French word to designate French people from African descent). It seems that, even in the twenty-first century, black leaders in France are hard to find, and one can wonder if the constant appreciation of African American culture and African American activists does not contribute to making the work of Afro-Caribbean activists even more invisible.

One of the issues is an institutional one: In French academia, few scholars are working on African or Caribbean literature or history, since there are no black studies or Africana studies departments in French universities. Therefore, most scholars working in black studies in France tend to work on African American literature or have a comparative approach. Writers, scholars, and thinkers from the postcolonial world are not given positions in French academia, hence the presence of several Francophone personalities in American universities, from Léon-Gontran Damas to Édouard Glissant, Abdourahman Waberi, Maryse Condé, and Alain Mabanckou.

The issue of visibility—or rather invisibility—in black communities in France has been raised by many commentators, including historian Pap Ndiaye in his book *La Condition noire* (The Black Condition), in which he writes that, as individuals, black citizens are extremely visible, but as a group or a community, they are invisible (Ndiaye 2008, 21). And yet, it seems that some progress has been made in the last few years to gain visibility in the public sphere and that women of African descent are leading social, political, and cultural activism. In the political world, the name Christiane Taubira obviously comes to mind, as her impact on French politics remains undeniable thanks to the 2001 Taubira Law, which forced the French government to recognize its role in the transatlantic slave trade. Her impact goes beyond the world of politics, since she has published several books, including *L'esclavage raconté à ma fille* (Slavery Explained to My Daughter, 2002), and she was also a contributor to the book *Black France/France Noire* (Keaton, Sharpley-Whiting, and Stovall 2012).

In the film industry, several women have come forward to advocate for the presence of more black characters on screen and insist on French people using the French word *noir* and not the English "black" in order to highlight the fact that the struggle of African and Caribbean communities in France is not the same as that of African Americans. The organization created by several black actresses of different backgrounds published a book in 2018 that denounces the lack of diversity in French cinema and on national television. Indeed, in *Noire n'est pas mon métier* (Being Black Is Not My Job), Sonia Rolland, Firmine Richard, and Aïssa Maïga, among others, insist on the (lack of) representation of French women of African descent in France (Collectif 2018). The book was inspired by Amandine Gay's documentary entitled *Ouvrir la Voix/Speak Up*, in which the interviewees were asked to give the names of five black actresses in France. Many interviewees were only able to mention one (Maïga). The latter decided to shed light on other French black actresses by gathering more than a dozen women who recounted their experiences as black actresses in cinema and, more specifically, on the stereotypical roles that are usually assigned to them (mostly, those of immigrants with a strong African accent). Other organizations, such as Mwasi, focus on the experience of black women in France. Inspired by the struggles of pioneer organizations like La Coordination des femmes noires (The Coordination of Black Women), a militant group created in the 1970s, they insist on telling the history of black women in France and on finding their own role models.[16] Even though they are familiar with the works of bell hooks and Angela Davis, they strive to look for inspiration in their own history. In the book *Black French Women and the Struggle for Equality, 1848–2016*, Silyane Larcher insists on the importance of telling the story of French women of African and Caribbean descent in France. Her introduction, cowritten with Félix Germain and entitled "Marianne Is Also Black," posits the need to put the emphasis on "black female experiences, a subject that for the most part has eluded French scholars" (Germain and Larcher 2018, xiii).

Therefore, it seems that, instead of relying on American figures or using the word "black" instead of *noir*, a new wave of cultural activists clearly see the need for a history that is their own and not merely the product of an American import. Rather than using African American models, they strive to find the roots of African and Caribbean history in France and create what can be called an Afropean consciousness that deals specifically with the struggles of Africans and Antilleans in the Hexagon. These efforts will undoubtedly contribute to a better visibility and understanding of the situation of French people of African and/or Caribbean descent in France, so that new heroes—whether political or cultural—can emerge. Since the French curriculum makes very little room for Afro-Caribbean culture and the French government makes little effort to put minorities in positions of power, cultural activism has become increasingly important in the last few years. Urban culture—and rap in particular—has been harnessed as an important source of counterpower since the 1980s but also more specifically since the 2005 riots and often contributes to creating new mythologies for a new generation of urban youth who might finally know who Frantz Fanon is, along with Malcolm X, to use rapper Rocé's words.

REFERENCES

Aidi, Hishaam D., and Manning Marable, eds. *Black Routes to Islam*. New York: Palgrave Macmillan, 2009.
Aïnouz, Abigaïl. "L'Âge d'or du rap français part en tournée dans les Zénith de France." *Les Inrockuptibles*, 12 December 2016. https://www.lesinrocks.com/2016/12/12/musique/lage-dor-rap-francais-part-tournee-11887593/
Akhenaton, and Éric Mandel. *La face B*. Paris: Don Quichotte, 2010.
Anonymous. "Seriez-vous prêts à voter pour un président noir en France?" *Le Figaro*, 5 November 2008. http://www.lefigaro.fr/elections-americaines-2008/2008/11/05/01017200811050QCMWWW00109-seriez-vous-prets-a-voter-pour-un-president-noir-en-france.php
———. "Le buste de Martin Luther King inauguré Place Eugène Varlin à Lyon 3e." *Le Progrès*, 3 April 2011. https://www.leprogres.fr/rhone/2011/04/03/le-buste-de-martin-luther-king-inaugure-place-eugene-varlin-a-lyon-3-e
———. "1965: France Bars Malcolm X." *New York Herald Tribune*, European Edition, 10 February 1965, 9 February 2015. https://ihtretrospective.blogs.nytimes.com/2015/02/09/1965-france-bars-malcolm-x/

————. "Diversité: Les blancs encore largement majoritaires à la télévision." *Ouest France*, 4 January 2018. https://www.ouest-france.fr/medias/television/diversite-les-blancs-encore-largement-majoritaires-la-television-5482887

Axiom. *J'ai un rêve*. Paris: Denoël, 2012.

Bibliothèque Municipale de Lyon. "Martin Luther King: Le rêve brisé?" 6 February–12 May 2018. https://www.bm-lyon.fr/expositions-en-ligne/martin-luther-king-le-revebrise/exposition/martin-luther-king-lyon-1966/

Bordenave, Yves. "A Paris, le pasteur Martin Luther King surveillé de près par la police." *Le Monde*, 1 April 2018. https://www.lemonde.fr/ameriques/article/2018/04/01/a-paris-le-pasteur-martin-luther-king-surveille-de-pres-par-la-police_5279302_3222.html

Bourderionnet, Olivier. "A 'Picture Perfect' Banlieue Artist: Abd Al Malik or the Perils of a Conciliatory Rap Discourse in France." *French Cultural Studies* 22, no. 2 (2011): 151–61.

Burlet, Laurent. "Le marathon des héritiers de Malcolm X en banlieue lyonnaise." *Rue89Lyon*, 10 May 2012. https://www.rue89lyon.fr/2012/05/10/marathon-heritiers-malcom-x-banlieue-lyonnaise/

Collectif. *Noire n'est pas mon métier*. Paris: Seuil, 2018.

Demay, Jonathan, and Médine. *Malcolm X: Sans lutte, il n'y a pas de progrès*. Paris: L'Harmattan, 2017.

Denis, Jacques. "Rap domestiqué, rap révolté." *Le Monde diplomatique*, September 2008. https://www.monde-diplomatique.fr/2008/09/DENIS/16290

Disiz. *René*. Paris: Denoël, 2012.

————. "En France on ne peut plus lire Malcolm X." *Good Morning Cefran: Mouv'*, 15 May 2015. https://www.youtube.com/watch?v=DqtI4rFhXck

————. "Je voudrais que tout le monde puisse lire Malcolm X, des frères Kouachi à ma mère." *France Inter*, 27 April 2015. https://www.youtube.com/watch?v=8SZJqq6B3D0

Elzas, Sarah. "Does France Need Its Martin Luther King, Jr.?" *RFI Podcast*, 19 January 2015. http://en.rfi.fr/americas/20150119-does-france-need-its-martin-luther-king-jr

Gay, Amandine. *Ouvrir la voix / Speak Up*. Arte, 2017.

Germain, Félix, and Silyane Larcher, eds. *Black French Women and the Struggle for Equality, 1848–2016*. Lincoln: University of Nebraska Press, 2018.

Ghio, Bettina. *Sans fautes de frappe: Rap et littérature*. Marseille: Le Mot et le reste, 2016.

Grey, Tobias. "A French-Rwandan Rap Star Turned Novelist from Burundi." *The New York Times*, 29 May 2018. https://www.nytimes.com/2018/05/29/books/gael-faye-small-country.html

Gueye, Sérigne M'Baye. *Les Derniers de la rue Ponty*. Paris: Naïve, 2009.

Haley, Alex. *The Autobiography of Malcolm X as Told to Alex Haley*. New York: Ballantine, 1964.

Hamé, Ekoué, and François Forestier. *Il y a toujours un lendemain*. Paris: Éditions de l'Observatoire, 2017.

Hammou, Karim. *Une histoire du rap en France*. Paris: La Découverte, 2012.

Jouili, Jeanette S. "Rapping the Republic: Utopia, Critique, and Muslim Role Models in Secular France." *French Politics, Culture & Society* 31, no. 2 (2013): 58–80.

Keaton, Trica Danielle, T. Denean Sharpley-Whiting, and Tyler Edward Stovall. *Black France/France Noire: The History and Politics of Blackness*. Durham, NC: Duke University Press, 2012.

Khiari, Sadri. *Malcolm X: Stratège de la dignité noire*. Paris: Amsterdam, 2013.

Kleppinger, Kathryn A., and Laura Reeck, eds. *Post-Migratory Cultures in Postcolonial France*. Liverpool: Liverpool University Press, 2018.

Laroche, Sophie. "'Une grande majorité des rappeurs sont des auteurs': Rencontre avec le magnétique Gaël Faye." *Konbini*, 14 April 2017. https://www.konbini.com/fr/entertainment-2/rencontre-avec-gael-faye-le-rappeur

La Rumeur. *Il y a toujours un lendemain*. Paris: Éditions de l'Observatoire, 2017.

Lino. "Malcolm X, prophète?" *Nofi Media*, 1 March 2018. https://www.youtube.com/watch?v=p-D0Ps_mMIM

Malcolm X. "There's a Worldwide Revolution Going On (Feb. 15, 1965)." *Malcolm X*, 10 January 2019. http://malcolmxfiles.blogspot.com/2013/07/a-worldwide-revolution-going-on-feb-15.html

Malik, Abd Al. *Qu'Allah bénisse la France*. Paris: Albin Michel, 2004.

———. *Sufi Rapper: The Spiritual Journey of Abd al Malik*. Rochester, VT: Inner Traditions, 2009.

———. *La guerre des banlieues n'aura pas lieu*. Paris: Points, 2011.

———. *Le Dernier Français*. Paris: Le Cherche Midi, 2012.

———. *L'Islam au secours de la République*. Paris: Flammarion, 2013.

———. *Place de la République*. Paris: Indigène éditions, 2015.

Malonga, Marie-France. "Television and Black Paris: Towards a Reception Theory for Terrestrial TV Programmes." *Journal of Romance Studies* 5, no. 3 (November 2005): 65–77.

Marable, Manning. *Malcolm X: A Life of Reinvention*. New York: Penguin Books, 2011.

McAuley, James. "Black Lives Matter Movement Comes to France: But Will It Translate?" *The Washington Post*, 8 August 2016. https://www.washingtonpost.com/world/black-lives-matter-movement-comes-to-france-but-will-it-translate/2016/08/07/7606567e-58cd-11e6-8b48-0cb344221131_story.html

Mwasi. *Afrofem*. Paris: Syllepse, 2018.

Ndiaye, Pap. *La Condition Noire: Essai sur une minorité française*. Paris: Calmann-Lévy, 2008.

Newkirk II, Vann R. "King's Death Gave Birth to Hip-Hop." *The Atlantic*, 8 April 2018. https://www.theatlantic.com/entertainment/archive/2018/04/fear-of-a-black-messiah/557474

Passi, and Steeve Balende. *Explication de textes*. Paris: Fetjaine, 2013.

Puccino, Oxmo. *Mines de cristal*. Vauvert, France: Au diable Vauvert, 2009.

Puig, Stève. "Redefining Frenchness through Urban Music and Literature: The Case of Rapper Writers Abd Al Malik and Disiz." In *Post-Migratory Cultures in Postcolonial France*, edited by Kathryn A. Kleppinger and Laura Reeck, 131–46. Liverpool: Liverpool University Press, 2018.

ROST. *Enfant des lieux bannis*. Paris: Robert Laffont, 2008.

Sayare, Scott. "A Rapper and Poet Pushes for a New French Identity of Inclusion." *The New York Times*, 24 August 2012. http://www.nytimes.com/2012/08/25/world/europe/rapper-abd-al-malik-pushes-for-new-french-identity.html

Shakur, Tupac. *The Rose That Grew from Concrete*. New York: Simon & Schuster, 1999.

Soprano. *Mélancolique anonyme*. Paris: Don Quichotte, 2014.

Spieser-Landes, David. "'Postcolonial Islam' Thought and Rapped: Abd al Malik's *Révolution Pacifique* From Within the French Nation." *Performing Islam* 4, no. 1 (May 2015): 35–59.

Starr, Joey, and Philippe Manœuvre. *Mauvaise réputation*. Paris: Flammarion, 2006.

Stille, Alexander. "The Justice Minister and the Banana: How Racist Is France?" *The New Yorker*, 14 November 2013. https://www.newyorker.com/news/daily-comment/the-justice-minister-and-the-banana-how-racist-is-france

Taubira-Delannon, Christiane. *L'esclavage raconté à ma fille*. Paris: Bibliophane, 2002.

Tellah L. "Who Is Malcolm X? Concert commémoratif le 19 mai au Bataclan." *Just Focus*, 18 May 2015. http://www.justfocus.fr/musique/who-is-malcolm-x-concert-commemoratifle-19-mai-au-bataclan.html

DISCOGRAPHY AND FILMOGRAPHY

2Pac. *The Rose That Grew from Concrete*. Uni/Interscope Ltd, compact disc. Originally released in 2000.

Brassens, Georges. "Le gorille." *La Mauvaise Réputation*. Polydor, vinyl. Originally released in 1953.

Collectif rap français. *30 ans après Martin Luther King*. On the One/Musidisc, compact disc. Originally released in 1998.

Disiz La Peste. *Le Poisson Rouge*. Nouvelle Donne Music, compact disc. Originally released in 2000.

———. *Transe Lucide*. Universal Music, compact disc. Originally released in 2014.

Gélas, Juan, and Pascal Blanchard. *Noirs de France: De 1889 à nos jours: Une histoire de France*. DVD Phares & Balises, 2011.

KDD (Kartel Double Detente). *Resurrection*. Columbia, compact disc. Originally released in 1998.

L'Algérino. *Les derniers seront les premiers*. 361 Records, compact disc. Originally released in 2005.

La Rumeur. *L'ombre sur la mesure*. EMI, compact disc. Originally released in 2002.

Malcolm X. Dir. Spike Lee. Largo International, 1992.

Malik, Abd Al. *Le face à face des cœurs*. Atmosphériques, compact disc. Originally released in 2004.

———. *Gibraltar*. Atmosphériques, compact disc. Originally released in 2006.

Malik, Abd Al. Featuring Mattéo Falkone. "Malcolm." Originally released in 2006. https://www.youtube.com/watch?v=9lSwzu_gmkE

Médine. *Arabian panther*. Because Music, compact disc. Originally released in 2008.

———. *Table d'écoute*. Din Records, compact disc. Originally released in 2011.

Montana, Alibi. Featuring Ol Kainry, Dany Dan, Nuby, and Sefyu. "Crie mon nom" (remix). Disques Durs, compact disc. Originally released in 2009.

Ol' Kainry and Dany Dan. Featuring Sefyu, Nubi, and Alibi Montana. "Crie mon nom" (remix). *Ol' Kainry and Dany Dan*. Nouvelle Donne Music, compact disc. Originally released in 2005.

Passi. *Les Tentations*. V2, compact disc. Originally released in 1997.

Puccino, Oxmo. *Opéra Puccino*. Delabel, compact disc. Originally released in 1998.

———. "Mines de cristal." *L'Amour est mort*. Musicast, compact disc. Originally released in 2001.

Roçé. *Identité en crescendo*. Universal Music, compact disc. Originally released in 2006.

Starr, Joey. *Gare au jaguarr*. Sony BMG Music Entertainment, compact disc. Originally released in 2007.

Chapter Seven

New Media, New Voices

Booba's and Sofiane's Uses of Social Networks to Promote Aspiring Rappers

Kathryn Kleppinger

.

When the highly provocative and controversial French rapper Booba released his first album with Lunatic in 2000, he quickly discovered that he could not rely on the traditional broadcast media to promote the music. In the days leading up to the album's release, the producers played the tracks for Laurent Bouneau, director of the high-profile radio station Skyrock (which advertises itself as "first in rap"), who pronounced it unplayable for the station.[1] In a comment that sparked a nearly twenty-year conflict between Booba and Skyrock, Bouneau supposedly called the album "rap du village," or "rap from the village." Booba interprets this phrase as a direct insult to his style—as though his music was provincial or unpolished—while Bouneau insists that his concern arose from a hyperviolent line of the song "Si tu kiffes pas" (If You Don't Like It) that portrays the death of a CRS officer in a positive light.[2] Regardless of the initial intent of Bouneau's comment, his refusal to play the album on the air created significant concern for the launch of the group's career. In a bold strategic move, Booba and his managers circumvented Skyrock's hold on the consumer market by creating an alternative print advertising campaign, primarily in the Paris metro. When the album sold well despite Skyrock's lack of support, Booba's team proudly proclaimed that they were "Number 1 without coke or Sky."[3]

While Booba's clash with Skyrock has continued through today and includes several songs criticizing the station as well as a book by Bouneau (with Tif Tobossi and Tonie Behar, 2016), it is also indicative of the end of an advertising and media promotion era. Skyrock's refusal to promote Booba's work could have prevented the artist from reaching a mass audience in 2000, but Booba and his team already sensed that listeners were open to learning about new music from different sources. Today, these sources have continued to multiply, in particular via the Internet, and young artists now have many online venues to promote their work. YouTube and the French site Dailymotion are prime examples of sites for aspiring rappers to share recordings of their work, although with millions of users and videos, it can be difficult to stand out. Booba recognized this challenge in 2014 and developed his own media conglomerate, OKLM. In 2016, another prominent French rapper, Sofiane, launched his own YouTube video series, called *Jesuispassé-chezSo* (I'veBeentoSo'sPlace) followed by another, *Rentre dans le cercle* (Go into the Circle) in 2017. Each of these programs provides a forum for new voices to reach audiences and bypasses the historically dominant broadcast media channels, such as Skyrock.

This chapter focuses on Booba's and Sofiane's respective social media projects to analyze how these rappers are influencing and changing French rap today. Ralph Schroeder's definition of social media is useful in this context: He identifies such platforms as Facebook, Twitter, and Instagram as "media for interpersonal (rather than institutional) active mutual engagement" and argues that "the main effect of social media is to reinforce bonds by means of sharing content and fostering constant tetheredness to others" (Schroeder 2018, 82). Use of social media is a relevant and effective tactic for these artists due to the popularity of several platforms in France. According to Statista, 43 percent of French people reported regularly using social media in 2017, spending on average 82 minutes per day. Of those who use social media regularly, 75 percent use such networks as Facebook (Anonymous, *Statista* 2019). These sites bring people together around mutual interests; strategic use to target audiences can create a community of supportive listeners who share a passion for discovering new music. As two of the rappers with the highest-paying recording contracts in French rap (Anonymous 2016), Booba and Sofiane are among the highest-profile artists active in the French rap scene today. They therefore have the following to attract significant attention with their online activities.

These sites also provide greater flexibility, as they are not subject to broadcast laws dictating what is appropriate for general consumption. Skyrock, for example, must follow national laws regarding language use and subject matter; the main argument against airing the Lunatic album in 2000 that was publicly put forward by Skyrock's leadership was that Skyrock had recently been taken off the air for twenty-four hours when a newscaster called the death of a policeman in Nice "good news" (Doucet 2014). And, as Karim Hammou has shown (2016, 75–76), playing rap on the radio, particularly in the 1990s, led to difficult discussions with advertisers, some of whom were not comfortable being associated with this form of music. With the ability to focus on a specific audience, online venues escape both the legal and commercial pressures of mainstream radio and therefore grant users a wider range of possibilities as they explore new music.

By facilitating Booba's and Sofiane's efforts to break the dominance of such radio stations as Skyrock, social media platforms have thus allowed these rappers to circumvent institutional sources of legitimacy by speaking directly with their audience. In other words, as Bimber, Flanagin, and Stohl (2005) have argued, individuals such as Booba and Sofiane "now have the potential to communicate and coordinate with others in ways that until recently were feasible almost exclusively for formal organizations" (375). Their use of these networks is a prime instance of John Branstetter's observation that, with new media, "the gatekeeping function of the media elite has been irreparably undermined" (71).

This aspect of social media use is particularly important with a genre such as rap, which has suffered from a negative reputation in mainstream society. As my analysis demonstrates, online platforms allow rappers to engage in what Jennifer Fredette (2018) has called "critical media engagement" (25): They directly address and counter the stereotypes to which they have been subjected in dominant media sources. By allowing the artists to speak for themselves and the audience to access new work without the intermediary of the record companies, social media has the potential to change nearly everything about how rap music is produced and promoted.

BOOBA AND SOFIANE: EARLY PROJECTS AND CAREERS

Élie Yaffa was born in 1976 in the Boulogne-Billancourt suburb of Paris. His father is Senegalese, and Yaffa took the stage name Booba, either in honor of a cousin named Boubakar or as a reference to the popular animated television show *Bouba* (Anonymous 2018). After earning commercial success with Lunatic, Booba subsequently released his own albums, starting with *Temps Mort* (Dead Time) in 2002. In 2004, Booba released his second album, *Panthéon*, and also launched two projects: his record label, Tallac Records, and a clothing line, Ünkut. From 2006 to 2017, he released seven additional albums and has lived in Miami, Florida, since 2007. In interviews, he frequently cites his admiration for American rap history, ranging from the relationships among early rappers to various radio stations involved in promoting rap in the 1970s and 1980s. He also follows current consumer lines by American rappers, such as P. Diddy and Jay-Z.

Booba has a controversial reputation in France due to his hardcore lyrics, criminal activities, and frequent conflicts with other rappers. His lyrics earned the attention of essayist Thomas A. Ravier (2003), who defined a new term, *métagore*, in his analysis of imagery in Booba's songs. Many of his early songs were written in jail: In 1998, Booba spent eighteen months incarcerated after an armed robbery of a taxi driver. In 2002, he was implicated but subsequently acquitted in a nightclub shooting after four months in prison. In 2005, he was again acquitted for car theft, and in October 2018, he was fined 50,000 euros and sentenced to an eighteen-month suspended jail term for a fight with the rapper Kaaris that occurred in the Orly airport in Paris (Paolini 2018). Booba is well known for such conflicts and has engaged in high-profile arguments (often called "clashs" in French) with several other prominent French rappers, including Rohff, La Fouine, and Sinik (Schmitt 2018). Booba's conflicts have also extended outside the rap world to include the magazine *Charlie Hebdo*; in 2015, he and cartoonist Luz engaged in a critical exchange of drawings in the aftermath of the terrorist attacks against the magazine (Kleppinger 2016).

While Booba is highly polemical, Sofiane's public persona is much calmer. Born in 1986 in Saint-Denis, Sofiane started performing freestyle rap at the age of twelve and released his first mixtape, *Première Claque* (First Hard Knock), in 2007. He released five additional mixtapes between 2009 to 2017 before releasing two albums, *Bandit Saleté* (Dirt Bandit) in 2017 and *Affranchis* (Emancipated) in 2018, both certified platinum. In addition to his writing and performing projects, he also founded INM Studio Publishing to bring together recording studios, publishers, and producers to facilitate the creation and production of rap music from conception to release. With his attention to all steps in the process as well as his continuing support of aspiring rappers through his online shows *JesuispasséchezSo* and *Rentre dans le cercle*, Sofiane has been called the "Quarterback of the Rap Game" (Anonymous, *BOOSKA-P* 2019).

In addition to his advocacy work for new rappers, Sofiane has also received attention for his participation in social justice causes. He was an active supporter of the calls for a full investigation of what happened to Adama Traoré, a young Frenchman who died in police custody in July 2016, and to Théo L., a young man sodomized by a policeman using a nightstick in February 2017 (Binet 2017). During a protest in support of Théo L., Sofiane mediated between a crowd of angry youth and a wall of police officers. In a video subsequently aired throughout the country, Sofiane is heard telling the youth to put their hands up and respect the directions of the police. The encounter concluded without incident after Sofiane told the crowd to maintain order so that "the youth can sleep at home."[4] After this incident, several mainstream newspapers covered the event and asked if he considered himself a spokesperson for the tough *banlieues* of France. As he replied to Quentin Girard (2017) of French newspaper *Libération*, "Spokesperson, that's not for me. Loudspeaker, why not."[5]

FRUSTRATIONS WITH TRADITIONAL MEDIA

While many previous studies have covered the long history of tensions between rappers and socially dominant media and political institutions, a 1
February 2018 appearance by Sofiane on the nightly infotainment French
television show *Quotidien* exemplifies the difficulties rappers face in mainstream media interviews.[6] In early 2018, Sofiane was in the midst of a court
appearance for an April 2017 violation in which he blocked the A3 autoroute
without authorization to film a music video. When he arrived onstage, host
Yann Barthès introduced him as follows: "There's an album, there are legal
cases. We'll start with the cases. A few days ago, you were in front of a judge
in Bobigny, accused of blocking the A3 autoroute for several minutes" ("Invité: Sofiane" 2018).[7] Sofiane accepted the introduction and replied, "I did
something stupid, I take responsibility for it and I hope I'm not giving people
bad ideas."[8] But Barthès continued with a look back on another video shoot
that attracted so many spectators that police were called in to control the
crowd. He then noted that Sofiane was risking up to four months in prison
and asked him, "Are you freaking out?"[9] Sofiane again accepted responsibility for both situations and replied, "I answer for my acts, I will take responsibility for the consequences."[10] At this point, Barthès finally transitioned to
a discussion of Sofiane's new album, *Affranchis*, by observing that releasing
an album at the same time as a court appearance could be interpreted as a
marketing stunt. Sofiane noted that he announced his album release well
before his court date was determined, a point that goes unacknowledged by
his interlocutors onstage. This presentation of Sofiane implies that he is
primarily a delinquent with legal troubles rather than a talented artist, and
Barthès's insistence on discussing primarily Sofiane's court appearance in-
scribes the rapper in a narrow frame of reference that relies on stereotypes of
delinquency and criminality.

In addition to the questioning Sofiane faced during the nine-minute appearance, a brief excerpt of his video for the song "Longue Vie" (Long Life)
was aired with subtitles (despite relatively standard vocabulary with very
little slang), as though he were speaking another language that viewers would
be unable to follow. And after the interview, Sofiane was subjected to a
performance by Jonathan Lambert, a humorist with a regular spot on the
show called *2217, Jonathan Lambert se souvient . . .* (It's 2217, Jonathan
Lambert Remembers When . . .). In these often scatological clips, Lambert
performs a sketch about what will be remembered about the guest of the day
in two hundred years. In the case of Sofiane, Lambert based his sketch—yet
again—on the blocking of the A3 autoroute and developed a story line of a
trucker caught in the traffic who is late to pick up his wife. The wife falls
asleep on the side of the road and is raped by a pigeon. While the clip was
intended to be funny (and Sofiane is a remarkably good sport about it, laugh-

ing on cue), it also implies that Sofiane's only enduring legacy will be for his traffic violation.

Given this type of reductive interview, with very little focus on the music, it is not surprising that Sofiane has shied away from most mainstream media interviews. As he explained to the French music and culture magazine *Les Inrockuptibles* after his intervention in the Febuary 2017 protest, "I don't go on France Inter or BFM TV because they just want a *rebeu* who knows how to string together more than three syllables. The token *bougnoule*, that's not me. And I also want to talk about music. . . . I'm very scared of political cooptation, of a billion things. There are traps in front of me" (Miclet 2017).[11] In another interview, this time with Mouloud Achour of *Le Gros Journal*, he noted that rappers are frequently treated as "guignols" (clown puppets) on talk shows, and he has no interest in playing that role (Anchour and Sofiane 2017). In each of these instances, Sofiane articulated a lucid analysis of the social positioning of rappers in the mainstream media. Either he risks being treated as a token because he is polite and well spoken, or he is expected to play a preordained part as a clown.

While Sofiane has mostly dealt with traditional media by maintaining a polite distance, Booba has adopted a more active, confrontational style. After his conflict with Laurent Bouneau of Skyrock in 2000, he included lyrics criticizing Bouneau in his song "Mon son" (My Sound), released on his *Panthéon* album. In an in-depth interview published in *Les Inrockuptibles*, Booba also addressed his media profile and the attention granted to the analysis of his lyrics in *La Nouvelle Revue française*: "I sometimes feel like they want to make me into a circus animal. When they cite *La Nouvelle Revue française* and then my worst punchlines in succession, I know that they want to make me out to be an idiot" (Fall and Doucet 2015).[12] In this comment, Booba demonstrated a nuanced understanding of the power dynamics of media presentations and the risk of being portrayed as a circus animal. He also pointed out that most media outlets take his lyrics out of context to make them sound exceptionally violent. He feels that the literary reading of his songs in *La Nouvelle Revue française* has done him a disservice by highlighting the supposed gore at the heart of his songs and providing fodder for spectacularized media portrayals of his work.

Like Sofiane, Booba also critiques the pressure he feels to act as a spokesperson or to comment on immigration, French identity, and integration. As Booba told *Les Inrockuptibles*, "I don't want to box myself in the stereotypes that the media want to slap on me. I don't want to say 'I am French.' No, I don't feel more French than anyone else. Tomorrow, if I want to, I'll go to Thailand. I will never be the spokesperson for the *banlieues*. Politicians are always talking about integration in their speeches but do you really think that, in the 16th *arrondissement* of Paris, they want a family of Malians living in their building?" (Fall and Doucet 2015).[13] Here, Booba pointed out the hypocrisy of calling for immigrant integration when those in power do not truly want to share their wealth and community with newcomers. He also noted that he does not feel any special tie to France and would just as easily go somewhere else. In this comment and those cited earlier, we can see how mainstream journalists approach these rappers with preconceived notions of what they are like and what they should discuss on air. Tellingly, these discussions rarely focus on their music and instead bring up legal troubles and conflicts with other rappers, as though the violence of some songs must represent the entire genre.

MEDIA PROJECTS

It is perhaps telling that when Booba announced the creation of his media project OKLM in 2014, he did so via Instagram. In an accompanying video, the rapper explains, "It's going to be a huge media platform that brings together all new stuff, musical as well as cultural. . . . What no one else is doing, we're going to do, our way, as it should be" (Oulac 2014).[14] The guiding principle of the site and the subsequent radio station (launched in 2015) and TV channel (launched in 2016) is that users submit their own content to the site's editors, who then select the best or most interesting submissions for promotion. While the site provides space for various forms of cultural expression, rap is clearly the primary focus. One tab provides links to a list of French rappers and featured music videos, while another tab provides users with a list of American rap videos. A third tab, called "Actualité" (Current Events), provides short articles about French and American rappers. Finally, a fourth tab, called "Le meilleur du web" (The Best of the Web), provides links to other genres of news, ranging from gossip to humor to strange events.

In his promotion of the site, Booba references his difficulties with Skyrock and sets up his media project as an alternative way to gain recognition. He frames himself as a "big brother" figure who is supportive of all new talent: "I want to create a real platform so that the new generation [of rappers] is not faced with the problems that I dealt with: the difficulty of signing with a record label, of getting airtime on the radio, etc. On OKLM, there's no inside track. If you are good, we'll post your video or sound. It's meritocratic. . . . For me, it's a revolution because it allows us to eliminate all the constraints of record companies, all the insider tracks like with Laurent Bouneau" (Fall and Doucet 2015).[15] This site, according to Booba, provides a new way to avoid the restrictions of record companies and radio executives. It also avoids the insider nature of record and radio deals so that access to an audience is based strictly on talent rather than on connections.

In perhaps his strongest statement against Skyrock, the OKLM radio station has brought back two programs that used to air on Skyrock but were subsequently canceled. Booba explains that *La Sauce* (The Sauce) and *Couvre Feu* (Curfew) were important programs during his youth because they aired new music and introduced listeners to new talent. In response to the question, "Is OKLM.com a way for you to counter the vision of rap defended by Skyrock?" Booba said, "The goal is to take back what they stole from us" (Fall and Doucet 2015).[16] He then explained that canceling the programs introducing new artists has stolen the sense of discovery from listeners and prevented new artists from reaching an audience. Elsewhere he described Skyrock's current editorial line by saying, "On the big rap radio Skyrock, you don't discover anything, they play sounds that have already been tested, that have millions of views. . . . They don't take any risk" (Delcourt 2016).[17] French rap radio has become homogenized, according to Booba, and listeners are caught in a cyclical logic where only the songs that have become hits are promoted in prime-time programming.

While Booba established his media project with a direct focus on critiquing the mainstream media and Skyrock in particular, Sofiane's two online video programs approach similar questions from a different angle. His first video series, *JesuispasséchezSo*, debuted in April 2016, and his second, *Rentre dans le cercle*, in September 2017. Each episode of *JesuispasséchezSo* lasts the length of a song, generally three to five minutes, during which Sofiane presents a new freestyle song from a different region of France. Episodes of *Rentre dans le cercle* are longer, generally around twenty minutes, and feature a wide range of participants, including writers, producers, and aspiring rappers. He developed these programs because, as he explained in an interview with the newspaper *20 Minutes*, "Being a rapper was never the end goal for me. I wanted to understand the musical chain from pen on paper to the store display bin" (Chapon 2017).[18] Sofiane's newest projects are a natural extension of his earlier work as an artist, when he developed an interest in the process of music production. *JesuispasséchezSo* allowed him to discover video editing, and *Rentre dans le cercle* brings together even more professionals from the rap music world to follow the creation of new music from its very beginnings, an artist with an idea.

In each of these programs, Sofiane encourages the promotion of new talent. As he explained in an interview on Booba's OKLM, "I created my own connections on *JesuispasséchezSo*. There are guys that people heard for the first time on *JesuispasséchezSo*, there are guys who were just starting to get attention online whom I invited to come get a few million views with me and that you can find in my other work, and I'm really happy about that" ("Interview Sofiane" 2017).[19] Here he emphasized how some of the artists who appeared in his brief videos became collaborators on future work, thus successfully launching a career. *Rentre dans le cercle* continues this process of discovery but focuses on developing connections and careers for new rappers. As he noted in an in-depth interview with Marie Richeux on the France Culture radio station, "It's the only place where you can see a completely unknown person come here straight from his parking lot and do a freestyle, on the heels of a diamond album that is on the front page of all the magazines right now. It's an exchange, a sharing" (Richeux 2018). [20]

Social Stakes of Social Media

The tag line for Booba's website, "Pour nous par nous" (For Us by Us), explicitly reinforces his opposition to socially dominant institutions. This line implies a community focus and that the rap community is creating its own media for itself rather than relying on media outlets controlled by outsiders. The host of the OKLM radio show *La Sauce*, Mehdi Maizi, raised a related point in an interview with *Slate*: "For a long time, the majority of people, and me first among them, thought that radios had no relevance in the Internet era. After all, why would we need a media that tells us what to listen to, at a given hour, when the web offers an infinite possibility of sounds? That said, I think that people have had enough of playlists and are looking for professionals who are capable of stripping down the work for them" (Delcourt 2016). [21] Maizi underscored the shift in consumer behavior, resulting from improved access to a wider range of choices, although he recognized that too many choices can create a different challenge. While Booba focused his commentaries on how Skyrock should not be the only arbiter of talent and promotion in French rap, Maizi observed that mainstream radio stations are no longer adapted to audience preferences. Instead, Internet-based channels have much more freedom to explore new music and present a range of options to users, who can decide what, when, and how much to listen to.

At the same time, the hosts of Skyrock are not under any illusions regarding the shift in listener behavior. Fred Musa, host of the popular Skyrock show *Planète Rap*, acknowledged that times have changed: "Skyrock can no longer play the role of tastemaker. This work is already amply done on the Internet. We are here to allow artists to reach a new level in their careers by playing them to our four million daily listeners. We are a popular media and we would be missing our target if we were still focused on discovery" (Delcourt 2016). [22] According to Musa, the role of radio has also evolved in reaction to the possibilities afforded by the Internet, and radio hosts recognize that listeners do not tune in to learn about new talent. Instead, Skyrock can help artists who are already gaining traction with listeners to expand their audience and further advance their careers after already reaching a baseline of popularity.

If this is indeed the case, that radio stations such as Skyrock act as an amplifier for artists who have already been discovered online, then Booba's and Sofiane's bets have paid off. Rappers who are discovered independently from the major institutional players have more freedom and flexibility to determine their own artistic profiles and are not obligated to follow rules or guidelines dictated by industry insiders. One of Booba's friends explained the stakes of Booba's conflict with Skyrock by noting that "Booba became a legend in the rap world because he successfully made two gold albums without Skyrock's help. . . . Today he is in an open war with this station because he believes that it's not their right to convey this culture given the way they treated him" (Doucet 2014).[23] The lasting impact on Booba of the initial conflict with Skyrock is that the radio station lost the credibility to act as a gatekeeper and storyteller for French rap. Booba continues to seek the last word in the fight; his website, thanks to the broader use of social media by French youth, has created a viable alternative to Skyrock's hold on the market.

Sofiane articulated the stakes of his own projects with a more economic focus in an interview with *Libération*. He observed, "Our big refrain is to repeat that rap is the music that sells the most in France. But who profits from it? The more that bosses from our world multiply, the more we keep control and reappropriate the financial benefits from our music" (Kefi 2018).[24] For Sofiane, the problem with institutional radio stations and record companies is that they funnel profits to outsiders rather than back into the rap community. By promoting leaders from within, the French rap community can support itself and maintain control over its own production. These internal leaders can then shape new generations of artists who speak more directly to listeners and who are not obligated to work through a music production system that does not understand them.

CRITIQUES OF THESE APPROACHES

Sofiane's earlier comment about promoting leaders from the inside does, however, touch upon one of the critiques that routinely arises in discussions of these new media projects. In her interview with Sofiane for France Culture, Marie Richeux began by asking about his high sales figures for his recent albums and whether these numbers give him greater liberty to do what he wants. Sofiane acknowledged her point, saying, "It allows a freedom of creation" (Richeux 2018).[25] In other words, Richeux gently observed that Sofiane is able to produce his new media programs precisely because he has already reached a certain status within the music industry. Sofiane did not disagree with her point, but he also responded with a different argument, saying that "we are a somewhat strange microcosm, we're the music that sells the most in France, and I think we're the one that is the least presented in the media. . . . Once the light is on you, you must act on it" (Richeux

2018).[26] In other words, Sofiane realizes that he has a certain responsibility now that he has become successful, and he has chosen to use his fame to facilitate the discovery of new talent. In this instance, the criticism that Sofiane is only able to develop these projects because he already successfully navigated the preexisting system is turned into a piece of background information that explains and justifies, rather than negates, Sofiane's engagement with the music industry.

Critiques of Booba, however, take a sharper turn in several commentaries about his new media project. As Maxime Delcourt notes in *Slate*, "Regardless of what he does or raps, the gesture is almost systematically situated in a marketing strategy" (Delcourt 2016).[27] Booba's long history as an entrepreneur, observes Delcourt, has created a reputation of self-promotion, so OKLM could be seen as yet another tactic in Booba's overall strategy of promoting his own work and identity. Digital marketing specialist Virginie Berger concurs and adds another dimension in a separate article: "He's positioning himself as the big brother of rap. OKLM allows him to put forward a positive process: 'I'm helping others, I'm sharing,' in opposition to his rather scandalous image. It's also a way to develop his productivity" (Oulac 2014).[28] In Berger's analysis, OKLM is more than a self-marketing vehicle; it is also a way to create an image of giving back to his community. For a rapper with a difficult reputation and who is known for his conflicts with others, supporting newcomers is a way to temper negative impressions of his behavior in other domains.

Booba's feud with Skyrock has also come under scrutiny, not least by those affiliated with the radio station. In an article for *Les Inrockuptibles*, David Doucet notes that Booba's name appears 172 times in Laurent Bouneau's 2014 book *Le rap est la musique préférée des Français* (Rap Is the Favorite Music of French People), and the adjectives used to describe the rapper include "calculateur" (calculating) and "égoïste" (egotistical) (Doucet 2014). Fred Musa agrees with his boss and claims that Booba's dislike of Skyrock is part of a broader marketing strategy: "I think it's above all a posture. Booba is extremely clever. He understood the existence of an anti-Skyrock current in French rap and he was able to position himself accordingly" (Fall 2015).[29] For these Skyrock insiders, Booba is using a clash with the radio station for his own benefit rather than as an inspiration to truly change the way music is made and produced in France.

CONCLUSION

Regardless of the motivations behind Booba's and Sofiane's respective projects, it is relevant to note that their programs are reaching an audience. After five years, OKLM has over 850,000 followers on Facebook and nearly

930,000 followers on Instagram, while in just over a year, *Rentre dans le cercle* has garnered nearly 33,000 followers on Facebook and 75,000 on Instagram. The reach of these sites confirms Lance Bennett's argument that such platforms can bring populations together around shared interests and that these projects can be deeply political: "The importance of these networks for forging generational identity and solidarity cannot be underestimated. Moreover, lurking just beneath the surface is the potential for vast networks of public voice on contemporary issues" (Bennett 2008, 11). With rap music's fundamental basis in denouncing inequalities, a public forum for such issues can serve as a site of action, as indicated by Sofiane's denunciation of police brutality in several of his *JesuispasséchezSo* episodes and subsequent mobilization for calls for justice for victims of police violence.

With Booba's and Sofiane's projects, we can see a profound shift in both the gatekeeping and consecration mechanisms in French rap. Audiences logging onto social media networks are influencing who and what is played, first in online shows and subsequently on mainstream radio stations, such as Skyrock. And, beyond determining which music is played, these sites are also changing the ways in which the music is discussed. Sofiane has been interviewed several times on Booba's website, for example, and the discussions are much longer (usually between thirty and sixty minutes) than any interview he has done with the mainstream media. In these conversations, he has the opportunity to discuss his inspiration along with his artistic vision and musical methods. These conversations are thus dramatically different from the interviews he has done with mainstream journalists, as they do not fixate on side stories, such as the incident involving the A3 highway. Social media platforms are thus creating an entirely new forum for the dissemination and discussion of new music, one that allows rappers to speak for themselves and to define their work in their own terms.

REFERENCES

Achour, Mouloud, and Sofiane. "Le bitumen avec une plume." *Le Gros Journal*, 29 May 2017. https://www.youtube.com/watch?v=0QvJp1xY3iQ

Anonymous. "Fianso signe chez Capitol pour une somme folle!" *Générations*, 7 November 2016. http://generations.fr/news/coulisse/38322/fianso-signe-chez-capitol-pour-une-somme-folle

———. "Le rappeur Booba aurait pu s'appeler . . . Jacky!" *Le Point*, 5 August 2018. https://www.lepoint.fr/societe/le-rappeur-booba-aurait-pu-s-appeler-jacky-05-08-2018-2241548_23.php

———. "What Kinds of Social Media Do You Use Regularly?" *Statista*, 17 August 2018. https://www.statista.com/forecasts/820540/popular-social-media-platform-types-in-france

———. "Average Daily Social Media Use via Any Device in Selected European Countries in 2017 (in Minutes)." *Statista*, accessed 15 January 2019. https://www.statista.com/statistics/719966/average-daily-social-media-use-in-selected-european-countries/

———. "Share of Individuals in France Participating in Social Networks from 2011 to 2017." *Statista*, accessed 15 January 2019. https://www.statista.com/statistics/384401/social-network-penetration-in-france/

———. "Sofiane." *BOOSKA-P*, accessed 15 January 2019. https://www.booska-p.com/biographie-sofiane.html

Bennett, W. Lance. "Changing Citizenship in the Digital Age." In *Civic Life Online: Learning How Digital Media Can Engage Youth*, edited by W. Lance Bennett, 1–24. Cambridge, MA: MIT Press, 2008.

Bimber, Bruce, Andrew J. Flanagin, and Cynthia Stohl. "Reconceptualizing Collective Action in the Contemporary Media Environment." *Communication Theory* 15, no. 4 (November 2005): 365–88.

Binet, Stéphanie. "Fianso, rappeur et pacificateur face à la police." *Le Monde*, 15 February 2017. https://www.lemonde.fr/police-justice/article/2017/02/15/fianso-rappeur-et-pacificateur-face-a-la-police_5079947_1653578.html

Bouneau, Laurent, Fif Tobossi, and Tonie Behar. *Le rap est la musique préférée des Français.* Paris: Points, 2016.

Branstetter, John. "The Challenge of New Media in French and American Politics: Concepts, Methods, and Opportunities." *French Politics* 9, no. 1 (2011): 69–86.

Chapon, Benjamin. "Après la polémique autour de son clip tourné sur l'A3, on a pu parler musique avec Sofiane." *20 Minutes*, 14 April 2017. https://www.20minutes.fr/culture/2049615-20170414-apres-polemique-autour-clip-tourne-a3-pu-parler-musique-sofiane

Delcourt, Maxime. "La radio de Booba OKLM a-t-elle gagné sa 'battle' face à Skyrock?" *Slate*, 13 November 2016. http://www.slate.fr/story/127451/radio-booba-oklm-battle-skyrock

Doucet, David. "Pourquoi Booba déteste autant Skyrock." *Les Inrockuptibles*, 24 October 2014. https://www.lesinrocks.com/2014/10/24/musique/booba-skyrock-11531775/

Fall, Azzedine. "Fred Musa: 'Détester Skyrock est une posture pour Booba.'" *Les Inrockuptibles*, 14 March 2015. https://www.lesinrocks.com/2015/03/14/musique/fred-musa-detester-skyrock-est-une-posture-pour-booba-11587093/

Fall, Azzedine, and David Doucet. "Booba: l'interview vérité sur toute sa carrière." *Les Inrockuptibles*, 15 March 2015. https://www.lesinrocks.com/2015/03/15/musique/boobainterview-verite-sur-toute-sa-carriere-11589515/

Fredette, Jennifer. "Difference-Conscious Critical Media Engagement and the Communitarian Question." In *Post-Migratory Cultures in Postcolonial France*, edited by Kathryn Kleppinger and Laura Reeck, 23–43. Liverpool: Liverpool University Press, 2018.

Girard, Quentin. "Sofiane: la voix désarme." *Libération*, 17 February 2017. http://next.liberation.fr/musique/2017/02/17/sofiane-la-voix-desarme_1549250

Hammou, Karim. "Mainstreaming French Rap Music: Commodification and Artistic Legitimation of Othered Cultural Goods." *Poetics* 59 (2016): 67–81.

Hélénon, Véronique. "Police: Rap Music in France and the Prosecution of Suprême NTM." *Black Renaissance* 1, no. 3 (1998): 233–40.

"Interview Sofiane." *OKLM*, 22 February 2017. https://www.youtube.com/watch?v=nRvjnov4YWs

"Invité: Sofiane, Le rappeur phénomène dans les charts et dans les tribunaux." *Quotidien*, 1 February 2018. https://www.tf1.fr/tmc/quotidien-avec-yann-barthes/videos/invite-sofiane-rappeur-phenomene-charts-tribunaux-2.html

Kefi, Ramsès. "Sofiane à la table des grands patrons." *Libération*, 23 April 2018. http://www.liberation.fr/apps/2018/04/sofiane/

Kleppinger, Kathryn. "When Parallels Collide: Social Commentary and Satire in French Rap before and after *Charlie Hebdo*." *Contemporary French Civilization* 41, no. 2 (2016): 197–216.

Miclet, Brice. "Qui est Sofiane, le rappeur de Blanc-Mesnil devenu porte-parole malgré lui." *Les Inrockuptibles*, 20 February 2017. https://www.lesinrocks.com/2017/02/20/musique/sofiane-rappeur-detre-exemple-porte-parole-11915127/

Oulac, François. "Que cherche Booba en créant OKLM.com, son site dénicheur de talents?" *Konbini*, 8 December 2014. http://www.konbini.com/fr/entertainment-2/booba-oklm-com-talents/

Paolini, Esther. "Booba et Kaaris condamnés à 18 mois de prison avec sursis." *Le Figaro*, 9 October 2018. http://www.lefigaro.fr/musique/2018/10/09/03006-20181009ARTFIG00008-le-jugement-des-rappeurs-booba-et-kaaris-attendu-ce-mardi.php

Ravier, Thomas A. "Booba ou Le démon des images." *Nouvelle Revue Française* 567 (October 2003): 37–56.

Richeux, Marie. "Sofiane: 'La lumière ne suffit plus, maintenant je veux être l'interrupteur.'" *France Culture*, 15 March 2018. https://www.franceculture.fr/emissions/par-les-temps-qui-courent/sofiane

Schmitt, Camille. "Booba: Rohff, La Fouine, Johnny. . . Ses 8 clashs marquants avant Kaaris." *RTL*, 2 August 2018. https://www.rtl.fr/culture/medias-people/booba-rohff-la-fouine-johnny-ses-8-clashs-marquants-avant-kaaris-7794304627

Schroeder, Ralph. *Social Theory After the Internet: Media, Technology and Globalization.* London: University College London Press, 2018.

DISCOGRAPHY

Booba. *Temps Mort*. 45 Scientific, compact disc. Originally released in 2002.

———. *Panthéon*. Tallac Records, compact disc. Originally released in 2004.

Lunatic. *Mauvais Œil*. 45 Scientific, compact disc. Originally released in 2000.

Sofiane. *Première Claque*. Karismatik, compact disc. Originally released in 2007.

———. *Bandit Saleté*. Capitol Music France, compact disc. Originally released in 2017.

———. *Affranchis*. Suther Kane Films, compact disc. Originally released in 2018.

Chapter Eight

Hip-Hop Based Education (HHBE) in Paris and Its Suburbs

Charles Norton

Hip-hop is a relatively new, urban, postmodern culture with very deep historical roots. Codified by Marc Lamont Hill (2009), Hip-Hop Based Education (HHBE) remains a burgeoning field in the United States and has also been adopted in France. As a graduate student at the University of Arizona, I conducted one year (academic year 2013–2014) of ethnographic fieldwork with students, engaged artists, and cultural associations in Paris to better understand how hip-hop cultures are being used in education and social engagement. This research is the foundation of the first academic work documenting HHBE in France (Norton 2015). Since completing my studies in Arizona, I have continued to collaborate with hip-hop educators and engaged artists to provide dynamic, accessible language and cultural education to youth and have expanded the scope of my HHBE research intercontinentally. This chapter shares some of the findings from the initial 2015 research and is enhanced by additional interviews and three more years of organizing and learning within my HHBE networks in Paris and beyond.

By exploring the relationships and interplay among the relevant infrastructure, institutions, and actors, this chapter examines how hip-hop cultures are implicated in education and social engagement in Paris and its neighboring suburbs. The opening sections provide a concise history of hip-hop culture and hip-hop in France, as well as my theoretical framework and research methods. The following section delineates the landscape of HHBE in Paris and its suburbs by describing the key infrastructure, institutions, and actors that make it function. The penultimate section showcases the work of one cultural association, one cultural center, one engaged artist, and one local government that are using hip-hop as a means for education and social engagement. The conclusion revisits the primary research questions and discusses the current challenges and future prospects of HHBE in France. Finally, this chapter closes out with an appendix of HHBE-related resources in Paris and its suburbs.

HIP-HOP ORIGINS

Hip-hop is a fusion of cultures and traditions that coalesced in poor, postindustrial, immigrant neighborhoods in New York City in the 1970s—neighborhoods that are not unlike the Parisian suburbs today. The story goes that Clive Campbell, a Jamaican American deejay better known as Kool Herc, organized block parties and gatherings in the community room at 1520 Sedgwick Avenue, a high-rise residential building in the Morris Heights section of the Bronx. Influenced by the Sound System culture of his native Jamaica, Kool Herc and other pioneering deejays used speakers, turntables, and microphones to blend samples of funk, rock, and punk and create a new genre of music that was dubbed "hip-hop" in 1974 (Calloway 2014). Not long after, the arts of graffiti, rap (or MCing), and break dance were incorporated with turntablism to form the fundamental elements of hip-hop culture. Although deejays were the originators of the genre, today rap music is the most visible element of hip-hop culture and perhaps its most ancient. Tricia Rose (1994) traces the roots of today's rap to the tradition of West African *griots*, a caste of poets, news bearers, and praise singers that has existed for more than one thousand years (Hale 1998). More recently, Henry Louis Gates Jr. has identified connections between rapping and other African American cultural traditions throughout the twentieth century (DuBois, Gates, and Chuck D. 2011).

Since its inception, hip-hop culture has been inherently linked to education and social engagement. Afrika Bambaataa (born Kevin Donovan), another hip-hop originator and onetime member of the Black Spades street gang in the Bronx, is both the son and nephew of social activists. After winning a writing contest where the prize was a trip to Africa, he returned to the Bronx, left the Black Spades, and began working to combat the gang-related violence that plagued his neighborhood. In 1974, he founded the Universal Zulu Nation and began recruiting local youth to practice break dance and other hip-hop arts as creative, competitive, and nonviolent forms of conflict resolution (Chang 2005). From the beginning of his movement, Bambaataa's goal was to develop and promote an inclusive culture to supplant the violence of gang life (George 2005).

HIP-HOP IN FRANCE

Hip-hop first arrived in France in 1981 via music and graffiti, and in 1984, Bambaataa visited Paris and founded a branch of his new movement. However, the Zulu Nation never proliferated in France, and break dance became the most prominent element of French hip-hop culture until the album *Rapattitude* achieved commercial success in 1990 (Bazin 2002; Vulbeau 1992). Later in the 1990s—with the ascension of artists like MC Solaar, NTM, and IAM—French hip-hop gained global recognition, showing the world that French rappers were poetic, diverse, and politically conscious. Beyond commercial success, the lyrical content and moral positions espoused by the second generation of French rappers were also significant: championing freedom of expression; (re)valorizing Arab identity, which continues to be maligned by xenophobic and racist politicians; and confronting and interrogating France's colonial legacy (Prévos 2002). Today France is the largest hip-hop market in the world outside the United States, with producers and consumers that represent every population, ethnicity, social class, and political orientation that exists in the country (Oliver 2019).

Contemporaneously, hip-hop became an important cultural and political force in France due to its popularity in ethnically diverse and marginalized suburbs and low-income neighborhoods.[1] Following numerous riots and civil unrest beginning in the late 1970s, hip-hop became a favored means of intervention between local elected officials and youth from the suburbs and other disenfranchised neighborhoods.[2] According to Lafargue de Grangeneuve, "at the turn of the 1980s and 1990s, a public politics of hip-hop was firmly established: the prominence of hip-hop as a political tool is primarily the consequence of the renewed emergence of the suburbs as a public problem" (2008, 10).[3] Although widely accepted as a tool for social engagement, not all artists believe that the "appropriation of hip hop by French authorities" is a good thing. According to Gaël Faye, a Franco-Rwandan engaged hip-hop artist and author, the misappropriation of hip-hop culture by local elected officials is one of the biggest challenges to HHBE and social engagement in France today (Norton 2015).

THEORETICAL FRAMEWORK: HHBE AND CIVIC ENGAGEMENT

Academic research about hip-hop history, social context, and linguistics began appearing in the 1990s (Roediger 1998; Rose 1994; Smitherman 1997). In 2009, Marc Lamont Hill articulated parameters of the field of HHBE:

> Scholars have shown how the elements of hip hop culture—rap music, turntablism, break dancing, graffiti culture, fashion, and language—can be used within classrooms to improve student motivation, teach critical media literacy,

foster critical consciousness, and transmit disciplinary knowledge. These foci and approaches, along with others collectively comprise the field of study I refer to as Hip Hop Based Education. (2)

According to Petchauer, there are three axes of literature focusing on hip-hop: "Historical/Textual" (the broadest and most widespread), "Social Commentary" (similar to Historical/Textual but written for a nonacademic audience), and "Grounded Literature" (focused on the creators and producers of hip-hop culture). This chapter contributes to "Grounded Literature," which Petchauer describes as "bridging the gap between local practice and theory" and states that "studies classified within this category serve as valuable contributions to educational research" (2009, 952).

Coupled with HHBE, this study also documents hip-hop based social engagement, focusing on initiatives that meet Zukin's definition of *civic engagement*, which is "participation aimed at achieving a public good, but usually through direct hands-on work in cooperation with others, typically in nongovernmental settings" (2006, 51). Thus, it is important to note that, although every project I observed and participated in during fieldwork was funded by government entities, all of my research took place in nongovernmental settings.

METHODS: PARTICIPANT OBSERVATION, ETHNOGRAPHIC INTERVIEWING, AND CRITICAL REFLECTION

As a study in applied anthropology, this research uses anthropological knowledge and methods to address practical problems (Van Willigen 2002). I used participant observation and ethnographic interviewing to document Hip-Hop Based Education and social engagement in the Paris metropolitan region.[4] During 2013–2014 fieldwork, I gave weekly English language and culture workshops with the HHBE Parisian cultural association 123...RAP!, used HHBE methods in courses I gave as a lecturer in English at the Université de Paris VII–Diderot, and attended more than twenty concerts and hip-hop events in the Paris region. From 2014 to the present, I have continued to provide intermittent pedagogical and curriculum support to 123...RAP!, and in 2017, I collaborated with 123...RAP!, Arizona-based engaged hip-hop group Shining Soul, and the American Cultural Center of Morocco to organize a seven-city, thirteen-event tour of HHBE language and culture workshops in Morocco and Paris focusing on Native American sovereignty, U.S.-Mexico migration, and artistic resistance to xenophobic politics. In 2018, I returned to Paris to conduct additional ethnographic interviews and facilitate an HHBE artist and practitioner roundtable at the Université de Paris X–Nanterre that brought together participants from Arizona, Morocco, Mexico, the Navajo and Hualapai Nations, and France to share their works and insights.

Following the models of hooks's (1994) and Freire's (1973) transformative and critical pedagogies, the third method employed in this research is critical reflection, which is an important tool for all teachers. The five years that have passed since beginning fieldwork have been especially valuable for reflecting on the data generated, comparing it with similar work in other research sites, and situating it within the broader contexts of global HHBE practices.

HHBE IN PARIS: INFRASTRUCTURE, INSTITUTIONS, AND ACTORS

Although HHBE is a newer research field, French educators have been using rap as a teaching tool in elementary and secondary schools since the 1980s, and French universities have offered courses on hip-hop topics since the latter half of the same decade (Durand, Milon, and Norton 2018). Not limited to formal education, artists and social animators in France have been using HHBE in community-based writing workshops since at least the early 1990s. According to Puma (1997), HHBE has been particularly successful in encouraging students from low-income and marginalized backgrounds to write and expand their vocabularies

> Rap is the first French popular music created in this [working-class] social milieu, for once triumphant. While whole generations of teachers have struggled in vain to try to interest children in literature, a few popular songs by MC Solaar or IAM are enough for a whole generation to be passionate about writing rhymes and frequent consultation of the dictionary! (8)[5]

Despite its early adoption by traditional educators, community-driven, youth-focused writing workshops remain the most common HHBE interventions in France today. These workshops are part of a larger network of public funding and support for hip-hop and other arts that is very different from the U.S. context, where profit-driven models are the norm and public funding for arts and education has been steadily declining. In order to better understand the primary institutions and actors of HHBE in France, we must first understand the financial infrastructure that undergirds this system.

Infrastructure

Paris is perennially one of the top tourist destinations in the world, and the city's arts and culture are among its most alluring features. While internationally recognizable icons like the Eiffel Tower and Notre Dame market themselves, lesser-known Parisian regions use hip-hop culture to attract tourists and the revenue they generate. Furthermore, the city's historic and prolific arts scene, combined with its relatively small size, have led to high operating costs for performing arts centers (Norton 2015). In order to encourage a flourishing, dynamic artistic culture, French and Parisian governments have devoted significant resources to creating a financial infrastructure to support this system. The two most salient features of this infrastructure relating to HHBE are tourism and financial subsidies. The 13th *arrondissement* is the epicenter of Parisian hip-hop tourism and is addressed in greater detail in the next section; however, artistic subsidies are part of the larger system within France's manifestation of the welfare state.

According to veteran hip-hop educator Ludovic Sauvajot, whom I interviewed in Paris in 2013, organizing concerts and events in the French capital is not financially viable due to the elevated cost of living: "Unless you are organizing a huge event like a Jay-Z and Beyoncé concert at Bercy, it is almost impossible to turn a profit from organizing concerts in Paris."[6] Thus, explained Sauvajot, in order to encourage the performing arts scene that is vital to tourism and French patrimony, the French governments at the national, regional, provincial, departmental, prefectural, and municipal levels actively subsidize artists, technicians, events, and centers for training and performing arts to make them financially viable. Although many artists and fans are grateful for this support (which even includes a provision where unemployed artists can get a salary from the French government), Sauvajot is ambivalent about these subsidies. On the one hand, the musical scene in Paris would not be as rich and dynamic without them; on the other hand, Sauvajot feels that this government funding has created entitled artists and performers

> Since the 1980s, state support of the music industry in France has created many well-equipped concert halls, but has also created a sense of entitlement, especially among younger artists. Nowadays, many artists are more concerned about the quality of their equipment than with performing a good show on a consistent basis.

Sauvajot's lamentation about this entitlement and how it affects the quality of artistic production in France has been expressed by other critics, as well. More than twenty-five years ago, Fumaroli (1991) and Schneider (1993) both argued that the same subsidies that facilitate HHBE in Paris today have historically contributed to a decline in the quality of the French arts across generic boundaries.

Institutions

This section identifies the key organizations and established practices that use the financial infrastructure described earlier to make HHBE in Paris possible. Following these institutions have been divided into three sections based on their functions and are listed with brief descriptions and examples. Examples of *Financial Institutions* have been drawn from the "Partenaires" page of 123...RAP!'s website; further examples are taken from other project data.[7]

Financial institutions provide the funding necessary to carry out HHBE activities in Paris:

- Governments (local, regional, national, and foreign) provide the bulk of funding for HHBE activities in Paris. For example, during the 2017–2018 academic year, 123...RAP! received funding from: the mayor's office of Paris's 18th *arrondissement*, Paris's city hall, the city of Saint-Denis, the Prefecture of Ile-de-France, Service Civique (part of the French Ministry of Education), and the U.S. embassies in Algiers (Algeria) and Paris (France).
- Private-sector foundations run by large corporate enterprises also contribute significant funding and support. 123...RAP!'s patrons include Fondation Batigère, Fondation BNP Paribas, Fondation HSBC pour l'Education, and Fondation Auchan pour la Jeunesse.

Beyond financial concerns, *host institutions* play an integral part in providing the physical space where HHBE formations take place.

- Cultural centers are found throughout Paris and its suburbs, often concentrated in low-income neighborhoods and targeting their services and outreach to local youth. Cultural centers partnering with 123...RAP! to provide space for workshops include Espace Jeunes Mahalia Jackson in Paris's 20th *arrondissement*; Centre Social et Cultural Rosa-Parks in Paris's 19th; La Maison Verte in the 18th; and Mains d'Œuvres in Saint-Ouen.
- *Maisons de quartier* (neighborhood houses) are similar to cultural centers but are usually smaller and more intimate and can be likened to after-school centers in the United States. Les Voisins-le-Bretonneux is a *maison de quartier* in the Parisian suburb of Versailles where Gaël Faye learned to process the traumas of being a refugee via creative writing and expression at after-school writing workshops.
- *Salles de concert et formation* (concert and instructional training rooms) are publically subsidized spaces where youth and emerging artists can receive artistic training and enjoy free or affordable access to performance space. Noteworthy concert and training rooms in Paris are the Centre Musical Fleury Goutte d'Or-Barbara in Paris's 18th and the resplendent, newly opened La Place in the center of Paris at Les Halles.

Educational institutions also play a role in the HHBE in Paris, which include primary and secondary schools and universities. The Université de Paris X–Nanterre has emerged as an important center for HHBE teaching and research based on decades of work from established professors like Alain Milon and Alain Vulbeau and emerging scholars like Charles Norton, Sidy Seye, and Aurel Fleureux.

Lastly, *interactional institutions* are not fixed spaces or organizations but the events through which HHBE initiatives are carried out. Obviously, HHBE activities are conducted in traditional classroom settings, but the majority of Parisian HHBE and social engagements transpire in the following two settings:

- *Ateliers* (workshops) is the general name used for HHBE learning meetings that take place outside of the formal education system. The most common workshops are organized around writing and poetic composition, are hosted in cultural centers or *maisons de quartier*, and are led by one or more of the following people: engaged artists, social animators, and volunteers (more on these HHBE actors in the next section). Workshops usually meet on a weekly basis during the school year (September through May) and, unless expressly stated otherwise, are free, open to the public, and target local youth for participation. When relating specifically to social engagement, these workshops have been an important tool for government intervention in what French policy makers call *quartiers sensibles*, or sensitive neighborhoods. These "sensitive" neighborhoods are usually low-income, ethnically diverse, home to large immigrant populations, and spatially marginalized and play host to persistent crime and/or civil unrest.[8]
- Festivals play a major role in French governments' efforts to engage and improve the quality of life for residents in *quartiers sensibles*. While hip-hop music and culture remain popular across French demographics, suburbs of major cities (especially Paris) are home to the largest concentrations of hip-hop performers, practitioners, and fans. Ironically, most hip-hop concerts and events take place within major cities (again, especially Paris), where the distance from the suburbs and cost of admission prevent many suburban residents from attending. French hip-hop festivals are different from US musical festivals readers may be more familiar with (e.g., Coachella and Burning Man). Rather than being organized around debaucherous weekends of music and partying, French hip-hop festivals are often months long; host diverse events at myriad sites; feature multimedia arts; and privilege community participation vis-à-vis open mics, cyphers, master classes, panel discussions, art exhibitions, and film screenings in addition to musical performances. Examples of French hip-hop festivals

include Festival Paris Hip Hop, Ile-de-France Buzz Booster, Festival Terre(s) Hip-Hop, and Festival Hip-Hop Art Mature.

Actors

The actors in Parisian HHBE are not very different from their counterparts in the United States, albeit with one major exception:

- Engaged artists are performing artists who regularly take on voluntary community outreach in addition to producing creative works. The most common form of their engagement is hosting writing workshops. However, as I show in the next section, these community engagements take many forms. Many well-known French hip-hop artists have been active in community service for years, and there is not adequate space here to list them all. However, a few examples are: Kery James, Demi Portion, S. Pri Noir, Pumpkin, Franglish, Hamé and Ekoué of La Rumeur, and Gaël Faye.
- Social animators are a class of cultural and educative workers who lead formations and training, usually with low-income, at-risk youth. While there is to my knowledge no direct equivalent in the United States, social animators in France combine elements of teaching, youth outreach, and social work.
- Volunteers are an important component of Parisian HHBE, despite the presence of paid social animators. Volunteers come from diverse backgrounds and contribute to HHBE operations as they are able and needed. University students (and, increasingly, professionals in other fields) looking to gain teaching experience and for new challenges form the majority of volunteers that I have encountered in my HHBE work in Paris.
- *Fonctionnaires*, or salaried civil servant office employees, are an emergent and extremely important category of HHBE actors. My research in 2013–2014 revealed that a lack of professionalization in Parisian HHBE institutions was a major challenge to overcome. Since then, two of the most important HHBE organizations in Paris, 123...RAP! and La Place, have hired full-time administrators to coordinate the various aspects of their respective organizations. This commitment to hiring full-time support staff is a significant positive development in Parisian HHBE and beyond.
- Lastly, HHBE would not be possible without students. Students in Parisian HHBE workshops are mostly ages eighteen and under. However, it is not uncommon for adults and older folks to participate in workshops and other interventions. Unfortunately, HHBE student participants are overwhelmingly male, so encouraging young women and girls to participate is an old challenge that needs more work (Norton 2015).

HHBE PARIS: ACTOR AND INSTITUTION SHOWCASE

Now that readers are more familiar with the major components of Parisian HHBE, it is helpful to present a few of the institutions and actors that have been particularly successful.

123...RAP!

Founded in 2012, 123...RAP! is a cultural association that has been using HHBE methods to offer free English-language, cultural, and artistic formations to Parisian youth for more than five years. 123...RAP! works to empower youth through four primary actions:

1. Weekly English-language and culture workshops. During the 2017–2018 academic year, 123...RAP! held five free, weekly workshops in cultural centers in low-income neighborhoods in Paris's 18th, 19th, and 20th *arrondissements* and the suburb of Saint-Denis. In the past, weekly workshops have also been held in the suburbs of Saint-Ouen, La Courneuve, Vitry-sur-Seine, Sartrouville, and Villiers-le-Bel.
2. Shorter-term and one-off engagements where 123...RAP!'s hip-hop educators bring workshops to local schools and businesses. Likewise, 123...RAP! also organizes one-off artistic and cultural training sessions led by engaged artists from regions across France and abroad.
3. Organizing end-of-the-school-year recording sessions and performances, which give students attending weekly workshops a chance to perform and share what they have learned with their own communities and beyond. Each year, 123...RAP! has engaged professional hip-hop artists to collaborate and guide students through their first experiences recording and performing. Past guest artists include Parisian MCs S. Pri Noir, Nakk Mendosa, Leo Seviyor, and Franglish, as well as veteran American solo MC and Crown City Rockers front man Raashan Ahmad.
4. Group trips abroad (London in 2015 and New York in 2016) give students opportunities to practice English with native speakers through linguistic and cultural immersion and, for most, experience international travel for the first time.

Most recently, 123...RAP! successfully debuted *Pimp Mon Anglais*, an HHBE MOOC (massive open online course) that is free and available to learners across the world (https://www.onetwothreerap.com/evenements-1/pimp-mon-anglais-elu-mooc-le-plus-original-de-2016).

La Place

After more than eight years of planning, La Place opened in 2016 along with the newly renovated canopy at Les Halles in the center of Paris. According to a 2018 personal correspondence with Anne Le Mottais, then–director of cultural action and public relations, La Place's mission is

> to promote all disciplines of hip-hop culture (dance, rap, DJing, graffiti, beat-boxing, and visual arts) through dissemination, transmission, and support for creation and accompaniment. Created as a place of expression dedicated to the hip-hop movement and its actors, La Place is a space where all hip-hop disciplines and practitioners can find space to practice, perform, and transmit their art and works.

The facilities at La Place include creative spaces (audio-recording studios, video-editing studios, and practice rooms), performance spaces (a large concert hall, dance studio, visual art gallery, conference room, cinema, and more intimate spaces for smaller gatherings or stand-up comedy), professional spaces (an entrepreneurial center and coworking space for hip-hop-centric businesses and professionals), and a café-bar for socializing and networking. In addition to world-class facilities, La Place also offers regular programs and training for emerging artists as well as the general public:

- master classes on hip-hop dance, graffiti, and navigating careers in the music industry;
- conferences, soirées, and performances;
- workshops and programs for young children and families;
- workshops for students on hip-hop history, performance, and empowerment (organized both at the center and on-site at schools); and
- hip-hop and artistic professionalization seminars.

Finally, La Place works toward culturally appropriate hip-hop public policy by developing partnerships with local, regional, national, and international partners; provides support for students and researchers interested in hip-hop cultures; creates bridges between public and private HHBE institutions and actors; and hosts foreign visitors.

Gaël Faye

Gaël Faye is a Franco-Rwandan MC, author, activist, and performer. Born in Burundi in 1982, he relocated to the Parisian suburbs at age thirteen as a refugee fleeing the Rwandan civil war. After learning to rap and write poetry as a teenager at a *maison de quartier* in Versailles, Faye earned a master's degree in economics and worked in the finance industry in London for several years before returning to France to pursue a career in arts and music.[9] He is a founding member of the live-band-backed hip-hop group Milk Coffee & Sugar and has achieved commercial and critical success with solo albums in 2013 (*Pili Pili sur un Croissant Beurre*, or Pili Pili Hot Sauce on a Butter Croissant), 2017 (*Rythmes et Botanique*, or Rhythms and Botanics), and 2018 (*Des Fleurs*, or Flowers). In 2016, Faye won the Goncourt Prize for his debut novel, *Petit Pays*, and in 2018 he won a Victoires de la Musique prize (the French Grammy) for the performance of his song "Paris Métèque" (Paris Half-Breed).

Faye is included on this list for his dedication to social engagement and accessibility to students and educators. He has mentored and performed with music students at the Sorbonne, composed the official theme song for the government of Rwanda's commemorative ceremonies of the twentieth anniversary of the Rwandan genocide, was the spokesperson for South African artist Bruce Clarke's *Les Hommes Debout* (Men Standing Up) arts and human rights campaign, and is the secretary of the Collectif des Parties Civiles pour le Rwanda, an organization that prepares legal actions against suspected leaders of the Rwandan genocide who have thus far escaped justice.[10] Faye also facilitates free writing, music, and professionalization workshops to students and emerging artists in France and Rwanda.[11] When I interviewed him in Meudon-la-Forêt in 2014, Faye identified his main goal as strengthening the capacity and infrastructure of the Rwandan artistic scene:

> It's true that more and more my goal is to invest my time and energy in the development of Rwanda's cultural resources and to build bridges between France and Rwanda. . . . For example, things that are very common in France require a lot of political and collective effort to accomplish in Rwanda: having access to concert halls and performance spaces, having trained sound engineers, being able to invite and attract artists from outside Rwanda to come there to perform, organizing nationwide tours for these artists and not just having shows in Kigali, etc. I have had a lot of success and made a lot of professional contacts in France; at this point in my life, it is important for me to leverage my success and professional network to develop the artistic infrastructure and institutions in Rwanda. (Norton 2015)[12]

The *Mairie* (Mayor's Office) of the 13th *Arrondissement*

Municipally, Paris is divided into twenty units called *arrondissements*, each with its own mayor, administrative offices, and staffs. Paris's arrondissements are numbered 1 through 20, with the 1st *arrondissement* being the oldest and located in the city center and spiraling out from there clockwise to end with the 20th *arrondissement* on Paris's east side. The 13th is a large *arrondissement* in the southeast corner of the city that was, until fairly recently, known mostly for its nondescript industrial infrastructure and diverse residential neighborhoods. Long home to illicit graffiti painted on the crumbling industrial buildings, as well as internationally acclaimed stencil and street artist Miss.Tic, within the past ten years the 13th has used public funding and its reputation as a haven for graffiti to raise its touristic profile by transforming itself into an international street art destination equal to New York and Lisbon. This success, recognized with mayor Jérôme Coumet's 2016 Marianne d'Or award for civic innovation, has been achieved through three main avenues:

- The Tour Paris 13 was an aging housing project, situated on the Quai d'Austerlitz, overlooking the Seine River, and slated for demolition. Prior to its razing in 2014, the 13th *arrondissement*'s city hall collaborated with Galerie Itinerrance and the building's owner to invite one hundred renowned street artists from sixteen countries to transform the tower into the largest street art exhibition ever realized. Free and open to the public during October 2013 (which the Mairie of the 13th branded as the "Month of Street Art"), the Tour Paris 13 encompassed 4,500 square meters of art, including thirty-six apartments (many of which were still-furnished four- and five-bedroom units) spanning the buildings' nine stories and basement. During the month that it was open, the Tour Paris 13 received more than thirty thousand visitors.[13]
- Capitalizing on the popularity of the Tour Paris 13, the Mairie of the 13th continued to collaborate with Galerie Itinerrance to commission numerous large, public murals by high-profile international street artists. These works are concentrated along the scenic aboveground section of the RATP's Metro Line 6, with the most acclaimed being Shepard Fairley's 2016 mural *Liberté, Egalité, Fraternité*, honoring victims of the coordinated terrorist attacks in November 2015 that killed 137 people.
- Carte de Parcours (Walking Tour Map) is a self-guided walking tour showcasing the best of Paris 13's street art, both new and old. A map and accompanying information about the route and artists is available for free online (http://www.streetart13.fr/).

CONCLUSION

This chapter demonstrates that Paris is home to a dynamic, thriving landscape of HHBE and social engagement by identifying and describing the infrastructure, institutions, and actors that make this possible. During the four years that have passed since completing my first fieldwork, the two largest HHBE institutions in Paris (123...RAP! and La Place) have both hired full-time administrators to improve organizational communication and coordination, which was the biggest challenge identified by earlier research (Norton 2015).

While progress has been made, other challenges remain. Although many volunteers and HHBE professionals are women, the overwhelming majority of engaged artists and workshop participants are men. Furthermore, during a 2017 interview, Randa Chekoun—123...RAP!'s director of communication and development—shared that the organization still has considerable difficulty finding Anglophone volunteer teachers, making learning aspects of HHBE workshops consistently interesting, and finding private-sector funding that is not earmarked for very specific activities. Chekoun also noted that, due to the age and minor status of most of 123...RAP!'s participants, it is difficult to organize group activities beyond workshops (e.g., going to concerts at venues requiring that spectators be adults). Despite these challenges, this research shows that Paris is nonetheless a global leader in HHBE due to its diversity of engagements, strong public funding and support, international reach and influence, and increasing commitment to professionalization.

APPENDIX: HHBE RESOURCES IN PARIS AND BEYOND

- 123...RAP!: Parisian HHBE cultural association, http://onetwothree-rap.com/, https://www.facebook.com/OneTwoThreeRap/
- Centquatre: Huge cultural center in Paris's 19th *arrondissement*, http://www.104.fr/
- Centre Musical Fleury Goutte d'Or-Barbara: Cultural center in Paris 18 that has offered robust hip-hop and urban arts training sessions and content for many years, http://www.fgo-barbara.fr/home
- Centre Social et Cultural Rosa-Parks: Cultural center in Paris 19, https://www.centrerosaparks.paris/
- Espace Icare: Cultural center located in the suburb of Issy-les-Moulineaux, http://espace-icare.net/
- Espace Jeunes Mahalia Jackson: Cultural center in Paris 20, https://www.paris.fr/equipements/espace-paris-jeunes-mahalia-jackson-17916
- Festival Paris Hip-Hop: Paris's longest-running annual hip-hop festival, http://paris-hiphop.com/
- Galerie Itinerrance: Urban art gallery in Paris 13, http://itinerrance.fr/
- Hiphopedia: Online hip-hop encyclopedia and space for discussion and exchange regarding Parisian hip-hop culture, https://www.hiphopedia.org/
- Hip Open: HHBE organization based in Toulouse, https://hipopen.net/
- La Bellevilloise: Venue and gallery in Paris 20, http://www.labellevilloise.com/

- La Maison du Hip Hop: Dynamic hip-hop cultural association located in Paris's 11th and 20th districts that has offered numerous HHBE and community outreach activities for years, http://www.maisonduhiphop.com
- La Maison Verte: Cultural center in Paris 18, http://blog.lamaison verte.org/
- La Place: Paris's premier hip-hop cultural center in the heart of the city, http://laplace.paris/, https://www.youtube.com/watch?v=CFG4yInqhUc
- Les Voisins-le-Bretonneux: *Maison de quartier* in Versailles, http://www.voisins78.fr/
- Mains d'Œuvres: *Maison de quartier* in Saint-Ouen, http://www.mainsdoeuvres.org/
- Mairie of the 13th *Arrondissement* in Paris, https://www.mairie13.paris.fr/
- Pimp Mon Anglais: Free HHBE MOOC developed by 123...RAP!, https://pimpmonanglais.com/
- *Quand deux fleuves se rencontrent*: Film depicting some of artist Gaël Faye's social engagement work in Paris and Rwanda, http://vimeo.com/82387913
- Street Art 13: Guide to street art tourism in Paris 13, http://www.streetart13.fr/

REFERENCES

Bazin, Hugues. "Hip-Hop Dance: Emergence of a Popular Art Form in France." In *Black, Blanc, Beur: Rap Music and Hip-Hop Culture in the Francophone World*, edited by Alain-Philippe Durand, 99–105. Lanham, MD: Scarecrow Press, 2002.

Benguigui, Yamina. *Mémoires d'immigrés: L'héritage maghrébin*. Paris: Canal+ Éditions, 1997.

Burbach, Roger, Orlando Núñez Soto, and Boris Kagarlitsky. *Globalization and Its Discontents: The Rise of Postmodern Socialisms*. London: Pluto Press, 1997.

Calloway, Sway. "Interview with Bambaataa." *Sway in the Morning*. New York: Shade 45 XM, 7 November 2014. Radio. https://www.youtube.com/watch?v=_ElDi4yFw_s

Chang, Jeff. *Can't Stop Won't Stop: A History of the Hip-Hop Generation*. New York: St. Martin's Press, 2005.

DuBois, Andrew, Henry Louis Gates Jr., and Chuck D. *The Anthology of Rap*. New Haven, CT: Yale University Press, 2011.

Durand, Alain-Philippe, Alain Milon, and Charles Norton. "Pédagogie Hip-Hop Trans Amérique." In *Heurs et malheurs du système éducatif en France*, edited by Marie-Christine Weidemann Koop, 95–114. Marion, IL: *The French Review* Book Series, 2018.

Faye, Gaël. *Petit pays*. Paris: Grasset, 2016.

Freire, Paulo. *Pedagogy of the Oppressed* (rev. ed.). New York: Continuum, (1970) 1993.

———. *Education for Critical Consciousness*. Vol. 1. London: Bloomsbury, 1973.

Fumaroli, Marc. *L'État culturel: Essai sur une religion moderne*. Paris: Éditions de Fallois, 1991.

George, Nelson. *Hip Hop America*. New York: Penguin, 2005.

Giroux, Henry. "Lessons from Paulo Freire." *Chronicle of Higher Education* 57, no. 9 (2010): B15–B16.

Hale, Thomas A. *Griots and Griottes: Masters of Words and Music*. Bloomington: Indiana University Press, 1998.

Hill, Marc Lamont. *Beats, Rhymes, and Classroom Life: Hip-Hop Pedagogy and the Politics of Identity*. New York: Teachers College Press, 2009.

hooks, bell. *Teaching to Transgress: Education as the Practice of Freedom*. London: Routledge, (1994) 2014.

Lafargue de Grangeneuve, Loïc. *Politique du hip-hop: Action publique et cultures urbaines*. Toulouse: Presses Universitaires du Mirail, 2008.

McKechnie, Lynne E. F. "Participant Observation." In *The SAGE Encyclopedia of Qualitative Research Methods*, edited by Lisa M. Given, 599–600. Thousand Oaks, CA: SAGE, 2008.

Norton, Charles. "Engagement social et éducation dans la culture hip-hop parisienne." M.A. thesis, University of Arizona, 2015. https://hcommons.org/deposits/item/hc:13555/

Oliver, M. "The French (Hip-Hop) Revolution." *DJBOOTH*, 28 June 2019. https://djbooth.net/features/2019-06-26-the-french-hip-hop-revolution

Petchauer, Emery. "Framing and Reviewing Hip-Hop Educational Research." *Review of Educational Research* 79, no. 2 (2009): 946–78.

Prévos, André J. M. "Two Decades of Rap in France: Emergence, Developments, Prospects." In *Black, Blanc, Beur: Rap Music and Hip-Hop Culture in the Francophone World*, edited by Alain-Philippe Durand, 124–37. Lanham, MD: Scarecrow Press, 2002.

Puma, Clyde. *Le rap français*. Paris: Éditions Hors collection, 1997.

Roediger, David. "What to Make of Wiggers: A Work in Progress." In *Generations of Youth: Youth Cultures and History in Twentieth-Century America*, edited by Joe Austin and Michael N. Willard, 358–66. New York: New York University Press, 1998.

Rose, Tricia. *Black Noise: Rap Music and Black Culture in Contemporary America*. Hanover, NH: University Press of New England, 1994.

Schneider, Michel. *La comédie de la culture*. Paris: Éditions du Seuil, 1993.

Smitherman, Geneva. "'The Chain Remain the Same': Communicative Practices in the Hip Hop Nation." *Journal of Black Studies* 28, no. 1 (September 1997): 3–25.

Spradley, James P. *The Ethnographic Interview*. Long Grove, IL: Waveland Press, (1979) 2016.

Van Willigen, John. *Applied Anthropology: An Introduction*. Westport, CT: Bergin & Garvey, 2002.

Vulbeau, Alain. *Du tag au tag*. Paris: Desclée de Brouwer, 1992.

Zukin, Cliff, et al. *A New Engagement? Political Participation, Civic Life, and the Changing American Citizen*. New York: Oxford University Press, 2006.

DISCOGRAPHY AND FILMOGRAPHY

Bozino, Nicolas, and Toumani Sangaré, dirs. *Quand deux fleuves se rencontrent*. France Ô. Originally released in 2014. http://www.les-docus.com/gael-faye-quand-deux-fleuves-se-rencontrent/

Faye, Gaël. *Pili Pili sur un croissant beurre*. Universal, compact disc. Originally released in 2013.

———. *Rythmes et botanique*. Universal, compact disc. Originally released in 2017.

———. *Des fleurs*. Universal, compact disc. Originally released in 2018.

Grandmaster Flash and the Furious Five. *The Message*. Sugar Hill Records, vinyl. Originally released in 1982.

Various Artists. *Rapattitude*. Virgin, compact disc. Originally released in 1989.

Chapter Nine

The Body Politic of Hip-Hop Dance

What Hip-Hop Dance's Relation with French Society and Institutions Tells Us about the Place of Popular Art and Its Political Stakes

Hugues Bazin,
Translated by André Pettman

The body politic refers to the relationship of the body to the public, to the stereotypes and the consequences of power over the body. What happens when a new body, a body dancing and thinking hip-hop, appears in the public sphere of the street, the media, and the theater scene? Understanding current issues means understanding how the body reacts in public space. Is the body ruled by it, or on the contrary, does it open a new space by spreading itself out through it? This immersion in space provokes a political thrust of a living art, an *art à l'état vif*. But have cultural institutions taken it into account in this political dimension, or have they simply seized upon it?

THE NATURAL BODY AND LIVING ART

The body is the original accessible material that we carry everywhere; hip-hop will make it a tool of expression even before the words exist to describe the cultural movement. In France, it is through dance that the generation of the 1980s appropriates the elements of hip-hop culture. This aesthetic grammar constitutes "style." Style describes both its individuality and the group to which it belongs. This is why it occupies a preponderant place in more or less ritualized processes of socialization. It facilitates entry into the circle of the initiated as an identification code and at the same time is the affirmation of an original personality as a code of distinction. This is what distinguishes "having a style" (developing a fashion) and "having style" (developing a lifestyle). By playing on these two repertoires in a balance between appearance and meaning, the superficial appearance of a form and the depth of a way of being, each seeks an agreement with its environment through freedom of movement.

Style borrows from different vocabularies and cultural heritages, both traditional and modern. The space-time of parties and "free parties" is where the deejay plays a central role, letting in musical trends from mix and electronic culture: disco, hip-hop, house, techno, jungle, trip-hop, ambient, dance. House dance, hype, and other components of hip-hop dance will draw from this energy of club culture and prior forms, such as musicals (tap dance and the famous acrobatic tricks of the Nicholas Brothers), R&B shows (from the famous dance steps of James Brown to those of the "King of Pop" Michael Jackson), rock and lounge dances (Lindy hop, Charleston), and jazz dances, which set all the parts of the body into action. Another inexhaustible source is obviously street dance forms and the combat of the ghetto: directly derived from gang life, the crip walk is a warrior celebration based solely on leg movements, much like uprock (or rocking), which is a direct confrontation of two groups face to face in a synchronized movement in the art of evasion, not to mention older inspirations from Brazilian capoeira to Asian martial arts. The historical spine remains structured by dance on the ground and standing dance. Break dance recomposes the figures of the circle on the ground with a preparation for the descent (top rock). Dancers establish a new hierarchy in the role of body parts by modifying the main points of support. Thus, rotations on the head (head spin, tracks), on the hands (the Ninety-Nine, the Scorpion, or the Thomas), or on the back or shoulders (the dome or crown) free the legs of their supporting role. Six-step is the basic sequence of break-dancing footwork that, depending on the imagination and virtuosity of the dancer, establishes a link between the main phases of the break. As for standing dance, it includes a great variety of styles based on muscle contraction and relaxation (boogie, moonwalk, vogueing, popping, locking, pointing, micro-drive, Tetris, etc.).

Hip-hop dance cannot be enumerated as a series of techniques. The whole creative game is at the level of expression: between the details and the major steps, between standing dance and dance on the ground, between the reference to academic bases and research in various fields, between the work on the material of the form and the exploration of universes of cultural recognition. Thus styles perpetually reconstruct themselves into new movements, such as the impulses of krump, which do not hesitate to rub up against baroque or more recently ghost flow, a fusion of the gestures of hip-hop, body tap, and bikutsi, a dance originating in Cameroon and developed by the choreographer Michel "Meech" Onomo. Initiation and creation are inseparable actions: "From micro to macro, ancestral to contemporary, intimate to global—so many passages, crossings, abandons, and offerings. From one space to another, from death to birth, from silence to emergence, from the hidden deep to its revelation, the rite to heal and to feel the sins/signs of the body? Everything leads me to desire reinventing a function of the constraint of ritual and initiation. Can the memory of the body soothe us?" (*Le Syndrome de l'initié* [Syndrome of the Initiated] 2018).

This "style" finally transforms the body into a medium, an appropriable material. It cannot be reduced to a mere transitory effect as its mediatization and its commodification can lead us to believe. In the beginning, the media were able to assimilate hip-hop into an adolescent effervescence. They saw only the superficial part of a fashion phenomenon in the explosion of the practice of dance between 1984 and 1985 thanks to the broadcast of the program *H.I.P. H.O.P.* (hosted by Sidney, first on French public radio, then on the TF1 television channel). But dance as an aesthetic form does not only find its reason for being in the pleasure of viewing it. It is not pure emotion detached from reality; it compels us to reflect on our relationship to the world. "There is a place in this world where I am at home, and that place is called my body. My body and the inside of my body. This little place goes everywhere with me in the world, it runs away when I run away and it stays when I stay and nobody can ask me to leave it, to change color, name, or feet. No one except death can tell me that I do not have the right, all of a sudden, to be where I am, that is to say, in my body" (*Corps pour corps* [Body for Body] 2017).

Hip-hop dance will make visible a body in public space, that of the explosive youth of the popular neighborhoods, an ebony, golden, mixed-race body of sons and daughters of immigrants from the former North African and Central African colonies and descendants of slaves living in France's Overseas Departments and Territories (DOM-TOM). This country has some difficulties, to say the least, facing up to its cultural diversity when, in fact, this youth is its greatest chance. It is an "invisible" population because it does not appear in the media, in socioeconomic decision-making bodies, or in political representation. It is their parents who came to work in factories and administrations and participate in the economic development of the country. These working families know what politics does to the body; it is a matter of life and death. While their parents wear themselves out working in factories, their children suffer discrimination. The submission of the body produces the same humiliation. The technology of power is exercised in the sensitive experience of pain, of the degradation of the body. Humiliation remains the privileged medium of erasing the subject in its very quality as a human being. To resist this domination is to analyze humiliation primarily as a decisive political issue.

If the dominated body is defined by deprivation, lack of access to the center, to places dedicated to evenings, hip-hop culture will create new popular centralities, making this repressed body, this body "in excess," the body of an inalienable freedom, a natural art in a lively state. "What is more solid and tangible than to unite for the sake of art? Sharing the same identity was for dancers so easy in the name of hip hop. I wondered why we could not, on a large scale, have united in this way . . . in our differences, and began then to think also about what makes up the body of France" (Slimani and Célinain 2018).

Making this body visible through dance disrupts the stereotypes plastered onto the "rich" and the "poor" bodies: beauty, health, success, and dynamism or the stigmas of labor, suffering, and life in the slums. The hip-hop body translates the dynamism of a creative youth that reconstructs aesthetic forms via imitation—creation—cutting—collage—recuperation—sampling that typify art forms for the people. It also reveals the relationship of economic and cultural domination, bringing to mind the darkest moments of French history that always confine part of the working class in a status of subcitizen. Dance brings this complexity to the fore. The body is the place where the intimate and the political are intertwined between the expression of feelings and the incorporation of oppressions. The "inside" is an operation of the "outside." The social conditions of production of the person are housed in these folds.

If dance expands perception to the whole of reality, political power will reduce this perception. It will recognize only the first side, that of a hip-hop aesthetic that will be recuperated by cultural institutions and the market economy. But it will refuse the second side, that which reveals the conditions of a social injustice and the richness of a multicultural contribution. Forty years later, it is the same pattern that takes place with dominated minorities. The recent victory of the French soccer players at the 2018 World Cup is a new illustration of this. This victory led to a garden party at the Elysée Palace. In front of the president of the republic, the football players sang and danced a mix of Creole hip-hop, the same working-class origin that gave birth to hip-hop. Political power wants to recognize this culture for its athletic and fun qualities as the marketing image of an individual entrepreneurial culture, without in any way acknowledging what comes from a collective resistance to territorial relegation and racial discrimination.

Working-class participants logically progress better in milieus that will privilege their skills independent of their origins. However, as soon as these athletic and hip-hop bodies—praised under the gilded trappings of official venues—return to their working-class neighborhoods, they are stopped, frisked, and patted down by law enforcement, cleared out of the bourgeois downtowns by municipal decrees and by the aggressive design of street furnishings that prevent young people from sitting or laying down (Bazin

2017). It is this feminine or masculine body—exoticized and eroticized in commercial and political messages—that is violated and martyred, reminding us that it is always the body of the dominated that is laid bare (literally as well as figuratively) and exposed to social violence, while the body of the dominant is protected. A young black or Arab person learns very early on in French streets not to run in view of police officers for risk of injury and pursuit because *if one runs, it means one is fleeing, and if one flees, it means one is guilty*. In 2005, two young men, Zyed Benna and Bouna Traore, died by electrocution in the Paris suburbs hiding in an electric transformer after being chased by the police. This was followed by several weeks of violent rebellion in numerous working-class neighborhoods of France and the imposition of a state-mandated curfew.

"The more we talk about the violence of the world, the more we defeat the violence of the world, the more we have a chance to produce beauty" (Louis 2018). This violence cannot be deconstructed as long as the body is seen only by its exterior sheath; no thought of the interior will be feasible. Since politics impacts the intimate, the intimate becomes political. This "reversal" of the corporeal sheath, if it is combined with the reversal of its environment, touches upon the conditions of oppression. Hip-hop dance has made it possible to overcome the grip of fear in this reversal between interior and exterior space. Where the city refuses meeting and expression, where others look away, hip-hop dance will establish the site of an improvised stage. This invisible body, repressed, folded, relegated to the peripheries, begins then to give rhythm to the heart of places where no one expects it. This fundamental act of appropriating its living space recomposes the unicity of its life course.

"Here I spent my time running, always faster, until exhaustion. After what? It is clear to me that this race was a flight, I left my life there. The entirety of my time spent on projects, thrown far beyond my present. And dance, dance that served as an escape. I drowned in it. It was the only door that had been opened for me, I dived into it" (Slimani 2015). It is the body that resists, the body that makes visible, the body that transforms social space via the disruption of the norm. If there really is a space where this confrontation between art and power takes place, it is the public space between those that practice space and those that want to control its wild, disorganized, unlikely, ungoverned character.

The street is a fight, a challenge. Hip-hop will make it a place of intermingling and a school seeking to codify its most warlike aspects to make it an art of evasion, using movements of linkage and of repetition of daily life. Unlike classical dance (vertical yearning), the street lowers the center of gravity toward the ground. At the lowest of slabs and building halls, concrete takes on the role of Mother Earth. By this reversal, the pivoting of the bases, movement draws its strength from the hardness of the materials and of social conditions. Banging into cement cements oneself. It is in this structuring force that a collective consciousness can be born.

"We are dead that come back to life and must feel like they exist. Once stripped of these artifices, the dancer is left with one body, which could be any body. The artifices that covered it were those which fashion or society think we need in order to identify ourselves or differentiate ourselves from the majority. What these 'detours' allow us to do is produce ourselves through culture as new subjects" (Miredin and Bénac-Giroux 2017). It is a stripped-down, radical experience of one's self and one's origin, until one understands that this experience and origin are no longer points in the past but of the future. Identity is not closed, endured, and reified in cultural traits assigned to the body. It is open and constructed, what the theorists of *antillanité* (West Indian-ness) call "rhizome culture," that is to say, something other than an assignment—precisely not a "thing" but a dancer, a person in motion who puts others in motion through their expression of their search.

The body is not thought before movement; rather, movement develops a notion of the body. Posture and gestures, how one moves and behaves: This "state of motion" informs us of the existence of whoever occupies the body and also of the social space that the body interiorizes, its constraints, its cleavages, and its fractures. The state of motion characterizes this self-consciousness of being in motion in those particular moments of existence that makes one's life a work in rhythm with the beat of the world, of singular situations. It is not necessarily an artistic work—it is first a human work—but, in all cases of expression, an enigma unique to our unfinished human condition, always in the making, never finished.

This thinking body is not produced by the words of a choreographic language. It creates a space that liberates the body of archetypes, either primitivist and sexist (the animal body) or ideological (the body of the rich or the poor). The dancing body is equally physical, lyrical, Baroque, and poetic and modifies the experience of minor art or the art of minorities by refusing to be locked into a choice between allocation and evasion. It is not a matter of being inside or outside society and its institutions but rather to create an in between so that a choice can emerge. One can attend choreographic centers and continue training in the street, perform in high-class environments, and continue to raise awareness in schools or prisons. This ability to invest in several levels of accessibility, several types of stages, is also characteristic of popular art (Bazin, Bornaz, and Slimani 2010).

The first choice as an act of resistance is to create spaces in which movement is possible, an initiative all the more necessary in situations of constraint or oppression. Hip-hop exhibits the lives of those who allow art to exist, this invisible population of which bourgeois art does not speak. What good is art if it cannot conceive the inconceivable? What do bodies say about the assignments and injunctions to which they are subjected? This raises the question of hip-hop dance as a "living spectacle," of its contemporary mean-ing and significance as a public forum and a place for a new cultural gram-mar that might be liable to think the world differently.

If popular art is born of the intersection of art and the people, then it cannot exist in anything but autonomous and subversive forms. Here lies the misunderstanding with the recognition of hip-hop dance by cultural institu-tions (government, national stages, conservatories). Popular art always seems to be defined and evaluated in relation or opposition to an immutable schol-arly art, an "artistic excellence." Thus, it is confused with an art of entertain-ment, mass-produced and commercial or ethnic and folkloric. Taking hip-hop into account in the artistic field is no exception to this rule. But the people are not simply a shapeless mass of consumers who just want to enjoy themselves (although there is never any totally passive consumption, and festivals also have a subversive dimension of a reversal of class hierarchies). Above all, the people are not defined by constituting a mass but rather by existing as a consciousness situated in social relations and notably in rela-tions of production. It is also in this sense that popular art is political and that we speak of the body politic of hip-hop dance where the body plays the medium between reflexive process and artistic process in an experience that is as aesthetic as much as it is political—what Richard Shusterman calls "soma-aesthetic" (Shusterman 2007).

A second criticism then arises: the utilitarian character of a social art, in opposition to "art for art's sake," which would be a purely disinterested form, where "beauty and value are impervious to any need and all functions be-cause they reside in a domain of absolute freedom" (Shusterman 2009). Already, we note that "noble" art is undoubtedly more dependent on the demand of political power, precisely that of the "nobility," even if we are today in a republic. Further, indicating a function of art is not to restrict its autonomy but to affirm that this autonomy is created in the consciousness of its involvement in society by disentangling its own frames of reference, as an artistic process and not as a piece of art. The body of hip-hop dance is a good example. As a thinking body and not a mere thought of the body, the somatic experience is without doubt one of the most intense, complete, and complex in what it demands in terms of cognitive, social, and political investment.

THE PITFALLS FOR POPULAR ART IN GAINING "RECOGNITION"

Hip-hop freed art from the confinement that separated it from life. But, once included in the field of visibility and decreed "a piece of art" by the institu-tion, the work loses this mediating force and this life-saving energy of an undisciplined, wild movement that invents itself. Like African statues that die once separated from the living organism and are displayed in a museum, hip-hop art has become the object of sociological, aesthetic, and economic exhibitions.

No sooner had the effervescent period of the 1980s in France ended than the term "urban cultures" was coined to try to identify and control popular cultures under the pretext of accompanying their practices of creation and transmission. They only seem worthwhile once studied as a dead language. This "botany of death is what we call culture," remarks Chris Marker (1961), a writer and filmmaker who fought all forms of colonialism. Hip-hop will be accepted and assimilated into the cultural institution once it becomes an exotic object under the watchful eye of official culture. Its subversive force is neutralized in an evolutionist conception that goes "from the street to the stage." It trades its autonomy for an apparent recognition that traps it in a dual neocolonial designation: ethnic and paternalist. We will say then that artists are "products of hip-hop" as one says of peoples from distant lands who have had to respond to the injunction "to open up" and "to mix" in order to "civilize" themselves. Thus it is that hip-hop choreographers are pushed to join in with contemporary theater if they want to see themselves onstage. But contemporary dance, in its certified, established form, lost its emancipatory promise a long time ago; as such, it is "a project whose collapse accompanies the end of the historical avant-gardes and the failure of the revolutionary project" (Duve 1992). One can only call oneself contemporary if one does not allow oneself to be blinded by the lights of the spectacle.

This way of describing dance companies as "descendents of" would signify that hip-hop is but an intermediary category toward an accession to "real dance"; it imposes a distinction between minor and major art. The aesthetic assignment to a point of origin (social and territorial) amounts to explaining the artistic work prior to its public reception. Yet it is up to the public to judge this function of art, which is to enlighten us about the complexity of a moving reality and to give us access to an intelligent vision of our relationship to the world. Despite this, the popular arts will rarely be considered as "fine arts" because, by "describing the judgment of taste and the experience of the beautiful and the sublime as aesthetic, theorists have also tried to develop and reform these experiences in certain directions" (Shusterman 1992).

The category of "urban cultures" thus corresponds, since the mid-1990s, to the concomitance between the phase of hip-hop's professionalization and its appearance as an object of study, motivated by a desire to control the production of popular art forms that is at once symbolic, aesthetic, and economic. Placing hip-hop in a "rational" field of activity restricts its ability to lay out alternatives. In fact, the stated urban cultures did not produce fundamentally new directions. But this was not its goal, since an official label allows, above all, lines of financing to be set out clearly by categorizing projects. In short, it is not a matter of transforming society but of responding to sectorial strategic goals for art field professionals, operators, and cultural institutions.

Hip-hop participants allowed themselves to be trapped by this paradoxical injunction. This strategic vision—that one should go through the institution to be recognized while refusing the process of academization—can only lead to a dead end. Seized in a contradictory situation between the "street and the institution," the hip-hop message fades or becomes confused, torn between the demand for a movement of subversive living and the statutory and economic need for legitimation by the institutional milieu of art or youth. An analysis that is not more strategic but more political would make it possible to separate academization and institutionalization. Hip-hop can very well, on the one hand, remain an autonomous form while establishing partnerships without running out of steam in institutional collaborations and, on the other hand, tackle the process whereby the academic form is not the aim of a living culture but its universalized transmutation, that is to say, the possibility for everyone to access it, recognize it, and appropriate it.

The professionalization of dance companies permits a certain visibility at the institutional level but not an improved legibility in terms of issues. Hip-hop is not understood as a total art. Its autonomy is relative and depends on other socio-professional strata. In other words, the fundamentally political hip-hop body, once placed onstage, has not brought a political dimension to the surface despite the success, the aesthetic influence, and the renown of several choreographers who are now in charge of their own national companies. The "living spectacle" should have a contemporary impact and significance as a public forum and a space for the creation of new aesthetic references. Has hip-hop created a "new theater" that would allow for reconciling political thought about culture (this pluralist France that has been calling for a different form of shared civic life) and a cultural politics (conceiving working on culture as resources for human and territorial development)?

On the contrary, "urban cultures," "street art," and other "arts of the street" are instrumentalized to make territories "more attractive" and reinforce the tourism economy (according to the World Tourism Organization, France is the third tourist destination in the world; this sector generates an annual revenue of $67 billion) (World Tourism Organization 2019). This policy legitimizes an ideology of "reconquering" working-class territories, further paring down the rare spaces that still allow the city to breathe. According to Philippe Gargov, it is a "large enterprise of urban uniformization, framing functions in public space, and gentrification of working-class neighborhoods" (Gonon 2015). This other technology of power is apparently less repressive but just as effective at expelling undesirables from public space and fabricating docile bodies, such obedience being necessary to augment the forces of the body in terms of economic utility.

But all processes of oppression generate a culture of resistance. Struggles reinvent themselves in light of the changes in the relations of production. Starting with the 2000s, many hip-hop dancers, disappointed by institutional assimilation and the commodification of space, have turned to the economy of "battles," a stage open for head-to-head competitions between individuals and groups featuring the same styles of dance. The arrival of digital culture and social networks favored this economy, as well as its inherent compatibility with the logic of competition.

The street that might have been thought to be abandoned is reappropriated by a new generation. A liberated and free act questions by its mere existence the political dimensions of the body in public space, following the example of krump sessions: free, expressive, energetic movements that draw on ancestral telluric forces and the contemporary street. This original link thwarts the industry of the spectacle to remind us that the public space of the street is the shared space of cultural mixing, meetings with otherness, inexhaustible experimentation with rhythms, and of this state of movement between people and the world, form and meaning, materials and symbols. These creative methods of subverting spaces and recuperating materials are a matrix of hip-hop disciplines (e.g., graffiti) that today join other practices of "urban hacking" (e.g., parkour) (Bazin 2005).

Street dancing turns the sheath of the city inside out, allowing every poor, oppressed passerby to take on the airs of a Charlie Chaplin or Buster Keaton so as to project a revolutionary soul into the celestial tramp, fiercely denounce living conditions, and be a factor of chaos within the established order. It is in this vein that choreographers in the Paris region, such as Bintou Dembélé, Mehdi Slimani, or Hervé Sika, do not give in to the pressure of the cultural industry and artistic institutions. They draw on the many rhizomes of popular art, working tirelessly on this awareness of the relations of domination that exist in the link between body movements and cultural movements, between proto-movement and meta-movement, between the mediation of forms (the aesthetic experience) and the mediation of works (the artistic experience).

They are representative of minority art and are not satisfied with merely being a "visible minority." They demand to be an "active minority," that is to say, occupying a central historical role in the direction of society that, until now, has been kept hidden by the official national narrative.

> I worked on the events of October '61, the Algerians drowned in the Seine; we were in the context of the Algerian War. Beyond the sheer horror, what struck me was the erasing from memory of those bodies that had been subjected to a violence without precedent in the streets of Paris, the most repressed European protest in contemporary history. Thousands of protesters were arrested, imprisoned, and tortured; hundreds lost their life. . . . It is our duty to revive this memory, and to do so in a calm, dispassionate way. And my medium—I think

that's why I've been dancing every day for years. Because I'm convinced that the medium of dance is the most beautiful gateway to restoring a body to these disappeared bodies. (Slimani 2011)

Dance is not only "performative" in the sense of a spectacle or of entertainment; it is also "perforative," a perforator in the sense of a weapon (Phillips Geduld 2008). It is in this way that dance invites us or engages us to think movement. Between living culture, in which teaching is done in vivo in a game of interaction, and a culture transmitted by passing through academic codification, it is important that the participants directly concerned—dancers and choreographers—draw on expertise to translate this thought of movement in terms of cultural politics, at the risk of being subjected to the alienating logics that deprive them of the meaning of their engagement. It is symptomatic that, after years of discussion, a national diploma in hip-hop dance does not exist and perhaps never will. In a negotiation between participants and institutions, each party must understand the other in their operations and objectives. This is not to refuse professionalization but to indicate that the modes of creation, transmission, and diffusion can take "poaching" paths and, consequently, their own ways of organizing, classifying, and prioritizing their modes of validation and judgment, distinct from those of the "art world" (production, diffusion, consumption, and valorization according to the established order of a socio-professional field) (Becker 1982).

For hip-hop, art is in the world and artistic work is inseparable from life, inseparable from this completion of movement. There is not a qualitative leap from hip-hop dancing in stairwells, subway slabs, and backrooms of neighborhood arts and recreational centers to when choreographers explore collective memory and the conditions of production of a culture. Art and the social form a whole that surpasses the categorical opposition between the world and the street and the world and art. "Regarding artistic creation, it is essential that the imagination escapes all constraints, that under no circumstances does it allow a procedure [to] be imposed upon it. Artists can only serve the emancipatory struggle if they have subjectively penetrated their social and individual content, if they have passed the meaning and the drama into their fiber and if they freely seek to give an artistic incarnation to their inner world" (Breton and Rivera 1938).

Thus, we cannot separate experience and thought, action and research, the sensible and the intelligible, because this would sever the role of popular experimentation. This is the principle behind an art of *bricolage*, of freestyle, and of improvisation, with their privileged moments of collective experimentation and of experiencing works-in-motion, where the process is as important as the result and where the access obtained to a certain mode of being outweighs the finalization of the work (Bazin 2013). It is an equilibrium vital and taut, precarious and ephemeral.

The art of bricolage opens the field to a personal and collective approach that is creative and imaginative and in which everyone can develop their own research, leave their own traces, and build their own references. It is not a matter of using culture to make social reparations or ensure proper compensations but of reordering the material of reality in a different vision of the world and, through this change of perspective, providing a handle-hold on the world, especially to those who are characterized as "without perspective," those who have been closed up in penitentiaries and mental institutions or have known social relegation (proletarian, identity, or territorial) and been "discarded." What the bricoleur-artist tells us is that each of us can be this cultural worker and, thanks to the metamorphosis of common creation into the singular realization, find a response to our expectations and achieve a form of universal aesthetic expression.

> In the world of bricolage, "we authorize ourselves"; it is different from the cultural hierarchy. We do not have to account for ourselves or negotiate our creativity. We are dealing first of all with *persons*. They are not necessarily marginalized, but they are ordinary people or have a commitment to the people. I believe that we can build society differently, through encounters and through acts that can be considered unimportant or ephemeral, but whose effects can be very profound on individuals and their entourage. Bricoleurs align these civic, ethical, and aesthetic dimensions. We need to invent our culture, since this causes the pre-established frameworks to be called into question. For a bricoleur, acting on the world is an act of creation; it is a way to reaffirm one's existence and prove the contribution that popular culture can make. (Sika 2012)

Taking into account the randomness of a work, the dialogue or the confrontation with raw materials, the preference of the intuitive process in the absence of a planned project, the refusal to belong to an academic school, the valorization by the *détournement* (subversion) of decommissioned or relegated positions: These should all be acceptable criteria for an artistic work. But we have seen through hip-hop dance that the autonomy of artistic production is conditioned by other political and economic criteria.

In the perspective of an "autonomous popular school," we must then seize knowledge and all other useful materials from where they are, distribute them, and share them with the rest of the world to oppose confiscatory maneuvers. The body politic of dance is a guerrilla fight in favor of free access to the space of this experience.

REFERENCES

Bazin, Hugues. "L'art d'intervenir dans l'espace public." *Territoires*, no. 457 (2005): 10–12.
———. "Art du bricolage, bricoleurs d'art." *L'art à l'épreuve du social. Les cahiers d'Artes*, no. 9 (2013): 95–113.

———. "Police des banlieues, contremaître du néocapitalisme." *Mediapart*, 13 February 2017. https://blogs.mediapart.fr/hugues-bazin/blog/130217/police-des-banlieues-contremaitre-du-neocapitalisme

Bazin, Hugues, and Naïm Bornaz. "Les arpenteurs ouvreurs d'espaces. Pour une apiculture politique, accompagnement du surgissement." *Arpentages* 2 (2014): 113–23.

Bazin, Hugues, Naïm Bornaz, and Mehdi Slimani. "Quels enjeux pour un art et une culture populaires en France?" *Cahiers de recherche sociologique*, no. 49 (Winter 2010): 123–45.

Becker, Howard S. *Art Worlds*. Berkeley: University of California Press, 1982.

Breton, André, and Diego Rivera. *Pour un art révolutionnaire indépendant. Mexico, le 25 juillet 1938. Manifeste de la Fédération internationale des Artistes révolutionnaires indépendants*. Paris: Service d'édition et de librairie du Parti communiste internationaliste (IVe Internationale), 1945–1947.

Corps pour corps. Opéra hip-hop & baroque. Choreographed by Hervé Sika. Cie MOOD/RV6K, 2017.

Duve, Thierry de. "Fonction critique de l'art? Examen d'une question." In *L'Art sans compas. Redéfinitions de l'esthétique*, edited by Christian Bouchindhomme and Rainer Rochlitz, 11–23. Paris: Éditions du Cerf, 1992.

Gonon, Anne. "La ville a-t-elle définitivement dompté les artistes urbains?" *Nectart*, no. 1 (2015): 128–36.

Louis, Édouard. "J'ai voulu écrire l'histoire de la destruction d'un corps." *Mediapart*, 16 May 2018. https://www.mediapart.fr/journal/france/160518/edouard-louis-j-ai-voulu-ecrire-l-histoire-de-la-destruction-d-un-corps

Marker, Chris. *Commentaires*. Paris: Éditions du Seuil, 1961.

Miredin, Jean-Hugues, and Karine Bénac-Giroux. "Entretien. Des poncifs aux contre-pieds: Les mises en corps des Noirs dans la danse-théâtre." *Tracés. Revue de Sciences humaines* 16, no. 30 (2017): 227–38.

Phillips Geduld, Victoria. *Dance Is a Weapon: New Dance Group, 1932–1955*. Paris: Centre National de la Danse, 2008.

Shusterman, Richard. *Pragmatist Aesthetics: Living Beauty, Rethinking Art*. Oxford: Basil Blackwell, 1992.

———. *Conscience du corps: Pour une soma-esthétique*. Paris: Éditions de L'Éclat, 2007.

———. "Divertissement et art populaire." *Mouvements*, no. 57 (2009): 12–20.

Sika, Hervé. Interview with the author. 2012. Cie MOOD/RV6K, Paris, France.

Slimani, Mehdi. "Propos chorégraphique *Les Disparus*." Cie No MaD, 2011. http://www.cienomad.com/choregraphies-2/les-disparus-2011/

———. *Écrits*. Cie No MaD, 2015.

Slimani, Mehdi, and Charly Célinain. "Entretien. 'C'Franc' mélange danse hip-hop et chanson française." *Le Courrier de l'Atlas*, 23 August 2018. https://www.lecourrierdelatlas.com/musique-c-franc-melange-danse-hip-hop-et-chanson-francaise-20445

Le Syndrome de l'initié (Les damné.es de la terre). Choreographed by Bintou Dembélé. Cie Rualité, Nanterre, 2018.

World Tourism Organization. "International Tourism Highlights 2019 Edition." https://www.e-unwto.org/doi/pdf/10.18111/9789284421152

Chapter Ten

"Beats Working"

Performance Economics in
The Roots *(2013) and* Divines *(2016)*

Felicia McCarren

In France, *le hip hop*—also called *la danse urbaine*—has been anything but American: included in French arts policy from the local level of subsidized dance classes in housing projects to the level of the *scènes nationales*, theaters with state subventions.[1] Rather than counterculture, *la danse hip hop* was seen, beginning with François Mitterrand's first term as president in 1981, as contributing to civic culture, as pedagogy for marginalized youth, and as an art form.[2] It has been taken seriously as both artistic and social work in a double institutionalization (by art/aesthetic and social/educational structures) that Roberta Shapiro has called *artification* (Shapiro 2012). In homage to its U.S. founders and not solely in imitation of them, French hip-hop developed a recognizable choreographic model with a rich vocabulary of moves, higher production values, and dancers with a range of techniques. It inspired dancers to move from their turf to performance spaces and eventually national stages for dance. It also developed a following, bringing young people who might never go to the theater into the big auditoriums where contemporary choreography is programmed.

French hip-hop is unique not only because of its choreographic development and its social charge but because of its economics. Other American forms of entertainment have been valorized in France and have even sometimes reached global markets via France (for example, early jazz). With hip-hop, the story has unfolded differently. New York "wild style" inspired French hip-hop dance from its beginnings in the 1980s, but the U.S. entertainment market has never been the only option for French hip-hoppers. A very different economics has supported French hip-hop dancers who—I have argued—have been far "freer" than their U.S. analogs: By that I mean, more likely to be paid for performances, compensated while developing as dancers, or commissioned for choreography as part of a cultural policy that in the United States some might see as approaching state art or "recuperation."[3]

Techniques du corps (body techniques), or the *pratiques* (practices) studied in the anthropology and sociology well known in the French human sciences corpus, anchor an intellectual valorization of physical expression that helps to explain the unique development and state support of hip-hop dance in France. In *French Moves* (2013), I studied the *sciences humaines* and the socialism that made possible the development of hip-hop into a form of contemporary dance. Here I consider how, in spite of shifting notions of work, the erosion of social support, and a new generation of dancers, French hip-hop dance can continue to be read as cultural politics, a cultural exception that has "protected" (in an economic sense) dance, cinema, and their performers in France.

In this chapter, following the trajectory of one dancer from the national theaters to the Cannes Film Festival and beyond, I explore, first, a rejection of American ways of working and of the commercial culture in a French hip-hop that was not capitalist in its roots and, second, the elaboration of the French form challenging definitions of work and value in performance.

In Kader Attou's hip-hop choreography *The Roots* (2013) and in Houda Benyamina's film *Divines* (2016), hip-hop dance represents work and comments on productivity and *précarité* (job insecurity) in the French context. The production of hip-hop dance both on the national stages, where *The Roots* has been programmed over the past few years, and in Benyamina's award-winning film—by this I mean the *contexts* of its production—also comments on the value of moving bodies in performing economies, set in a French history of productivity and "performance" that has historically maintained ergonomic protections in the workplace and unemployment insurance for performing artists. French *politique culturelle* (cultural policy), with its public arts budgets for community development promoting a reflective, embodied expression of multicultural minority identity, should not be confused with the "free market" of the global entertainment industry. In my reading, this *politique culturelle* has produced hip-hop choreography more interesting than that often relegated to a backdrop in the spectacles of touring hip-hop or rap stars.

The cultural stereotype of living to work—rather than simply working to make a living—differentiates the United States from France. At his swearing-in ceremony in May 2017, French president Emmanuel Macron swept aside criticism of his attitude after the first round of presidential elections two weeks earlier, one that appeared to show him taking victory for granted, intoning gravely that he would be at work that very evening. Work has been a major theme of his presidency, as it had been during the campaign: He wore the suit that you can afford, he said, by working, not one donated by a wealthy friend, as rival candidate François Fillon did, and he has mobilized an American vocabulary of entrepreneurship, casting France as a "start-up nation." Since his election, he has gone on record against the "do-nothings" (*fainéants*) who have resisted economic reforms.[4] In a 25 April 2019 press conference, Macron urged "working more" (*travailler davantage*) as imperative to improving economic conditions in France. Indeed, in 2015, then–presidential candidate Jeb Bush described the U.S. Congress's nonproductivity through the metaphor of the "French working week."[5]

These two very different cultures of work produce two very different ideas about the significance of art and the role of performing artists in relation to their publics. My subtitle "performance economics" refers both to the work performances and productivity demanded by national economies, as well as to the very different economics of performance in the two nations.[6] In this chapter, I explore this cultural contrast concerning work as defined in performances of *la danse hip hop*, moving from the national stages for dance to Netflix, in Kader Attou's 2013 choreography *The Roots* and Houda Benyamina's 2016 film *Divines*: how it is defined, how it is measured, and how it is changing.

My title refers to American-style show business at the antipodes of the French *politique culturelle*. In a well-known *Doonesbury* cartoon from 1974 caricaturing the Motown star Gladys Knight with her backup singers, the Pips, Gary Trudeau's frames depict a stereotype of the performing artist who feels lucky to have a moment in the spotlight.[7] "Beats working," claims one of the Pips singing and dancing behind Gladys Knight; as the expression goes, "It beats working for a living." Of course, this view of the entertainer is also a raced image: The black performers known and loved all over the world lived through segregation at home, with a long history of unequal opportunity. If the cartoon jokes about the good money paid for just a few steps, it is haunted by the long shadow of slave labor or of the chain gang, in which people who looked like the Pips did not own the products of their labor nor even their own bodies.

In the *Doonesbury* cartoon, the performers themselves tell the joke; gloriously calling up their talent just as it is needed. This cool, this ease, are at the heart of the image of America that circulates around the world, in cultural products reflecting black popular music and culture. This is, after all, what distinguishes the United States from Europe: these forms created and exported (and valued) elsewhere—but not only in monetary terms. This cartoon summarizes an entire era: Cultural workers in the United States—African American cultural workers—are indeed working; James Brown, nicknamed "the Hardest Working Man in Show Business," complements this caricature of the Pips. But these performers do not make it look like work—their grace, their talent, are as naturalized as the traits are racialized. Between the extremes of working too hard or not at all, the *Doonesbury* cartoon suggests that this kind of performance, even if well paid, *does not count* in the United States as work. Dance has always had this problem of not being considered "work" in modernity: neither a *work of art* that exists as an object nor the *labor* that is dancing, as dance scholars Frédéric Pouillaude (2017) and Mark Franko (2002) have shown. But in France dance has more recently been taken seriously as state-supported cultural work. The U.S. *cool* that has always been represented by dancing that "beats working" becomes, in France, not only work but also art, not highly paid, perhaps, but precious and productive in and of the nation. French hip-hop reappropriated the dances of mythic minority and often unknown U.S. dancers, paying them homage and taking their work from a realm considered entertainment to the level of state-recognized art. If dancing is, in the United States, an image for *not* working (getting paid to do something that "beats working for a living"), in France it can be seen as one image for work itself.

Kader Attou is an autodidact dancer from the first generation of hip-hoppers, the son of immigrants, and now the director of a regional choreographic center, the CCN–La Rochelle. In *The Roots*, he comments directly on labor in France: its colonial history, its postcolonial legacies, and its current challenges for and against the American idea of living to work. Performed by eleven young men, *The Roots*, created by Attou in 2013 in collaboration with these dancers, produces images of both work *and* play, represented in the dancing and by the example of dance itself, as physical effort and as diversion. In a recent work on this piece, I describe how it allows dancers to move beyond the stereotypes of *banlieue* associated with hip-hop to a broader range of expression, beyond identity politics and closer to what I have called an identity *poetics* (McCarren 2018). In the choreography's different moving sections, I emphasize here two details from the piece: both focused on one of its featured dancers, Kevin Mischel. From an opening solo in *The Roots*, Kevin leads the ensemble cast, and through his performance in *The Roots* from its creation in 2013 and subsequently in the film *Divines* (2016) (as well as in the 2018 release of the film *Break*), his dancing records the unique development of French hip-hop and sketches a new arc for hip-hop dancers in France, an unusual trajectory.

In *The Roots*'s opening scene, in the choreography's opening move, Mischel is sitting downstage in a high-backed armchair. He stops a record by Break Machine playing on the turntable. In this musical gesture—the choice to turn away from the historical hip-hop score toward other musical forms inspiring the dancers—Attou's choreography sketches the entire history of French hip-hop. Pioneer hip-hoppers Attou and his close collaborator Mourad Merzouki—also a self-taught dancer and director of a national choreographic center (the CCN-Créteil near Paris)—began in the early 1990s rejecting images of rap music and culture.[8] Attou has always pushed aside the American pop influence even as the choreographer pays homage to New York as the capital of diversity and of what he calls *his dance*: "New York is for me 'the place.' I cannot dissociate New York from hip hop. From Block Party to the emergence of graf, rap and my dance, a part of myself belongs to this city" (Birmann Bloom 2018).[9]

Yet the choreography reveals a profoundly French workplace, far from the New York block party and even further from the unpaid rehearsals of most U.S. dance performance.[10] It registers the benefits of ways of working that are supported by regional and state structures rather than corporations or short-term grants. Attou describes the process of collaborating with dancers, eliciting from them their stories in movement. The choreography's dramatic score makes room for these individual moments of memories expressed by the dancers moving with their music.[11] *The Roots* also serves as an example of what rehearsal time makes possible: the variety of styles of dancing represented by the group of dancers that might be found all over the world but that are here staged in a choreographic narrative by Attou. This innovation is exemplified by Mischel, dancing a new trend—a more fluid, less percussive form of popping, with melting, gummy-bear bending legs and fluid torso, often taking the dancer down to the floor and up again rather than mechanical moves of angular standing forms with their so-called Egyptian or robotic resonance.[12] The most significant innovation, however, is the theatricalization of this form. Fifteen years ago, this particular style of dancing would not have carried a hip-hop choreography, and it was a challenge for choreographers to integrate standing styles with break-dancers in the same scenes. Dancers creating this style whom I saw auditioning for contracts in touring hip-hop choreographies in 2000, for example, were of great interest to choreographers in the way they extended and fused forms, but they did not get leading roles. The fusion that has happened in France is not simply a matter of choreographic invention but an investment of time, composition workshops, and personal development afforded to dancers, such as those in Attou's company Accrorap, based now at the CCN in La Rochelle.

In France, the *régime d'intermittence* (intermittent worker program) protects performers with unemployment insurance and allows them to accomplish this kind of work—the training, preparation, and creation that is mostly done outside of periods of contractual employment. Being an *intermittent* allows dancers the time to work at their art and to experiment, permitting French hip-hop's unique, globally recognized choreographic development at the opposite end of the *entertainment* spectrum: valorized by the French state, offering a living to dancers performing nationally, and touring internationally to represent French culture. Rather than *avoiding* work or making money "without working" (again—dancing "beats working for a living"), the

French context deems performers capable of producing something valuable that contributes to the common good.[13]

Hip-hop dance does a lot of significant social and cultural work in France.[14] Yet *intermittence* is far from perfect. As Antonella Corsani and Maurizio Lazzarato (2008) have shown in their study *Intermittents et Précaires*, the *intermittents du spectacle* represent those who mostly work *when not employed* (70). In this way, the *régime d'intermittence* becomes the model for the "discontinuity of employment" that marks the working life of a growing number of people in many different domains. This particular status has served as emblematic, introducing this concern: how to provide social protections, rights such as medical insurance, for people who work on short-term contracts. In one survey of *intermittents*, Corsani and Lazzarato heard different perspectives on the economics of this type of contract: "Is it a new form of work or a new form of hiring? *Intermittence* has two faces—one *libertarian* (in this context, *focused on individual freedom*), the other *ultra libéral* (free-market economy). The regime of *intermittence* covers the whole range between 'I work when I want, where I want, as I want' and 'I work when I can, where they want, as they want.'"[15] Another respondent explains:

> In addition to everything that can be seen, the visible part of the iceberg—what we perform in the show—there is the invisible part, the submerged part of the iceberg, often the major part of what we do. This includes the time of conceiving, preparing, and documenting . . . and for the most part this time is paid very little or not at all. How can we evaluate the artist's work to decide what is really necessary, or what is needed just in this context, for his work to be accomplished? It seems to me that the two are indissociable, just as researchers in medicine, or in physics or literature, are not paid for their discoveries but for their research time. (Corsani and Lazzarato 2008, 59)[16]

That dancing might be considered important enough to receive funding that in the United States would be earmarked for science or social science research is surprising, and as I have described elsewhere, it is even more surprising when hip-hop choreography is commissioned by the French Ministry of Defense (McCarren 2017).

Divines also shows the positive side of *intermittence*, as something that can change the lives of young dance artists. In Benyamina's film, awarded the *Caméra d'or* at the Cannes Film Festival in 2016, Mischel's character Djigui represents once again the history of *la danse urbaine* (urban dance): Not only has he metaphorically turned off the American music and worked on his own to develop his own style, but he crosses over from self-taught hip-hop moves to a contract with a dance company that allows him to quit his day job and go out on tour. Far from a U.S. idea of success ("I got the job!"), passing this audition earns the dancer in the film the very *statut d'intermittence* that dancers like Mischel have represented.

Divines displays the dancer's constant practice and his struggle to extend his movement vocabulary to match the commissioned choreographer's expectation. He rehearses whenever he can. This is not a competition or battle but a three-week-long internship: artistic development that Djigui undertakes while holding down his job at the Carrefour supermarket, American style. He even discusses the challenge in mastering some movements while sparring with Dounia, the love interest who has mocked his dancing in public but secretly admired and filmed him rehearsing. In a scene in which she interrupts him practicing on the stage, he shows her the movement he finds too difficult while trying to engage her. When he gets the contract, Djigui remarks with ebullience, "I got the job—for the lead role in the piece!" He says to Dounia, "You have no idea how this will change my life." This is the kind of breakthrough that in the United States would be seen in monetary terms; yet here, what Djigui means is that, starting from this first contract, he will be able to gain the status of *intermittent* that will valorize his dancing through his entire career, whether he is employed or not.

Yet, in the extra-diegetic context of its production, *Divines* also demonstrates shifting work opportunities for hip-hoppers. The success of *Divines* in 2016 garnered Mischel media attention that then translated into other kinds of performances: modeling and advertising for luxury brands. Suddenly, on YouTube there were videos of Mischel not dancing at all but arriving at sponsored fashion events, with banks of photographers asking him to turn his face their way. Other dancers have monetized their visibility. For example, Paris Opéra Ballet *étoile* Jérémie Bélingard, both dancing and not dancing, in ads for Hermès and Miss Dior; Benjamin Millepied (*étoile*, choreographer, and director) in ads for Air France and others.[17] These two options, then—in the diegesis of *Divines* and in the context of its production—suggest two alternatives, the "socialist" and "capitalist" (*ultra libéral*) solutions to the part-time work of an *intermittent du spectacle*. Against the "invisible" work that a dancer has to do every day in between contracts, that remains unpaid but supported by *allocations*, there is the option of hypervisibility. So even as Djigui represents the pinnacle of success in socialist *intermittence* in the film, the film's own success catapults Mischel toward brand advertising that can only be described as spectacularly "capitalist," even if not exclusively American.[18]

This kind of commercial success may not be unusual in the world of the Paris Opéra or in the history of ballet, but it is rare in the "associative" world of French hip-hop dance.[19] U.S. hip-hop goes for the money; in France, too, a younger generation focuses, like Benyamina's character Dounia, on "money, money, money" and abandons other "national" values in its pursuit. The actress playing Dounia, Oulaya Amamra, has said in an interview that her generation growing up in the *banlieue* no longer thinks in "associative" terms and no longer sees NGO *associations* as the solution. However, this has clearly been filmmaker Benyamina's focus, in her NGO *1000 visages* whose mission was never to teach youths from the projects to become artists in order to sell luxury goods.[20]

Hip-hop dance in *The Roots* reflects both the personal enjoyment and satisfaction of dancing (in the homestyle party that concludes the more somber piece), in addition to the dignity that *intermittence* can give to artists, regardless of artists' generalized job insecurity, or *précarité. Divines* also idealizes the "sacred" side of dance, which Djigui himself rhapsodizes, while seducing Dounia: "When I dance," he says, "I let everything around me flow through me. . . . Dancing does not lie. . . . It's sacred." This scene of seduction in which the young people dance together takes place after hours in the closed superstore where Djigui has been working as a security guard. Djigui courts Dounia amid the stuff that he has been guarding and that she has been stealing; they are surrounded by products that have come on the boat from China. He holds the keys to the storehouse full of cheap plastic goods and junk food. But as he turns off the lights, he is clearly abandoning his old post, and this represents much more than all the treasure around him. Dancing and musing on his calling and new career, legitimized as a dancer, Djigui has the confidence to connect with Dounia, and he gains her confidence along with her admiration for his art. His dance and his discourse about his dancing represent a spirituality (the filmmaker also calls it "beauty") that is a soulful state of mind, not the money or the commodities that Dounia has been chasing. So even as the performer himself moves toward commercial success—broader visibility and more lucrative contracts—the performer's *character* emphasizes the fulfillment of personal development made possible by *intermittence*.[21]

Such juxtapositions that represent contradictions in the French context would not necessarily ring false in the United States. Why not brand modeling and luxury goods along with social justice? Sponsorship of luxury products as a *form* of social justice? The world of luxury has long been the province of hip-hop stars, asserting their rights as celebrities to the kind of exclusion that they may themselves have been subject to before "breaking through." In this career trajectory, hip-hop dance and *intermittence* become a platform for other, more remunerative kinds of performance. This might be a generational change invoked by *Divines*'s Amamra, an anti-French or postcolonial sentiment on the left that strangely resonates with another "new spirit of Capitalism" on the center-right (Boltanski and Chiapello 2018).[22]

Crossing over as a dancer into the world of money-making performance—selling one's image (the image of one's body) and sponsoring products for global markets—may be one way of "beating working"—easier than *performing* dance, *doing* the work that does not pay. Who can blame the dancer then for saying—as Mischel has recently—that he does not want to dance anymore, that he wants to act "full-time"? However, the real "cheating" or "beating" work comes from pretending to be a dancer without doing the work ("playing one on TV," as we say in the United States). Recent well-known cases of body doubles in cinematic dance scenes represent the substitutions that take dance work away from the bodies that create it and put another face on it—sometimes straightening a queer image or whitening a black image.[23] However, *Divines* focuses on the work of rehearsal: The actor's dancing is his own, not doubled by someone else. Djigui takes the motif further when he says to Dounia, "Dancing does not lie."[24] In a physical competition, he provokes her by crowing, "Is that all you've got?" The performer who does not "have" the moves will not get the job.

This hip-hop dance, both onstage and on-screen, highlights what can broadly be called capitalist and socialist approaches to work, imaged by dance. The economic reforms proposed in France are not simply American but will undoubtedly affect the status of culture, trending toward a global capitalism that emphasizes not the public good but the profitability of art.[25] French hip-hop has, for the most part, told a different story over the past thirty years: the legitimacy of the dancer's work validated in France via the legal status of *intermittent du spectacle*, which has become a broader model for a socialist conception of work. Yet whereas in France dance artists have been relatively protected, the possibility of new markets and U.S.-style capitalism are now being cast as liberatory for performers: This is the "Macronomics" of French president Emmanuel Macron and part of the discussion around the 2018 film *Break*, also audible in the debates surrounding *Divines*.[26]

Dance performers are "performant"—productive—in French culture in ways that U.S. dancers never could be; their nation gives them a political, civic charge. They are cultural agents at the service of the nation, not just players—or winners—in a market. *Intermittence* can support them for their entire career, not just for the time of one show. In France, where dance has been "protected" from market forces, I have suggested, dance may be "freer" precisely where work is less free because of the *code du travail*, because of social programs and employer obligations. In France, dance may be programmed both to divert and to teach the public something: to produce something valued by dancers as well as by their public and even their politicians.[27]

The French work system is in chaotic transition, and the shift to liberal policies for firing and new possibilities for hiring take a small step toward the American idea of the market as the definition of all things. This "Americanization" is also reflected in the dance world, from hip-hop to the opera ballet, as some dancers cross over from state support to a global market via movies and media (fashion, product endorsements) to the financial measure of success. Yet the *endurance* of *le hip hop*, with urban dance now anchored at two of the regional choreographic centers in France, reminds us that the U.S. dancing that "beats working" becomes, in France, not only work but also art.

French hip-hop represents the movement that continues to work to give youth the freedom of expression that can take them from the projects to the stage, and that beats the idea of freedom as working for "money, money, money."

REFERENCES

Amar, Jules. *Le Moteur humain et les bases scientifiques du travail professionnel.* Paris: Dunod, 1923.

Anonymous. "Jeb Bush Says Sorry for Mocking French Working Week." *BBC News*, 4 November 2015. http://www.bbc.com/news/world-us-canada-34720806

———. "Interview with Marc Fouchard." *Les GIFstoires du cinéma*, 8 July 2018. https://m.youtube.com/watch?v=TYHTq5qEiHA

———. "Le film événement de cet été *Break*." *Iconic People Web TV*, 16 July 2018. https://m.youtube.com/watch?v=y_7GvAlHbkI

Benyamina, Houda. "À Cannes, j'ai le sentiment d'avoir été au festival de Calais. Interview." *YARD*, 5 September 2016. https://www.youtube.com/watch?v=PY2Rqtf5RJE&app=desktop

Birmann Bloom, Nicole. "Hip Hop Choreographer Kader Attou." *Cultural Services French Embassy United States*, January 2018. http://frenchculture.org/performing-arts/7245-hip-hop-choreographer-kader-attou

Boltanski, Luc, and Eve Chiapello. *The New Spirit of Capitalism.* Translated by Gregory Porter. London: Verso, 2018.

Corsani, Antonella, and Maurizio Lazzarato. *Intermittents et Précaires.* Paris: Éditions Amsterdam, 2008.

de Royer, Solenn. "À Athènes, Macron assure qu'il ne 'cédera rien' sur les réformes." *Le Monde*, 8 September 2017. https://www.lemonde.fr/politique/article/2017/09/08/a-athenes-macron-assure-qu-il-ne-cedera-rien-sur-les-reformes_5182994_823448.html

Franko, Mark. *The Work of Dance: Labor, Movement, and Identity in the 1930s.* Middletown, CT: Wesleyan University Press, 2002.

Institut du Monde Arabe. *HIP HOP du Bronx aux rues arabes.* Foreword by Jack Lang. Catalogue of the exhibition. Paris: L'IMA, 2015.

McCarren, Felicia. *Dance Pathologies: Performance, Poetics, Medicine.* Stanford, CA: Stanford University Press, 1998.

———. *Dancing Machines: Choreographies of the Age of Mechanical Reproduction.* Stanford: Stanford University Press, 2003.

———. *French Moves: The Cultural Politics of le Hip Hop.* New York: Oxford University Press, 2013.

———. "Dancing D-Day." In *The Oxford Handbook of Dance and Politics*, edited by Rebekah J. Kowal, Gerald Siegmund, and Randy Martin, 329–46. Oxford: Oxford University Press, 2017.

———. "Somebody or Anybody? Hip Hop Choreography and the Cultural Economy." In *Post-Migratory Cultures in Postcolonial France*, edited by Kathryn A. Kleppinger and Laura Reeck, 185–201. Liverpool: Liverpool University Press, 2018.

Meriah. "*Flashdance*, 30 Years Later: B-Boy Recalls Girling Up for Final Scene." *Yahoo! Entertainment*, 15 April 2013. https://www.yahoo.com/entertainment/bp/flashdance-30-years-later-b-boy-recalls-girling-170107851.html

Piketty, Thomas. "De la productivité en France et en Allemagne." *Le Monde*, 5 January 2017. http://piketty.blog.lemonde.fr/2017/01/05/de-la-productivite-en-france-en-allemagne-et-ailleurs/

Pouillaude, Frédéric. *Unworking Choreography: The Notion of the Work in Dance.* New York: Oxford University Press, 2017.

Shapiro, Roberta. "Du smurf au ballet: l'invention de la danse hip hop." In *De l'artification: Enquêtes sur le passage à l'art*, edited by Nathalie Heinich and Roberta Shapiro, 172–92. Paris: Éditions de l'École des Hautes Études en Sciences Sociales, 2012.
Stiegler, Bernard. "Performance et singularité." In *La performance, une nouvelle idéologie?* edited by Benoît Heilbrunn, 209–10. Paris: La Découverte, 2004.

FILMOGRAPHY AND CHOREOGRAPHIES

Aliker. Dir. Guy Deslauriers. Kréol Productions. Originally released in 2009.
Amélie. Dir. Jean-Pierre Jeunet. UGC. Originally released in 2001.
Black Swan. Dir. Darren Aronofsky. Fox Searchlight Pictures. Originally released in 2010.
Break. Dir. Marc Fouchard. Nynamor. Originally released in 2018.
Divines. Dir. Houda Benyamina. Easy Tiger. Originally released in 2016.
Flashdance. Dir. Adrian Lyne. Paramount Pictures. Originally released in 1983.
La Haine. Dir. Mathieu Kassovitz. Les Productions Lazennec. Originally released in 1995.
Polina, danser sa vie. Dirs. Valérie Müller and Angelin Preljocaj. UGC. Originally released in 2016.
Récital. Compagnie Käfig. Choreographer Mourad Merzouki. Originally created in 1998.
The Roots. Choreographer Kader Attou. 24 images, Maison de la Danse, CCN de La Rochelle. Originally released in 2013.
Un Break à Mozart. Choreographer Kader Attou. Originally created in 2016.
Un break à Mozart 1.1. Choreographer Kader Attou. Originally created in 2017.

Chapter Eleven

Illegal Mural Expressions

Graffiti as an Act of Resistance?

Alain Milon,
Translated by Sarah Glasco

In this reflection on one aspect of urban resistance, only illegal mural expressions is addressed, with France as the context. However, it is not the technicality of the graffiti artist's act that is of interest here but rather its anthropological and political significance, the way in which the artist's gesture expresses and translates an act of resistance. To avoid any confusion and controversy, I treat only illegal mural expressions in their most common forms (tag, graffiti, stencil, mosaic, drop shadow, gravitti or glass etching, poster hijacking, collage), setting aside political and pornographic graffiti. Without highlighting these expressions beyond all artistic context, it is preferable to articulate that, by their very existence, they have the advantage of raising the issue of the face of a city. Are they indeed the face of the city or instead actually scars?

Graffiti as an illegal mural expression constitutes primarily an out-of-frame form in the sense that, a priori, its very nature prohibits it from any entry into an institutional framework, such as public or private commission, for example. Furthermore, it cannot be limited to what gallery owners/art dealers, the fashion industry, or advertising make of it; however, the *frame/ out-of-frame* opposition does have its own limitations. All one need do is look at what pop art does with it. The wall as exhibition space shows all too well that art is no longer an expression confined to institutional places. It becomes a way to question the entity of the artist as author or coauthor, the place of the work in the public space, the heritage of a territory, its democratization, and even its duplication. All of these questions go far beyond the simple *frame/out-of-frame* opposition.

In general, the graffiti artist agrees to remain *anonymous* (the signature is a pseudonym even if it is less the case because of the commodification of graffiti and the appearance of *street art* as a market sector), without any *authorial claim* (it is more the figure of the actor intervening in the staging of the public space than that of the author of a work that one finds in illegal mural writing), *ephemeral* (the graffiti artist accepts that his/her work is erased), often *collective* (belonging to a community), and *in situ* (the street as a place where one rushes or swarms: *rue*, the word for "street" in French, yields the verb *ruer*, or "to come running" in English).

The city is above all a body that exists outside of all "museumification," even if one can produce patrimonial interpretations of it therein. This is why I show preference for graffiti's intention over its artistic value—in other words, to reflect upon how graffiti artists interact with the cities they live in.

IS THE FACE OF THE CITY ITS LANDSCAPE?

Citing the invasion of city walls, degradation, visual pollution, infringement of personal freedom, and uncivil acts conjures a singular reality: Graffiti exist and, as such, actively contribute to urban decay.

This mode of expression questions me; it calls out to me because it sparks our imaginations of the city in the same way that it challenges our perceptions of property and purity. And yet, is this form of expression, often seen as a scarring of the cityscape, actually any more visibly dissonant and degrading than certain products of urban planning in Paris like Les Halles or the modern business district La Défense, the new neighborhood Paris Rive Gauche in the 13th *arrondissement*, the Parc de la Villette, or even certain spaces reserved for advertising?

Graffiti is a political production in the sense that it participates in public life. Its primary function is to challenge the institutional parties in its own way in order to alert them here and there to dysfunction, discontent, and urban maladjustments. But they are also artistic practices which, in extreme cases, tackle narcissistic and graphomaniacal behavior: showing off their name, their signature, their pseudonym, their brand, and their logo to as many people as possible like a sort of endless delirium in which graffiti artists would imagine themselves talking alone with the city, using their most exploitable supports like the façade, the wall, the storefront, the sidewalk, the freighter truck, or the 4x3–meter advertising billboard. All these surfaces are like immaculate pages, a sort of blank sheet of paper to cover, repeatedly and ceaselessly; the wall becomes almost an incentive to write on it. This super-imposing of graffiti is part of the deep-seated nature of the city's face; in a sense, this urban palimpsest becomes the invisible memory of a place. Ephemeral and destined not to last, illegal mural expressions remain fleeting. Nevertheless, they are present and reflect the different movements of the city.

By signing the walls, graffiti artists illuminate the city. They show its excesses, its aberrations, and its weaknesses while imposing an expression on its inhabitants that they did not want. It is the forced character of this mode of expression that leaves the inhabitants feeling ill at ease with what they consider to be mural contaminations. The declination that graffiti artist ZEVS offers by making clean graffiti is interesting from this point of view.

Producing graffiti with a high-pressure jet on a dirty wall is akin to making clean graffiti. In the same vein, invisible graffiti (graffiti made with an ultraviolet paint that can only be seen at night or with specific lighting) reflects the same questioning on the place of contamination in our cultural imagination. The clean graffiti actually raises the question of the limits of contamination. It is also interesting to note that, in the event of a penal sanction, one of the criteria used is the degree of lability of the stain; in other words, the easier it is to erase the graffiti, the less severe the punishment.

But how exactly would one describe these urbanistic scars? Are they mere ocular assaults that collide with our urban imagination, or do they rather contribute to shaping the face of the city? In order to answer this type of question, one must first eliminate the artistic alibi.

WARNING: GOOD GRAFFITI VS. THE BAD!

To say whether or not graffiti is artistic only takes into account a single artistic reading of mural expression with its limitations and weaknesses. Behind the judgment of tastes, the spectator must first and foremost submit to a *principle of acceptability* and the hierarchies therein: recognizing one expression as artistic while refusing another as such.

Accepting or tolerating graffiti because of its calligraphic or pictorial qualities, its artistic forms, the colors of its lettering, the graphic research of its layout, or the composition of the whole in order to refuse tags due to their artistic deficiency or their speed of execution: None of this explains the phenomenon itself. It is preferable to recognize an aesthetic nature in all these expressions in the sense that the aesthetic is defined above all as the study of the sensitive and affective behaviors of man, not a judgment of taste imposed on the artwork. And all the more so because judgments of taste lead to absurd situations. Such graffiti produced as a result of an order would represent solely the act of commissioning a work of art, whereas the same graffiti illegally placed would be considered graffiti in the legal sense, meaning an illicit expression resulting in the corrosion of the medium.

It is not a matter of dismissing the question of artistic value but recognizing that we cannot make it the first criterion in understanding this phenomenon. By the same token, the problem is not whether or not it is a cultural, countercultural, or subcultural form. It is there, and as such it is part of the face of the city. If one is satisfied with a singular artistic reading, graffiti is then reduced to the typical amalgamations of the mass media: Bad tags are pitted against good graffiti or the conduct of vandals versus the work of the artists. This kind of opposition does not explain anything; it only serves to perpetuate other stereotypical generalizations related to graffiti expressions, in particular those that associate the tag with crime rates or those that deem the tagger a teenager who lives in a bad neighborhood, comes from a single-parent home, and is flunking out of school. To avoid such often-fruitless debates, it is preferable to illuminate the issue of these illicit traces, not on the grounds of artistic judgment, but rather on the metamorphoses and movements of the city.

Graffiti as an illicit mural expression is still, in fact, a visual assault to the extent that it is imposed without consultation as urbanistic projects may be, imposed most often without any dialogue whatsoever with the inhabitants. And if some may consider it visual pollution, then we must move beyond reasoning and include advertising propaganda in all its forms in public and semipublic spaces. This is actually the question posed by anti-advertisement activists via their suburban actions in particular. All this is the same visual assault, an aggression that is part of the very body of the city. The city is violent, graffiti is violent, as is urban development–produced displacement. Everything is violent, and the speed of the flows aids in accentuating this violence.

PERCEPTION OF PROPERTY VS. PURITY: CHROMOPHOBIA OR CHROMOPHILIA?

We have seen that, because it is imposed unsolicited, graffiti is often experienced as a symbolic aggression. It both clashes with and touches deeply our perceptions of property. Painted on façades, carved into windowpanes, sprayed onto iron curtains, glued on urban road signs, contoured on sidewalks, sealed on walls, cut onto billboards, graffiti undermines public and semipublic spaces by affecting everyone's idea of the city and eventually their perception of place.

This image is based on the idea that we have possession of a good, which does not mean that the act of appropriation is imaginary, of course. In these conditions, graffitiing a public space amounts to undermining the integrity of that space while degrading the place and symbolically the social stakeholders behind it—that is to say, the owners of private property as well as the institutional agents for public spaces.

In Judeo-Christian tradition, this perception of property is often accompanied by a perceived image of purity and cleanliness. In the case of illegal mural expressions, these often go hand in hand. In antigraffiti arguments, we often compare these urban stains to the playful behaviors of a young child with his own feces; thus, these defilements would be reminiscent of Freud's anal-sadistic phase.

Beyond these psychoanalytic caricatures looms the question of chromophobia versus chromophilia. It is this same image that often leads one to think that the city must have a smooth and immaculate skin on which each scar would be felt as a defacement and an attack on the body, not unlike France's *Défense d'afficher* (Post no bills) law of 29 July 1881. This *Défense d'afficher* is often understood as the *Défense d'uriner* (No urinating) or *Défense de cracher* (No spitting) inscribed in the logic of nineteenth-century hygienist theories, theories that governed the construction of closed public places like the Paris metro, for example. Graffiti artists experience these multiple *No . . .* orders as *No Writing*, to which the graffiti (ironically) responds. How is one supposed to appreciate the work of these city highlighters in those conditions? And if we speak of "highlighters," it is in the sense that highlighting a text ultimately accentuates its defects and qualities, protrusions and particularities, with a phosphorescent color, as if to signal to the passerby the singularity of this place or that. By highlighting the city, graffiti artists distract/appropriate it or rather make it "speak" in a different way. It remains to be seen if this is a real language or a signature placed freely with no ulterior motives.

POLITICAL SLOGAN OR DEVOID OF MEANING?

Graffiti is here, and it must be dealt with. As a sign of the *presence* of anonymous authors, inhabitants, visitors, travelers, and wanderers in transit, must it be reduced to something devoid of meaning? In his chapter "Kool Killer or the Insurrection of Signs," from *Symbolic Exchange and Death*, Jean Baudrillard ponders the meaning of this kind of mural expression: "Invincible due to their own poverty, they resist every interpretation and every connotation, no longer denoting anyone or anything. In this way, with neither connotation or denotation, they escape the principle of signification and, as *empty signifiers*, erupt into the sphere of the *full* signs of the city, dissolving it on contact" (1976, 121–22).

Recognizing neither denotation or connotation, these visual forms have no meaning for Baudrillard, but I do not see how empty signifiers could dissolve the city's own signs. Even if these forms had the power to distort the city, which remains to be seen, they are neither neutral nor empty. For those who condemn them, for example, they are in fact bearers of the ability to completely alter the deep-seated identity of the city.

Regardless of whether we accept or reject them, they contribute to the establishment of urban public space. As such, they are as important as any other visual or audible gauge. From this point of view, a sociolinguistic reading of these expressions provides an additional illuminating perspective. Above all, it makes it possible to avoid generalities concerning the problems of the suburbs and the malaise of the housing projects—graffiti being a measure of this discomfort.

Illegal mural expressions are expressive in their content in the sense that whatever the circumstances, they express something that manifests a sense of well-being or uneasiness. From this point of view, they are meaningful, and even if for some they contribute to the disintegration of the artistic signs of the city, they succeed, however, in expressing something through this dissolution. According to the typology established by John R. Searle in *Expression and Meaning*, one can add other qualities to these kinds of visual expressions. We can say, for instance, that these mural expressions are *assertive*; in other words, they point out to the rest of the community how things are, even if graffiti artists express this in a hieroglyphic code that only insiders can understand. But, at the very least, this urban form reflects their perceptions of the city.

These expressions are also *promissive* in that they define the framework of a political claim in the broader sense. Even if they do not have an agenda, graffiti artists propose another reading of the appropriation of the public space. Drop shadows, stencils, poster hijacks, and mosaic are all examples. Regardless of the coherence of the project, the presence of such an awareness deserves to exist. More than just a gratuitous act, graffiti embody a sort of civil program complete with a personal reading of the urban layout by its author. This reading translates a social reality in its own way.

But the most important quality is perhaps the *directive* nature of mural expressions in the sense that they force the stakeholders of urban life to react and intervene. In this way, we can speak of urban resistance in the very act of highlighting.

GRAFFITI AS AN ACT OF RESISTANCE?

As we have seen, these mural expressions are plurivocal. They range from pure and simple gratuitous acts to clearly identified political claims. In the most common case, the approach is part of a psychological interpretation in which the tagger tags because everyone does it. Thus, graffiti makes clear a quest for status and is part of a communicative approach. From this point of view, the "pen name" often reveals the graffiti artist's state of mind. But this stance is not very significant, even if it is quantitatively the most widespread. Then comes a more elaborate approach that is found with many taggers-turned-graffiti-artists when they create advertisements of sorts in which the tag serves as a logo. In fact, not all taggers are graffiti artists and vice versa. Moreover, there are taggers who have more elaborate approaches than some graffiti artists.

Some graffiti artists use their signature as a logo to promote their brand (clothing, accessories, etc.). Their signatures are placed as would-be advertising posters to attract potential target markets. The comment of Futura 2000, one of the first New York taggers, shows this awareness: "After seeing a name fifteen or twenty minutes, it stays in our head—this is the principle of advertising" (Desse and SBG 1993, 63). This logo-like signature can be classified as a veritable marketing strategy. But, again, this kind of approach does not really elucidate what urban mural expression actually is.

That said, the psychoanalytical reading is more interesting, for it asserts that graffitiing leads to a staging: "I graff' my 'pen name.'" This posture also reflects the limits of the graffiti phenomenon, since in most cases the graffiti theme is constrained by the variation of artists' lettering. The public display of the "pseudonym" and the explicit discourse on the artist's identity, place, influence, or charisma contribute to excessive self-promotion. These artists' "egotrips," coupled with narcissistic behaviors, usually end in childish quarrels like, "I graffiti better than you." It is worth recalling Freud's (1982) differentiation between primary narcissism, which he defined as "an early state in which children are exclusively focused on their ego-libidos," and secondary narcissism, the only pathological one and which consists of "the libido turning against the ego because it is stripped of its object investments" (Laplanche and Pontalis 1967, 263).[1]

There is also a psychiatric interpretation of the phenomenon that implies that graffiti is responding to a kind of graphomaniacal delirium: The artist tags his or her name everywhere, on all media and in all possible forms. The tag then assumes a certain onomatopoeic value that consists of the infinite repetition of its pseudonym in a sort of egotrip. We express more than we mean, we vociferate more than we dialogue, we scream more than we communicate under calligraphic variants. What matters is the speed and violence of expression, a sort of stammering or stuttering. The tagger's cry is onomatopoeic and echolalic: CKC (Cruel Killers Crew), KOP (Kontrol of Paris), PAC (Partisan au Carton), UV (Ultra Violent). Each time, the expression is fast and punchy. A cry is uttered, but it must be euphonic. We write but with a calligraphic application. They write but with a calligraphic quest in mind. This way of writing while shouting their name is found in the vocabulary of the taggers to describe their actions. Tagging a surface is also attacking it, turning it inside out, fucking it up, tearing it, smashing it, or burning it.

The final interpretation of this phenomenon is political. It expresses a clearly stated claim. The episode at the Louvre-Rivoli metro station that took place on 30 April 1991 by three graffiti writers explains this position well. And, even if the event is a bit dated, it has the advantage of summarizing the various analyses of this phenomenon. The warning was clear: The aim was to challenge political stakeholders on issues related to exclusion and urban violence. At the same time, the legislature was examining a bill in the National Assembly on the reform of the Nationality Code. The signature of the graffiti writers was formulated as follows: "Whoever provokes the wind, suffers the storm."[2] But behind this "decoration" of the Louvre station, several things were said about museum art, street art, the role of institutional factors, the media coverage of the graffiti movement, the extreme right, etc. First, tagging the Louvre-Rivoli station was the means to have this new form of expression recognized while returning to the question of art made accessible to all. After all, we know that André Malraux was responsible for the transformation of this station into an exhibition space. In the Louvre station, the work is no longer in an institutional place with regard to Malraux's warning: "If you give them a wall, they will not make masterpieces, they will create a style" (Dufresne 1991, 143).[3] In other words, what was aboveground—recognized art—had to go underground into the subway, and what was previously below—the wall graffiti—had to go back up into the open.

Second, some graffiti artists have used this mode of expression to convey a message, a message that can be found on certain dedications: "Graffiti is and must remain a shitty word, an insult to the constipated mind" (MDC DÖC, taken from Salvador Dali's formula).[4]

Third, the stakeholders in the Louvre station project also asked about the political relegation of this mode of expression. Oeno, one of the three graffiti artists responsible for the "decoration" of the station, recounts, in his own way, how it was expedited:

> The guys bombarded the subway with tags, but not the painted ones. Because the painted subways were more beautiful, but it was such an indication of a takeover of some parts of society that it was not tolerable. Seeing the painted cars, people thought that it had to have been authorized, or that we were doing whatever we wanted in the subway. The guys from the RATP had all the painted subways sent away to be cleaned and ran only the dirty subways covered with tags.[5] I said to myself: "You guys do not want to see the difference between the beautiful and the ugly, and neither do I, so badaboom!" It became a war, and, as with any war, there were bombs, and that was the case with the graffiti: the bombs were being dropped everywhere! . . . There was supposed to be sixty of us, there were only fifty, and in the end 47 bailed on us. So we were even more furious! We didn't even use pseudonyms. We just wanted to make an impact. Since it was the day before May 1, the goal was to make the news before [Jean-Marie] Le Pen's parade.[6] It came off like we wanted! We made the front page and Le Pen was pushed to the second. Just for

that, stealing the show from Le Pen the day of his own party, it was a big day
for hip hop. (Milon 1996)

This testimony shows that such an approach is not reduced to mere vandal-
ism or a gratuitous act. Underneath it all, we see the face of relegation.

Those relegated to the margins, unlike the banished or the exiled, keep
their rights while simultaneously living outside their city. They become sec-
ond-class citizens in a way. But, by maintaining the legal possibility of
enjoying their rights without actually being allowed to live on their own
territory, they end up losing both. Even if this exile does not entail the loss of
civil rights, is it still possible for them to live anywhere they want? While
less serious than deportation, since there is neither confiscation of property
nor suppression of political rights, relegation nevertheless forces one to give
up part of his or her citizenship. When applied to graffiti artists, this leads to
a kind of reversal: They are in their own space but with the impossibility of
being able to use their mode of expression. This is reminiscent of the relegation of the citizen who has everything—nationality—except the essential—
citizenship; in other words, one can have a French ID but remain a second-
class citizen (have a homeland but few rights). This relegation is also remi-
niscent of the way we treat a city's residents on whom we impose plans of
urbanization without consultation. This relegation is all the more interesting
because it leads to a double relegation: I relegate while being relegated.

Graffiti artists are excluded from traditional artistic forms but relegate in
turn by imposing visual imprints on inhabitants that are subjected to hieroglyphic codes and comprehensible only to insiders. Symbolic violence responds to another symbolic violence. This double relegation is also found in
a city's inhabitants on whom urban arrangements are imposed but who, in
turn, relegate these places of residence themselves through multiple forms of
vacancy of these spaces: from the refusal to use them to ruining them. Urbanization is also part of a broader symbolic violence that can be found at all
levels, for instance, in urban planning imposed on residents, and often by
polluting a place's image with slick advertising. This is also what the anti-
advertising collective wants to express by graffitiing the commercial spaces
of the subway: "Why condemn tags when we willingly accept the soft porn
proliferated by some advertising campaigns and which ultimately embodies
the same visual pollution?" The economic response provided by the institutional stakeholders is only one way of removing the question of the occupation of public or semipublic space. But beyond these considerations regarding the judicial aspects of illegal mural expressions looms the bigger question of the appropriation of the wall, a difficult question to treat and all the
more difficult as the graffiti becomes part of the body of the city.

Who owns the wall, and who owns the city? This question is not a legal
one, as if one could be content to break up the city into multiple parcels, but a

symbolic one. In addition to this question, another surfaces, namely, that of who owns the graffiti. The person who did it? This makes little sense insofar as the author claims anonymity. Does it belong to the person who contributed to it first if it is a collage? Or to the wall's owner? To the community? And who, in fact, is the recipient? The inhabitants, the community, or strangers just passing through? "Writing" in the street, regardless of "the writer," means accepting anonymity and implicitly that it disappears immediately. The case of the Paris subway's electrical switchboard panel doors painted over by C215 and then torn off is interesting because "the artist" had to stop his activity. However, isn't this just the result of the double blind that illegal mural expressions are in when they claim to be an art? While graffiti artists use the street with its constraints (where they are obliged to use pseudonyms that are less and less of an alias because of the media coverage of the phenomenon; acceptance of the ephemeral nature of the work, etc.), those who put their work out there are also those who most often aspire to artistic recognition. It is undoubtedly the schizophrenic position of the urban artist who accepts the stakes of the street without truly accepting them. This is the same ambiguity found with art dealers. Reducing the issue of illegal mural expressions to street art already basically constitutes subscribing to the market logic of gallery owners. Who is talking about urban art but collectors like Gallizia, the Cartier Foundation in 2009, or the advertising world? Did the Cartier Foundation have anything to say about graffiti other than its market value when it organized its "Born in the Street" exhibition in 2009? This is true for most of the painted walls of Paris that are purely decorative and serve no other purpose. All one need do is to linger in the rue de Ménilmontant in Paris at the Jérôme Mesnager wall or the sculpture of Ben; these are false acts of resistance and in truth decorative works. But much more than the commercialization of these mural expressions, the position the artists are put in is the larger problem at hand.

To only consider the most publicized cases—the defacement of Banksy's works, for example—we see how it reveals the double-talk of these artists and the way in which they appropriate this space. Let us also note that, even if the wall legally belongs to a landowner, the appropriation of a place is more than just a case of ownership. It is above all symbolic, and nobody owns the urban landscape. Remember Immanuel Kant's warning when he deemed advertising and publicity (public-city) to be diffusion by shared public space (2006). In the case of Banksy, it is quite symptomatic. One cannot claim responsibility for a graffiti practice while also claiming copyright and demanding royalties. Acts of resistance do not adhere to commercial logic. The problem with graffiti is no longer even that of artistic practice; it becomes rather that of the place and function of copyright. It is not uncommon to see some urban artists making graffiti while simultaneously demanding legal protection. It becomes absurd. Graffiti is interesting when it is considered part of a rationale for urban resistance. The fact that certain "artists" experience identity issues is a completely different problem that does not pertain to a critical analysis. Ultimately, if the commodification caused by street art were to disappear, it would have the advantage of freeing mural writing of any speculative rationale, thereby confirming its mission of urban resistance.

REFERENCES

Baudrillard, Jean. *L'échange symbolique et la mort*. Paris: Gallimard, 1976.

Desse (Desdémone Bardin), and SBG (Sébastian Bardin-Greenberg). *Freestyle*. Paris: Massot & Millet, 1993.

Dufresne, David. *Yo! Révolution rap: L'histoire, les groupes, le movement*. Paris: Ramsay, 1991.

Freud, Sigmund. *La vie sexuelle*. Translated by Denise Berger et al. Paris: PUF, reprinted 1982.

Kant, Immanuel. *Anthropology From a Pragmatic Point of View*. Cambridge: Cambridge University Press, 2006.

Laplanche, Jean, and J.-B. Pontalis. *Vocabulaire de la psychanalyse*. Paris: PUF, 1967.

Milon, Alain. "Les expressions murales illicites: Le graff comme acte de résistance." In *Machines de guerre urbaines*, 77–92, edited by Manola Antonioli. Paris: Editions Loco, 2015.

Searle, John R. *Expression and Meaning: Studies in the Theory of Speech Acts*. Cambridge: Cambridge University Press, 1979.

Chapter Twelve

Of Melody, Markets, and Mobilization

A History of Hip-Hop in Dakar, Senegal

Catherine M. Appert

On 19 June 2018, a music video titled "7 Minutes contre le CFA" (7 Minutes against the [West African] CFA Franc) appeared on its own YouTube channel. Its description, in French, reads,

> SEVEN minutes of music, TEN artists coming from SEVEN countries, unite around the same Pan-African combat. They are rappers, singers, or slam poets, expressing themselves at the mic in Wolof, Bambara, English, or French, and they have all decided to lend their pens and voices to a common cause: the economic sovereignty of the Francophone West African countries where the Franc CFA, the currency of dependence on France, cracks its whip. (my translation)

Over a reggae beat, with a French-language hook performed by Senegalese singer Daba, artists from throughout West Africa sing and rap, some in indigenous languages, but most in French. In addition to shots of Bamako, Cotonou, and Lomé, the music video features aerial and street views of Dakar, the capital city of Senegal. Here, in the onetime administrative center of colonial French West Africa, contemporary hip-hop narratives about imperialism, language, cultural globalization, urbanity, and blackness intersect with colonial histories and the specificity of Francophone connections.[1] In protesting France's continued economic influence over its former colonies, the artists involved in "7 Minutes contre le CFA" joined an ongoing struggle spearheaded by activist Kémi Séba, who was imprisoned in 2017 for his performative burning of a Franc CFA note in Dakar's Place de l'Obélisque (Anonymous 2017). This large public plaza has frequently been a site of both performance and protest, from the defunct annual festival 72H of Hip Hop to the youth rallies of 2011 and 2012, in which members of the movement Y'en a Marre (Enough Is Enough) protested corrupt electoral politics. In 2017, rappers associated with Y'en a Marre joined the fray to speak out against the CFA and Senegal's broader dependence on imported goods (Ndao 2017). Nearly a year later, "7 Minutes contre le CFA" was released. The song's anticolonial message was at once grounded in Senegalese history and Pan-Africanist in scope. Its musical and linguistic features—a melodic French-language refrain over a globally familiar reggae beat—speak to a particular history of the intersections of musical style, commercial concerns, and social engagement in Dakar where, over decades of hip-hop practice, musical aesthetics have intersected with debates over commodification and the role of political activism in constructing and contesting local hip-hop authenticity.

INTERNATIONAL FLOWS

In the 1980s, as certain global circulations waxed and others waned, hip-hop arrived in Dakar, riding global flows of media that originated in the United States but also following transnational Senegalese movements between (and within) West Africa, Europe, and North America. A vibrant hip-hop scene developed in the intervening decades; in 2018, a series of events and celebrations commemorated Senegal's "30 Ans du Hip Hop" (30 Years of Hip-Hop). This history takes us back to 1988, the time when the first Senegalese rappers were beginning to record original music, so that the beginning of what local hip-hoppers refer to as "Rap Galsen" (an inversion of the first and last syllables of "Sene-gal," inspired by the linguistic practices of North African youth in France) is considered to have begun not with the music's arrival in Dakar but rather with its localization and adaptation.[2]

These corresponded to a particular historical moment. The former French colony's first twenty years of independence were marked by cultural policy that valued French humanism and *Francophonie* under President Leopold Sedar Senghor, so that, despite its diminished formal domination, France's cultural legacy remained strong. Perhaps contradictorily, however, the French colonial policy of assimilating a select, elite urban population into French culture (and sometimes citizenship) meant that, conversely, to this day nonelite and rural Senegalese have never fully adopted the French language. Thus, unlike other West African countries formerly colonized by France, French is not a lingua franca in Senegal, despite its status as a national language. When Abdou Diouf succeeded Senghor as president in the early 1980s, he initiated a shift to Wolof-centric cultural policy that privileged indigenous African values over the assimilated French ones of Senghor while retaining French as the language of governance and education (Kringelbach 2013, 100). That same decade saw the Western imposition of structural adjustment programs, a surge in youth and student demonstrations against government corruption, and intensifying transnational networks of Senegalese migrants.

At the same time, accelerating flows of technology and media moved alongside and sometimes against those transnational networks to carry hip-hop from the United States around the world. Senegalese youth initially danced to this new music, imitating the images of break dancers they saw in movies like *Wild Style* and *Beat Street*. Within break-dance crews, certain members began to move to the back or side of the performance to take the mic as MCs, imitating the vocal performance of U.S. and French rappers. Soon, a localized hip-hop scene began to emerge, with young rappers producing original lyrics to imported instrumentals and eventually creating their own original instrumental tracks to rap over.[3] It is no coincidence that many of those crews emerged from neighborhoods in the area known as "SICAP" (short for Société Immobilière du Cap-Vert), which were constructed to accommodate a growing population of civil servants and military officials, beginning in the 1950s under colonial rule and extending to after independence in 1960 (Ndiaye 2011, 57). These were the young people who spoke French and had access to both globalized media and immediate family members who would bring cassettes and videos home from the United States and France.

It did not take long for hip-hop's global flows to change directions—not toward the United States, however, but to France. In 1992, Senegalese-French rapper MC Solaar visited Dakar to perform at the French Cultural Center, and the two young men who comprised the duo Positive Black Soul (PBS) were offered a spot as the opening act. The show would change the trajectory of DJ Awadi and Duggy Tee's careers, as they soon headed to France to record their first international album with Mango, a subsidiary of Island Records. That first album, *Salaam*, sounded the confluence of these transnational movements. Its songs open with bits and pieces of Senegalese languages, instruments, music, and soundscapes, only to transition into hip-hop beats that closely adhere to contemporaneous U.S. hip-hop styles. They rapped and sang in French, Wolof, and English, with lyrics ranging from broad social commentary to Pan-African sentiments to feel-good anthems.

Back in Senegal, Positive Black Soul mentored up-and-coming group Pee Froiss, who created music in a similar style, as did other groups, including, among many, Daara J, Jant Bi, Sunu Flavor, and Black Mboolo. This wave of hip-hoppers shared a distinctive stylistic model for their "soft" music (Benga 2002, 83): hip-hop beats or R&B instrumentals, sometimes flavored with local musical elements, mixing indigenous and colonial languages, with catchy melodic refrains sung in R&B or Jamaican toasting styles. They were thus "international" both in terms of the geographic scope of their circulation and in regard to their characteristic musical style. Their incorporation of indigenous languages and musics signaled novelty in world music markets; at the same time, their style was identifiably international to Senegalese audiences, not only in its incorporation of elements of contemporary hip-hop, but also in how it drew on familiar sounds of reggae and R&B that were already popular in Senegal (Appert 2018).

For example, Sunu Flavor's 1996 song "Nell Fess," an egotrip off their album of the same title, is performed in Wolof, with just a few French and English phrases thrown in.[4] A synthesized xylophone and twangy plucked instrument invoke, without replicating, the sounds of the indigenous *bala* and *xalam* or *ngoni*, respectively, embedded in a beat that layers sharp hip-hop snare hits with sustained synthesized chords. The refrain's nasal reworking of U.S. R&B singing was distinct to mainstream Senegalese hip-hop in this period; the vocal style appears in countless songs, including Black Mboolo's 1998 "Mbindane du Diaam" (A Domestic Worker Is Not a Slave). There, it melds with indigenous *griot* (bardic) singing styles, as the group's members admonish families to treat their maids, often young girls from rural villages, with respect.[5] Their focused social intervention rides an R&B beat made sensuous by a rich bass line and noodling guitar.

As Senegalese hip-hop's international wave swelled, a countermovement grew in Dakar's working-class neighborhoods, themselves a concrete legacy to colonial development. The French constructed the first of these, Médina, in the early twentieth century when, after a prolonged struggle with indigenous residents for the land in what is now the Plateau section of downtown Dakar, an outbreak of plague provided an excuse for them to forcibly relocate African inhabitants into the "hygienic" concrete fixtures in Médina (Bigon 2009). The urban population swelled in the mid-twentieth century, leading to the development of the SICAP neighborhoods just beyond Médina, and eventually to the rise of *banlieues*, the overcrowded, underserviced working-class neighborhoods on the outskirts of the city (Vernière 1973).

In the 1990s, young rappers across Dakar's working-class neighborhoods dubbed themselves "the hardcore" and claimed their imposed underground status as a marker of hip-hop authenticity. Claiming hip-hop as a music born of black American urban struggle, groups like Médina's Rap'Adio and the Guédiawaye *banlieue*'s Wa BMG 44 produced music that rejected French and the doubly "international" musical aesthetic of their SICAP peers, not only refusing to incorporate musical markers of "Africa," but also rejecting the melodic elements of R&B and reggae that marked international groups' music. Rap'Adio's "Xibaaru 1-2 Ground" (News of the Underground), from their seminal 1998 album *Ku Weet Xam sa bop* (You Know Yourself in Solitude), goes so far as to parody the songs and singing styles of many of the international groups listed earlier (Appert 2018, 41–42). Beyond clashing other rappers, hardcore lyrics dealt primarily with Senegal-specific political issues. Yatfu's "Stop! Agresseurs," from their 1998 album *Fenku* (Rise), presents a social critique similar in scale to Black Mboolo's "Mbindane du Diaam" discussed previously. The track starts with the sound of police sirens, giving way to an instrumental whose few pitched elements have been chopped and looped to become part of a dense percussive texture. There is no singing, no melodies; they communicate in forceful rhythmic rapping over the unchanging beat, indicting muggers in the streets of Dakar by appealing to social norms of hard work as a mark of manliness.

International and hardcore hip-hop, then, were nearly parallel movements. In retrospect, they give the impression of being consecutive because the working-class rappers who dubbed themselves "underground" had fewer resources to record and disseminate their music; were less visible in mainstream media; and produced music that, in its adherence to a strict U.S. hip-hop aesthetic, did not appeal to international audiences. But across categories, rappers shared an interest in social commentary; a reliance on an urban Wolof inflected with French; and, of course, an engagement with U.S. hip-hop styles.[6]

THE NEW MILLENNIUM

By the turn of the century, *Rap Galsen* was a dynamic and diverse musical movement that at times splintered along lines of socioeconomic status, audience, and musical style. The relative majority status of underground artists, who, mentored and inspired by the early hardcore, performed a rough and sometimes vulgar version of hip-hop, meant that hip-hop remained marginalized in mainstream media and elite performance spaces. Into the 2000s, rappers across divisions of mainstream and underground engaged in social movements and political agitation. This came to a head in the period leading up to the 2000 presidential elections, where many rappers put their efforts behind opposition candidate Abdoulaye Wade, who aimed to wrest power from the Parti Socialiste that had been in power since independence in 1960. When Wade won the election, not only rappers but also their local communities and international commentators lauded Senegalese hip-hop for its instrumental role in this momentous power shift. By 2007, however, many Senegalese, including a majority of rappers, were disillusioned with Wade. Again, rappers mobilized to effect a change in power, but Wade won reelection.

All along, hip-hop continued its stylistic development. The generation of rappers that had come up under the hardcore's tutelage formed their own groups and collectives. In the first decade of the new millennium, their sound continued to evolve in step with U.S. hip-hop norms while maintaining an emphasis on Wolof-language social critiques and a hardcore musical aesthetic that often alienated them from their elders in Senegalese society. This continuous intergenerational conflict—between adults who think rap is bad and the youth who hope to convince them that it is not—is the topic of hardcore group Keur Gui's 2009 song "Guiss Guiss you Woro" (Opposing Views). Even so, hip-hoppers' continued involvement in electoral politics aided in the broadening social acceptance of their musical activities.

At the same time, a parallel local hip-hop mainstream continued to thrive, intermingling with the hardcore artists, sharing stages at open-air concerts and festivals, and collaborating on tracks. The same year that Keur Gui released "Guiss Guiss," Da Brains had a hit with their song "Link," a light-hearted, Wolof-language hip-hop number that mixes harmonized singing and rapping to ask a young woman for her contact information on a long list of social platforms. Still other artists, like Nix and Canabasse, created music following the newest trends in U.S. mainstream hip-hop, with sleek music videos and French and Wolof lyrics.

Twenty years into its development, and with a history of concrete political engagement under its belt, underground hip-hop had less to prove than it once did. When young rapper Profete released "Niom Leu" (It's Them) in 2011, it had become fairly standard for underground rappers to have a song or two on their albums with a sung hook. "Niom Leu" opens with the voice of reggae singer Youssou Makkan J riffing in a wordless high falsetto over synthesized piano and strings; the bass enters, and then the drums and Profete come in together. He raps about the struggles of people working in Dakar's informal sector: mothers selling peanuts, children begging, women selling their bodies. The song indicts the government for its failures to live up to its promises.

By the time this song came out, rappers still identifying as underground—a category that now encompassed multiple generations—increasingly incorporated singing and even traditional instruments in select tracks, producing songs that were more musically "commercial" than would have been possible ten years before (Appert 2015). Many rappers remained adamant, however, that, as with "Niom Leu," the incorporation of traditional instruments and/or of singing operate within strict conceptions of hip-hop meter, an understanding that they expressed in terms of the "squareness" of hip-hop beats as opposed to the triple internal rhythms of much indigenous music (Appert 2018, 172–74; Appert 2016). It was this metric difference, as much as a difference in lyrical message, that continued to distinguish mainstream and underground hip-hop in the twenty-first century.

The underground's opening to singing and traditional music in the second decade of the twenty-first century was at once a process of localization typical both of hip-hop as a genre that has always centered on ideas of place (Forman 2002) and of popular music globalization more broadly. It was also, however, part of a conscious process of commercialization. By emphasizing the metric distinctions between hip-hop and indigenous musics, hip-hoppers were able to relocate hip-hop consciousness in their lyrical content while moving toward musical styles that appealed to broader national and foreign audiences. In a parallel vein, rappers spoke about the relationship between language, global intelligibility, and local relevance. They recognized Wolof's necessity to their primary goal of reaching Senegalese audiences, even as some became more open to using French and English to extend their reach. The desire for internationalization had to do both with extending the range of their messages and with a need-based desire to benefit financially from their labor as artists. Ultimately, however, aesthetic considerations led many to continue to record almost exclusively in Wolof, prioritizing a skillful flow in their first language over a broader lyrical intelligibility. Here, the globality of hip-hop *music* exceeds that of the French (or English) language (Appert 2018).

A contemporaneous local mainstream has continued to thrive. Several artists have built successful careers with songs ranging from contemporary U.S. hip-hop styles with Wolof (and sometimes French) lyrics to songs that blend R&B and local pop styles to imitating current Nigerian and Ghanaian pop music. On the one hand, songs like rapper OMG's 2018 "Boss Lady" sound like a Wolof-language remake of contemporary U.S. hip-hop styles with a bit of U.K. grime vocalization and a sung hook in the mix. The mainstream duo Ahklou Brick's 2016 "Fayma Money" (Pay Me Money), featuring Elzo Jamdong and Dip Doundou Guiss, has a trap-influenced beat, although the lyrical flow would be more at home over the East Coast–style beats that were so popular in Senegal in the first decade of the century. On the other hand, many current mainstream artists, much like the earliest rappers to be popular in Senegal, draw on international musical styles while blending them with local elements, in ways that appeal to Senegalese youth living in a global city. In particular, they increasingly favor the triple feel of indigenous music and mix it with contemporary trap styles from the U.S. South. Ahklou Brick's 2018 song "Sama Logo Bi" (My Logo), for example, layers a trap beat with a synthesized xylophone that invokes the Mande *bala*, or wooden xylophone with gourd resonators—a sound signaling indigenous music to Senegalese listeners (Appert 2018, 164).

But this trend has increasingly extended beyond the mainstream. A few underground hip-hop artists, notably Fata El Presidente, long ago shifted to rapping over the rhythms of Mbalax (Senegal's preeminent popular genre, based in indigenous rhythms), to criticism from hardcore hip-hoppers. More recently, rapper M.A.S.S., known as part of the first generation of underground hip-hoppers, released several Mbalax-inspired tracks, including "Wodou Wodou" (Tie a Wrap) in 2017. In 2018, rapper and beatmaker Iss 814, who came up through the underground scene in the Guédiawaye *banlieue*, released "Noce" ("Dakar Trap #1," reads the rest of the video's title on YouTube), which similarly melds a synthesized xylophone with a trap beat.

This points to how, in the second decade of the twenty-first century, this turn toward increased musical localization—itself a kind of internationalization—and linguistic openness has loosened the categories that previously governed *Rap Galsen*. Less and less are "underground" artists concerned with maintaining a strict distinction between hip-hop and other genres. They, too, increasingly draw on indigenous rhythms, now without necessarily altering them to fit hip-hop beats. They also experiment with contemporary Nigerian and Ghanaian popular styles. The result is that it is much harder to tell underground and mainstream hip-hop apart stylistically than it used to be.

CONCLUSION

When a coalition of artists released "7 Minutes contre le CFA" in 2018, they mobilized a set of aesthetic and linguistic practices that have emerged from a complex matrix of global connections and movements: colonialism, globalization, transnationalism, and diasporic and Pan-African identification. Of course, "7 Minutes contre le CFA" is not only a Senegalese hip-hop song but a collaborative Pan-African anthem. Yet, produced in Senegal, with a predominance of Senegalese artists, the song speaks to the entwined musical and social histories that have shaped *Rap Galsen* over the last thirty years—histories that are, themselves, necessarily inseparable from colonial domination. "7 Minutes," after all, is performed primarily in French for its intersecting international audiences where, ironically, a shared colonial history provides a means of communicating across a wide range of African countries as well as across continental divides.

For if the relationship between France and Senegal nuances narratives of hip-hop globalization to mark France as an important node, then hip-hop globalization equally complicates the relationship between Senegal, France, and other Francophone African countries. Multidirectional and complex flows of people, power, and capital brought hip-hop to Senegal and Senegalese hip-hop to the world. Colonial influence on Senegalese culture and urban geography in turn influenced hip-hop, as I have outlined here, so that early divisions in the hip-hop community centered on a critique of certain kinds of internationalism as an embrace of colonialism and instead claimed black American music as a nonimperial medium of global connection. And so we see in the history of *Rap Galsen* a consistent movement toward understandings of internationalism that have to do with musical style more than language, until a song's potential for global impact is not limited to its embrace of colonial languages but may rely on its ability to tap into global circulations of African and African American musics. This was true when rappers in the 1990s positioned hip-hop as a global musical expression of racialized urban struggle in which they heard and participated in a diasporic resonance of experience, and it remains true as hip-hoppers increasingly turn toward the globally circulating Afrobeats of their Anglophone West African neighbors.

REFERENCES

Anonymous. "2017: L'année où l'Afrique a déclaré la guerre au CFA/La France sur la défensive." *Dakaractu*, 25 December 2017. https://www.dakaractu.com/2017-l-annee-ou-l-Afrique-a-declare-la-guerre-au-Cfa-La-France-sur-la-defensive_a144326.html

Appert, Catherine M. "To Make Song without Singing: Hip Hop and Popular Music in Senegal." *New Literary History* 46, no. 4 (2015): 759–74.

———. "On Hybridity in African Popular Music: The Case of Senegalese Hip Hop." *Ethnomusicology* 60, no. 2 (2016): 279–99.

———. *In Hip Hop Time: Music, Memory, and Social Change in Urban Senegal*. New York: Oxford University Press, 2018.

Benga, Ndiouga Adrien. "'The Air of the City Makes Free': Urban Music from the 1950s to the 1990s in Senegal—Variété, Jazz, Mbalax, Rap." In *Playing with Identities in Contemporary Music in Africa*, edited by Mai Palmberg and Annemette Kirkegaard, 75–85. Stockholm: Nordiska Afrikainstitutet, 2002.

Bigon, Liora. *A History of Urban Planning in Two West African Colonial Capitals: Residential Segregation in British Lagos and French Dakar (1850–1930)*. Lewiston, NY: Edwin Mellon Press, 2009.

Forman, Murray. *The Hood Comes First: Race, Space, and Place in Rap and Hip-Hop*. Middletown, CT: Wesleyan University Press, 2002.

Kringelbach, Hélène Neveu. *Dance Circles: Movement, Morality, and Self-Fashioning in Urban Senegal*. New York: Berghahn Books, 2013.

McLaughlin, Fiona. "The Ascent of Wolof as an Urban Vernacular and National Lingua Franca in Senegal." In *Globalization and Language Vitality: Perspectives from Africa*, edited by Cécile B. Vigouroux and Salikoko S. Mufwene, 142–70. London: Continuum, 2009.

Ndao, Sidy Djimby. "Sénégal: Lutte contre le F CFA, le rappeur Thiat appelle à boycotter les multinationales françaises." *Koaci.com*, 17 September 2017. http://koaci.com/senegal-lutte-contre-rappeur-thiat-appelle-boycotter-multinationales-francaises-113112.html

Ndiaye, Mariéma. "Analyse du processus d'élaboration du budget dans une société de gestion immobilière: cas de la SICAP SA." M.A. thesis, Centre Africain d'Études Supérieures en Gestion, Dakar, Senegal, 2011.

Swigart, Leigh. "Cultural Creolisation and Language Use in Post-Colonial Africa: The Case of Senegal." *Africa: Journal of the International African Institute* 64, no. 2 (1994): 175–89.

Vernière, Marc. "Campagne, ville, bidonville, banlieue: Migrations intra-urbaines vers Dagoudane-Pikine, ville nouvelle de Dakar (Sénégal)." *Cahiers ORSTOM: Série Sciences Humaines* 10, nos. 2–3 (1973): 217–43.

DISCOGRAPHY AND FILMOGRAPHY

Ahklou Brick. "Sama Logo Bi." Musee Records. Web. Originally released in 2018. https://www.youtube.com/watch?v=3nrqsQSMjgM

Ahklou Brick, featuring Elzo and Dip. "Fayma Money." *A.D.B.D.* Hoside Studio, compact disc. Originally released in 2016.

Beat Street. Dir. Stan Lathan. Orion Pictures. Originally released in 1984.

Black Mboolo. "Mbindane du Diaam." Independent, cassette tape. Originally released in 1998.

Daba, Mouna, Kamal Radji, Romeij MC, Black Moojah, Saah Karim, Nit Doff, Jah Moko, Elom 20ce, and Samayone. "7 Minutes contre le CFA." Amoul Bayi Records. Web. Originally released in 2018. https://www.youtube.com/watch?v=OO-s94Rf36k

Da Brains. "Link." Independent. Web. Originally released in 2011. https://www.youtube.com/watch?v=w-7HCQQ2U_8

Iss 814. "Noce (Dakar Trap #1)." Web. Originally released in 2018. https://www.youtube.com/watch?v=XNJgGD84pS0

Keur Gui. "Guiss Guiss you Woro." *Nos Connes Doléances*. Independent, compact disc. Originally released in 2009.

M.A.S.S. "Wodou Wodou." Rep'tyle Music. Web. Originally released in 2017. https://www.youtube.com/watch?v=omi6ItbPhl0

OMG. "Boss Lady." DD Records. Web. Originally released in 2018. https://www.youtube.com/watch?v=i6kWbE2IZjI

Positive Black Soul. *Salaam*. Mango/Island Records, cassette tape. Originally released in 1996.

Profete. "Niom Leu." 4MyDogs Records. Web. Originally released in 2011. https://www.youtube.com/watch?v=ZnMOZW27yw0

Rap'Adio. *Ku Weet Xam sa bop*. Fitna Prod, cassette tape. Originally released in 1998.

Sunu Flavor. "Nell Fess." *Nell Fess*. Dakar: Independent Release, cassette tape. Originally released in 1996.

Wild Style. Dir. Charlie Ahearn. Rhino Entertainment. Originally released in 1983.

Yatfu. "Stop! Agresseurs." *Fenku*. Independent Release, cassette tape. Originally released in 1998.

Chapter Thirteen

Rap Music in Quebec

An Essentially Hybrid Genre

Maxime Delcourt,
Translated by Patricia Frederick

Beginning in 2010, numerous Francophone rap artists have appeared onstage to remind us that the genre is not only confined to France. Emerging talents from Belgium, Switzerland, Morocco, and Quebec have combined ambition with youthful enthusiasm to escape all stereotypes. A new generation of rap artists raised in the era of YouTube and Spotify algorithms is proving capable of amplifying the Quebec hip-hop scene. Occurring at a crucial moment for Francophone rap, the emergence of these different national scenes created an explosion from all corners of the French-speaking world, one categorized by diverse esthetics and approaches. A quick glance at the discography of Alaclair Ensemble, Dead Obies, Loud Lary Ajust, or Sans Pression makes it immediately clear that what characterizes Montreal rap has little to do with what is produced in France or Belgium. However, some common points have existed since the movement began.

IN THE NAME OF HUMOR

Simultaneously in the United States and France, a number of powerful figures emerged in the early 1980s to lay the groundwork for rap music in Quebec. Local rappers Butcher T, Andrew Carr, and Michael Williams followed trends and were satisfied with replicating U.S. musical styles in popular Montreal area locales.[1] In 1983, an artist with comedic talent, Lucien Francœur, achieved distinguished national recognition in Canada with the 45 "Rap à Billy" (Billy's Rap), similar to the fervor later in 1989 over Belgian

Benny B's "Vous êtes fous" (You're Crazy) or in France with "Auteuil, Neuilly, Passy" by the French humorists Les Inconnus in 1991. Although its success was short-lived, the early misadventures of Lucien Francœur and other artists associated with the same comedy movement paved the way for future generations' ability to doubt the record industry so that they might focus on self-management: a *Do It Yourself* attitude that would never compromise musical vision. This comedy movement included "Ça rend rap" (This Is Rap) by Rock et Belles Oreilles in 1985, "Le Pape du rap" (The Pope of Rap) by Daniel Lavoie in 1990, and "Rapper Chic—Je rap en français" (Chic Rapper—I Rap in French) by Le Boyfriend in 1991.

The constraints of the Quebec rap scene—such as its wavering between English and French, the quest for a larger audience while maintaining its underground authenticity, and territorial rivalries with the rest of Canada—ironically turned out to be its very strengths. Due in part to its isolation, the evolution came about on the fringes of a record industry, favoring radical approaches while refusing to compromise. The proximity of Montreal to New York City lured local rappers with an obsession for the American dream to reproduce certain U.S. codes that almost gave their music a sense of parody. Nevertheless, these artists clearly supported stronger ties to France. In order to better understand this, one needs only consult Dubmatique, Sans Pression, or even Manu Militari and Koriass, names synonymous with the founders of Quebec rap music. According to them, there was without a doubt an abundance of intense connections between the two countries during the early 1990s. This period was characterized by the growing popularity and rapid expansion of rap culture and Francophone hip-hop throughout Quebec, thanks to groups like Frenchie B, Mélomane (Stratège) or MRF (Mouvement Rap Francophone).

RAPPERS AND ACTIVISTS

The rappers Kool Rock and the deejay Jay Tee, who form MRF, pioneered Quebec rap by launching local hip-hop productions. This was achieved in part by finding inspiration in French rap codes, as well as in the early works of American artists such as Ice-T and Public Enemy, and by drawing inspiration from one of the most sampled artists in history, James Brown. Kool Rock and the deejay Jay Tee cunningly used the beat from Brown's "Funky Drummer" on their single "MRF est arrivé" (MRF Has Arrived) in 1990. Quebec rappers then began to organize, gaining greater confidence in their skills and embracing their uniqueness in the name of establishing a community. Anecdotally, community centers and small specialized graffiti, vinyl, or streetwear shops in Montreal and elsewhere were still around in the 1990s, in large part because Quebec rappers were working so collectively. The rappers became an exception; they were activists prepared to militantly defend the behind-the-scenes mentality beneath the shadow of an emerging industry.

Included in this collection of artists is Cédric Morgan, cofounder of the defunct record label MontReal and the main orchestrator behind the strong sense of cohesion among Quebec rappers.[2] This Canadian was also host for the renowned hip-hop program *Dubmatique* on the CIBL airwaves in the early 1990s. This mythical show ended up inspiring the members of a band who chose its name as their own. Dubmatique's first album, *La force de comprendre* (The Power to Understand), released in 1997, sold more than 150,000 copies and went on to receive the Gala ADISQ (Association québé-coise de l'industrie du disque, du spectacle, et de la vidéo) award in the category "Alternative Rock Album" (because a hip-hop category did not yet exist).

DUBMATIQUE, A TEXTBOOK CASE

To anyone closely involved in the Quebec scene, it is no secret that Dubma-tique not only spearheaded an entire generation but also symbolized the vast richness and cultural diversity of the region. One of the duo's members, Jérôme-Philippe Bélinga (a.k.a. DiSoul), grew up with a Quebecois mother and a Camerounian father and spent twelve years of his childhood in Dakar. It was there, in the heart of Senegal's capital, that he met Ousmane Traoré (alias OTMC), who had returned to live in Senegal in the early 1990s after a youth spent in France. Together, they formed Trouble MC, esthetically remi-niscent of MC Solaar, who had authored the French rap hit of the time "Bouge de là" (Move). After several years of playing in Senegalese night-clubs and sharing the stage with local stars like Positive Black Soul, the two partners returned to Canada to attend college. They stumbled upon the CIBL show *Dubmatique*, contacted host Morgan, and adopted the program's name as a moniker. The platform allowed them to introduce freestyle to the radio. It was the beginning of a strong symbiotic relationship of reciprocal support between the duo and the show. As a result of this nearly unprecedented media explosion, Dubmatique quickly became the prime example for Mon-treal rap groups. The duo was organized, with a manager, a well-run show, and an established producer (DJ Choice) who brought coherence to the entire project.

Meanwhile, in the United States, groups like De La Soul and A Tribe Called Quest were actively fighting for another form of hip-hop. Dubmatique was familiar with these two groups' approach but radically supported the "Peace, Love, Unity, and Having Fun" principles that were valued by Afrika Bambaataa and the Zulu Nation. It should be noted that it was rare back then for hip-hop artists to make much money. In 1995, for the first recording of about ten of its songs, Dubmatique made only CAD $10,000. Because of their intensity and passion, DiSoul and OTMC did not get bored with putting words (without vulgarity) to music. On the contrary, they interspersed them with positive values.

This was not to everyone's taste. Purists most notably criticized Dubmatique for lyrics not focused enough on social problems, although at the same time they failed to recognize something of an antigang statement in a title like "Soul Pleureur" (Soul Cryer). The problem was that other more politically active groups were beginning to emerge, and media outlets in Montreal were quick to oppose these styles of rap. When Sans Pression came on the scene in 1999 with two openly political pieces, including "514-50 dans mon réseau" (514-50 in My Network), he made a real impact, thanks in part to support from the tireless Morgan. After this first album, most of Quebec rap would embrace this realist style, tackling themes that were rooted in the street and its excesses.

Born in Buffalo, New York, an American of Congolese origin, Kamenga Mbikay (stage name Sans Pression, or "No Pressure") was also a member of the group Treizième Étage (Thirteenth Floor) and a close collaborator of Yvon Krevé and Joe BG, who chose a much more abrasive, direct, and aggressive attitude. This would inspire other rappers—notably Muzion, whose *Mentalité Moune Morne (Ils n'ont pas compris)* (in Creole and in French, "They Just Don't Get It") from 1999 on ViK Recordings/BMG constantly flirted with social critiques—but few at the time were lucky enough to be as successful. *514-50 dans mon réseau* sold more than thirty thousand copies, a record back then for a rap production in French. It was also produced entirely independently with a linguistic mix of *Joual* (working-class slang in Quebec), Creole, and *Franglais* (a French-English mishmash).

NEW ERA

Thanks to these successes, rappers seemed to gradually gain confidence in their skills and the richness of their origins. In the mid-1990s, some MCs were looking to promote the use of patois expressions and local jargon, tapping into inspirations and references from American and French music as well as European and West Indian. One needs to mention, for instance, the important role that IAM and their albums played in Quebecois artists coming to accept their own cultural origins. With the typical sing-song accent from the South of France, phrasing that sounded different from that of NTM, Assassin, or any other Parisian groups, and with regional slang used and quoted in texts, Akhenaton, Shurik'n, and other rappers from the Marseille crowd, doubtless unknowingly, freed up Quebec artists, as well. These latter artists were just beginning to grasp the idea that it was possible to rap with an accent, that it was no longer necessary to imitate Parisians and New Yorkers.

Interviews with Quebec rappers and hip-hop activists reveal, however, that international rappers' appearances at local venues were more important than their records in forging connections.[3] When asked, almost all mention MC Solaar's 8 October 1992 concert at Montreal's FrancoFolies Festival. Likely more than anyone else, MC Solaar was the catalyst for a new kind of energy; he incited different local talents to meet up and believe in their potential.

QUEBEC–FRANCE: A CONSTANT EXCHANGE

Relationships that sprang up between French and Quebec rappers are easily explained in myriad ways. There were numerous collaborations between artists of the two countries.[4] The role played by certain producers—most notably Cédric Morgan and Vladimir Bazile—established direct links between France and Quebec. Local print media shops placed French media (*Radikal*, *Affiche*, *R.E.R.*) and local fanzines (*24karat*, *Influence*, *la Taupe*, or even *Up Front*) on the same shelves.[5] Key as well was a compilation like *Freestyle Canada*, orchestrated by Cut Killer, the Parisian deejay and producer who brought together a significant showing of the Montreal underground (Complys, Dubmatique, Replik, Traumaturges, Division Blindée, Vice Verset, Royal Hill, Rain Men, Roufou 91, Acropole, Mathematik, Cavaliers Noirs, X-Horde, and RDPIzeurs). Lastly, the oldest French-language hip-hop show in America, *Nuit Blanche* (All-Nighter), took advantage of widespread local enthusiasm to showcase a diverse group of French artists. In an article published in 2000 in the Canadian newspaper *Voir*, for example, journalist Rose-Laure Météllus was insistent that *Nuit Blanche*'s number one concern had long been to spread local rap music. Led by open-minded TV host Dice-B every Monday night at 11:30 p.m., the show's small team transformed the studio into a spontaneous meeting ground where well-versed rappers and promoters decided on the spot how the program would take shape.

Another important means of support was the independent radio station Kachot, which, like many underground FM stations in the 1990s, was intent upon backing the rapidly growing local talent (such as Rico Rich, Ricky D, Duke Eatmon, Ernest B, Panama, and Gilbert Mosambo). Very small scale and with no other goal than to play songs by IAM and other French rappers it liked, Kachot, like Quebec rap itself, become more professional as the years went by. Thus, beginning in 1995, it became the rallying point for an entire scene that was looking for visibility, helped by an organization that could promote it in the best way possible.

Because rap is a musical esthetic in its own right, it makes sense that beyond promotion and broadcasting, connections between France and Quebec were due in large part to a shared view of the hip-hop movement, an obsession with certain themes (easy money, protest, hedonism, nightlife, temptations), the explosive spread of the Internet in the early 2000s, and a similar culture. If there is no doubt that the battle of freestyle was born in the United States, it was by contrast the WordUP! Battles in Quebec that directly influenced the creation of the Rap Contenders in France, occasionally joined by certain MCs from Montreal, like Obia le Chef.

Just as in the United States and France, Quebec rap music can potentially be divided into subcategories, without any real rivalry or conscious decision between stylistic preferences. In the alternative or minimalist rap defended by Frenchie B; protest rap symbolized by the Cavaliers Noirs, Jyhad, or Judge Dread Mathematik; hardcore lyrics by Black Taboo, Sudan, or Ravette; or even those adept in *Franglais* (Alaclair Ensemble, Dead Obies, PAPA) and street rap (Le Voyou), what stands out most is that all of these scenes in Quebec are mutually influential. All appear systematically filled with spontaneous elements; with energy, self-assurance, freshness, and style; with many parts that make each new song unpredictable and desirable; and more appealing each time one listens to them.

OFFBEAT RAPPERS

Shifting easily between two cultures, able to waver between influences or poke fun at the orthodoxy of both great nations of hip-hop (America and France), and soundly refusing to choose between Francophone rap codes and New York hip-hop codes, Quebec rap has been able to remain strong since its beginnings. These traits are also what drove certain rappers to the point of caricature, like Roi Heenok, who always had fun exaggerating gangsta rap codes like those from the United States's West Coast. Born in Haiti, Henoc Beauséjour was the first Quebecois rapper to easily cross borders at the beginning of 2000, aided at that time by the huge growth of the Internet in the West.

To understand his success, it should be emphasized that Roi Heenok is more than just a rapper. He is a genuine character. Extravagant and outrageous, almost to the point of being ridiculous, he fascinates not only rappers (he collaborated notably with artists like Alibi Montana, Sofiane, La Fouine, and Raekwon of the Wu-Tang Clan) but filmmakers.[6] Never before in the history of Quebec rap has a rapper had the nerve to use American gangsta rap lingo to flirt repeatedly with male stereotypes; make references to terrorism; and show video images of guns, white powder, and endless stacks of dollars.

Before the arrival of someone as radical as Roi Heenok, no Quebec rapper in Montreal's musical industry seemed talented enough to export his music in any lasting way to the world's B-boys. But things have changed since then. Thanks to a label like Disques 7ième Ciel, founded in the early 2000s and very influential, Quebec rap had enough of an identity to allow for the birth and exportation of its finest artists: Alaclair Ensemble and its many spinoffs (KNLO, Eman x Vlooper), Brown, FouKi, Obia le Chef, Dramatik, and even Anodajay.

Let's consider for a moment the case of Alaclair Ensemble. Originally from Lower Canada, from Quebec City and Montreal, this six-member collective defines its music as being "post-Rigodon" (i.e., post seventeenth- and eighteenth-century Provençal). Theirs is a traditional music of the future, a savvy mix of rough flows, with influences from the 1990s (one of the group's rappers, Maybe Watson, claims inspiration from De La Soul) and oral traditions from Quebecois culture. Obviously, this did not come together easily. Groups like Alaclair Ensemble or Dead Obies, signaling the rebirth of the Montreal scene of the early 2010s, have been accused of furthering the Anglicization of the Quebec province, whose economic capital is bilingual.[7] Francophone on the east side and Anglophone on the west, Montreal has for decades been at center stage of constant cultural tensions. Rather than considering this bilingualism as a natural creative boon to the region, as a way for artists to increase their wide range of rhymes and musical rhythms, allowing words to become more fluid and precise, Quebec columnists and other polemicists used this scene's success and blending of languages to claim that these were idle undertakings, a form of colonization, and a suicidal infatuation with English.

FRANGLAIS AS A SYMBOL OF FREEDOM

Such accusations, whether appearing in newspaper headlines or not, say nothing about the underlying richness of this language bipolarity. To understand it, it is helpful to consider the cases of Loud and Lary Kidd, two rappers that previously formed Loud Lary Ajust but who now work on their own. An analysis of their words demonstrates how Quebec rappers are able to switch from English to French from one sentence to the next, in an almost utopic quest for the perfect rhyme. Rather than going by standard American rules, especially those set in Atlanta—a center for an entire artistic generation since the early 2010s—and the popularity of Young Thug, Gucci Mane, or Future, Loud and Lary Kidd clearly established new rhyming schemes. They were constantly looking for variations in flow, focused above all on the consonance of the two languages along with the energy this could bring to a musical piece. In fact, Loud and Lary Kidd found the perfect intersection between French and English literary constructs: on the one hand, a taste for complex grammatical structures and, on the other, through the play of assonance and phrasing, which became more flexible, more fluid, and less choppy, a deliberate accentuating of the melody's rhythm.

In one of his articles for *Radio Nova* from November 2014, journalist Jean Morel rightly claimed that, through this approach, Loud and Lary Kidd had not only invented a new language but created new sonorities and rhyming schemes that allowed rap to be reshaped yet again and invented a sound unique to Montreal.

In 2018, many people championed this new sound, this new way of approaching melody and writing. Whether on the Internet or in the media, barely a month went by without the arrival of new faces seducing rap connoisseurs on both sides of the Atlantic. If Spotify's statistics are to be believed, this is how FouKi's debut album *Zay* came to be listened to more in France than in Montreal. The same was true for Rowjay, whose largely egocentric lyrics have something of the high-popular Atlanta-sound productions. Equally true for all of the producers—Kaytranada, QuietMike, Atamone, to name a few—who systematically joined the avant-garde in order to bring an undeniable freshness to Quebec hip-hop, which in turn became more unified than ever. Lary Kid appeared on FouKi's first project; Rowjay introduced the beatmaker Freakey! to his close friend Hamza, a rapper from Brussels, Belgium; the members of Dead Obies created their own studio in the Montreal neighborhood of Hochelaga; Obie le Chef collaborated with the Belgians Caballero & JeanJass; Monk.E featured Ugandan rapper Ruyonga on "Boda Boda Molotow"; and, in addition to his partnership with the singer Cœur de Pirate, Loud invited both Lary Kidd and 20Some of Dead Obies to appear on his first solo album (*Une année record*, A Record Year).

A DIVERSE AND UNIFIED SCENE

Eventually, women also proved their ability to write Quebec rap lyrics. According to journalist Olivier Boisvert-Magnen, however, few of them managed to make it professionally or even earn a place in Quebec billings, but more recently dozens of free-spirited female rappers have joined the Montreal scene. Unfortunately, the public and media have failed to take much notice of them even though some of these artists have been around since the 1990s and 2000s (e.g., J.Kyll, ex-member of Muzion and Sarahmée), but nothing seems to deter the outpouring of women rappers like Naya Ali, Marie-Gold, and Tyleen who, through their many projects, have connected with different musical genres, each time further decreasing the opposition between male and female rappers. Exiled from the foursome Bad Nylon, Marie-Gold claims a rather rare position in the world rap scene: At once writer, singer, and beatmaker, this female artist from Montreal is now entirely independent. This allows her to speak openly about her sexuality, to sample a song by pianist Bill Evans—at a time when electronic music is predominant—to play around with the standards of femininity, while still being recognized as a liberated woman, equal to men and ready to sit at the table with the greatest names in Quebec rap music.

These Quebec rappers and producers have become so trendy that the magazine *Voir* devoted entire weekly columns to the most interesting and timely of them. No longer can we not be charmed by these singers with their carefree style who talk about sex to heal the wounds of bad relationships. Successful in developing an essentially hybrid universe, they systematically target pop music and emotional gimmicks with refrains meant to seduce listeners.[8] Although the songs' content has retained its initial political impact, today's heavy, secretive, and even convoluted lyrics are giving way to an airier style that is based largely upon double meanings, offbeat flows, and powerful punch lines.[9]

In 2018, there are countless international media outlets—mostly French (*Tracks*, *Libération*, *Radio Nova*, or *Les Inrockuptibles*) but also Belgian (*Check*, *Focus Vif*) and American (*Pitchfork*, *Complex*, etc.)—that have become interested in Quebec rap music, which sets this unique Internet rap apart from that produced elsewhere in the world. For a while, the radio program *Plus on est de fous, plus on lit!* (The More Crazy People There Are, the More We Read!) even gave weekly play to a rapper of Obie le Chef's caliber, allowing him to show off his knowledge of words and love of language.

While these artists are not yet topping European and American charts, the quality of their releases makes it clear that Dead Obies, Rowjay, White-B, Alaclair Ensemble, and Loud (who performed numerous times in France in 2018) could change that state of affairs. They prove that it always pays to be constantly active. The new generation of Quebecois rap music is taking over quietly, writing songs that resist French rap standards and doing it with the ease of old masters who have absorbed decades of hip-hop and anticipated the future. They help us understand the social, cultural, and collective motives of a generation that prefers all-nighters to everlasting dreams, slick rhymes to easy words, ego-trips to heavy political lyrics. Obviously, this esthetic might amuse those who cling to the notion of a so-called original spirit, but the imagination found in songs like "Devenir immortel (et puis mourir)" (Become Immortal [and Then Die]) by Loud or "Mode de vie" (Way of Life) by White-B or "Make-up" by FouKi is perfectly embodied by this new group of rappers whose flow is created by easygoing lyrics inspired more by pop culture and their own regional character than by movies or skateboards.

In conclusion, it is clear that Quebec rappers—from the earliest hip-hop movements to later generations—have proudly and convincingly laid claim to *Joual*, the Quebecois French slang that makes these artists unique, allowing them to assert themselves as icons of Quebec musical expression and definitively establishing Quebec rap as part of the international music scene.

REFERENCES

Boisvert-Magnen, Olivier. "Il y a 20 ans: Dubmatique—La force de comprendre." *Voir.ca*, 9 June 2017. https://voir.ca/musique/2017/06/09/il-y-a-20-ans-dubmatique-la-force-de-comprendre/
———. "Elles pis leurs homies." *Voir.ca*, 16 August 2017. https://voir.ca/musique/2017/08/16/elles-pis-leurs-homies/
———. "Rap local: Sarahmée, sans restriction." *Voir.ca*, 2 March 2018. https://voir.ca/musique/2018/03/02/rap-local-sarahmee/
———. "Limoilou, terre sacrée du hip-hop québécois." *Voir.ca*, 30 March 2018. https://voir.ca/musique/2018/03/30/limoilou-terre-sacree-du-hip-hop-quebecois/
Bompart, Mario. "Le franglais dans le rap québécois: une créolisation qui fait débat." *Lesinrocks.fr*, 4 April 2015. https://www.lesinrocks.com/2015/04/04/musique/le-franglais-dans-le-rap-quebecois-une-creolisation-qui-fait-debat-11701415/
Genono. "Avertis tes chums: 'Les Boss du Québec' est le livre ultime du rap québécois." *Noisey*, 20 January 2015.
Gomez, François-Xavier. "Le rap exprime beaucoup avec trois mots." *Libération*, 10 December 2014. https://next.liberation.fr/musique/2014/12/10/le-rap-exprime-beaucoup-avec-trois-mots_1160978
Lamort, Kapois. *Les Boss du Québec: R.A.P du Fleur de Lysée (analyse socio-historique et sociologique du hip-hop dans la société québécoise*. Montreal: Production Noire, 2014.
Météllus, Rose-Laure. "Le hip-hop à la radio: Système D." *Voir.ca*, 6 January 2000. https://voir.ca/musique/2000/01/06/le-hip-hop-a-la-radio-systeme-d/
Morel, Jean. "La controverse du rap québécois." *Nova*, 27 November 2014. http://www.nova.fr/novamag/38124/la-controverse-du-rap-quebecois
Papineau, Philippe. "Quand IAM a fait école." *Le Devoir*, 17 June 2017. http://www.lapresse.ca/arts/musique/disques/200908/06/01-890167-cinq-albums-qui-ont-defini-le-rap-quebecois.php
Renaud, Philippe. "Cinq albums qui ont défini le rap québécois." *La Presse.ca*, 6 August 2009. http://www.lapresse.ca/arts/musique/disques/200908/06/01-890167-cinq-albums-qui-ont-defini-le-rap-quebecois.php

DISCOGRAPHY AND FILMOGRAPHY

Benny B. "Vous êtes fous!" *L'Album*. Vie Privée, compact disc. Originally released in 1990.
DawaMafia. *D'où je viens*. Disques RER, streaming. Originally released in 2018.
Dead Obies. *Montréal $ud*. Bonsound Records, compact disc. Originally released in 2013.
Dubmatique. *La force de comprendre*. Tox, compact disc. Originally released in 1997.
Fonky Family. *Si Dieu Veut*. Small, compact disc. Originally released in 1997.
FouKi. *Zay*. Disques 7ième Ciel, compact disc. Originally released in 2018.
Francœur, Lucien. *Jour et Nuit*. Pelo, vinyl. Originally released in 1983.
Gavras, Romain, and Mohamed Mazouz, dirs. *Les Mathématiques du Roi Heenok*. Kourtrajmé. Originally released in 2008.
Lavoie, Daniel. "Le Pape du rap." Trafic, vinyl. Originally released in 1990.
Le Boyfriend. *Rapper chic (Je rap en français)*. Station 12 Records, compact disc. Originally released in 1991.

Les Inconnus. "Auteuil, Neuilly, Passy." *Bouleversifiant*. Lederman, compact disc. Originally released in 1991.

Loud. *Une année record*. Joy Ride Records, compact disc. Originally released in 2017.

MC Solaar. "Bouge de là." Polydor, vinyl. Originally released in 1990.

MRF. "MRF est arrivé." Blat Productions, vinyl. Originally released in 1990.

Muzion. *Mentalité Moune Morne (Ils n'ont pas compris)*. ViK Recordings/BMG, compact disc. Originally released in 1999.

Obia le Chef. *Souflette*. Disques 7ième Ciel, compact disc. Originally released in 2018.

Rock et Belles Oreilles. "Ça rend rap." Kébec-disc, vinyl. Originally released in 1985.

Sans Pression. *514-50 dans mon réseau*. Musicor, compact disc. Originally released in 1999.

———. *La Tendance se maintient*. Thirteen Deep Recordz, compact disc. Originally released in 2008.

White-B. *Cerbère*. MTLSIDE, compact disc. Originally released in 2017.

Zoxea. *Dans la lumière*. KDBZik, compact disc. Originally released in 2004.

Chapter Fourteen

Alaclair Ensemble's "Postrigodon"

An Inclusive Rewriting of "Lower Canada's"
History Applied to Hip-Hop

Ariane Gruet-Pelchat,
Translated by Matthew Kemp

The province of Quebec is a complex location for hip-hop. The rap music created by newcomers frequently deals with the poverty, racism, and exclusion that they experience in their attempt to integrate into Quebec society. By contrast, Francophone whites represent the more affluent majority, but they have still struggled with an identity crisis due to their low demographic weight in a predominantly Anglophone Canada. Noting a schism in Quebec's hip-hop milieu stemming from different realities between visible minorities and the white population, Roger Chamberland wrote in 2002, "It is very difficult, even impossible, for White French groups to attain some legitimacy if they do not display some ethnic hybridization" (Chamberland 2002, 125). Yet, predominantly white and Francophone artists are now achieving popular success and gaining legitimacy in the Quebec hip-hop scene without shying away from their middle-class origins and preoccupations. Moreover, this difference is exemplified, and indeed celebrated, by their use of what is for some an unsettling multilingualism, deconstructing a long-lived linguistic protectionism.

This chapter examines the particular case of the group Alaclair Ensemble, which has been widely credited with the revival of the Quebec rap scene with its first album, *4,99*, released in 2010. Mainly composed of middle-class, majority ethnic white Francophone members (the only member of an obvious mixed-race heritage has a distinctly Quebec accent), the group projects a troubadour image and uses completely over-the-top and often almost childish language, which breaks from practically all dimensions of authenticity associated with hip-hop and ethnicity. However, in conceiving Alaclair Ensemble's performance as a musical uchronia, we observe a group that renders obsolete the monosemic visions of both hip-hop and Quebec, which in turn calls into question the very notion of authenticity within the two contexts.

HIP-HOP, IDENTITY, AUTHENTICITY, AND *AUTHENTICATION*

In a post-structuralist context, identity is not conceptualized as something that exists in itself but more often as a discursive construction (Entwisle 1999, 22–25). For linguists Mary Bucholtz and Kira Hall, there is an "analytic value of approaching identity as a relational and sociocultural phenomenon that emerges and circulates in local discourse contexts of interaction rather than as a stable structure located primarily in the individual psyche or in fixed social categories" (2010, 18). They propose a theoretical framework from which three elements are useful in understanding the discursive formation of Alaclair Ensemble's identity:

> 1) identity is built through our relationships with others (the *relationality* principle), notably through strategies of *adequation* and *distinction* (Bucholtz and Hall 2010, 599);
> 2) it is indexed by language, for example, through the allocation of labels (the *indexicality* principle);
> 3) it depends on perceptions of others, on broader ideological processes, and on the interactional negotiations at stake (the *partialness* principle) (Bucholtz and Hall 2010).

Similarly, authenticity is an identity construct that is validated in a particular and discursively claimed context (Entwisle 1999, 29; Fraley 2009, 43); Bucholtz and Hall thus prefer to speak about the process of *authentication* (2010, 24). Authenticity, which is very important for the hip-hop scene, is a "multivalent notion" (Terkourafi 2010, 12) that can be interpreted in different ways. Must rappers describe their own reality or return to a fictional "street," one that is larger than life, as the imaginary world of hip-hop demands? For Mickey Hess, "Hip hop fans expect artists to lyrically express an authentic hip hop identity by revealing personal truths representing a legitimate geographical background linked to lived experiences that reach back to cultural origins of predominantly Black urban neighborhoods" (quoted by Fraley 2009, 43). Cecelia Cutler adds to these elements that of skills and notes seven dimensions that are discursively used by rappers to authenticate themselves in the hip-hop movement: social/psychological, political/economic, racial, gender-sexual, social/locational, cultural, and talent/skills (Cutler 2010, 302). Lastly, for Marina Terkourafi, authenticity is claimed on two levels: in the local context and in connection with the global hip-hop movement (2010, 7–8).

In general, authenticity requires a harmony between a person's experiences and their discourse, which automatically disqualifies most whites who have grown up in a privileged environment. As a result, a common reaction is the exaggeration by these rappers of other aspects of hip-hop authenticity, with the aim of creating such a harmony or *adequation* (Bucholtz and Hall 2010) with the experiences of the black community (Fraley 2009; Cutler 2010; Lee 2008). However, you will see that Alaclair Ensemble creates a fantasy universe in which these traditional dimensions of hip-hop authenticity lose importance in favor of the Quebecois identity question, which is also strongly shaken up.

LANGUAGE AND IDENTITY IN QUEBEC

We need to look in more detail at what makes the province of Quebec a distinct society within Canada. Originally a French colony, the territory of what was New France was ceded to the English in 1760. In 1791, troubled by the demographic weight of Francophones, the British Crown proceeded to carry out an ethnic redistricting: Lower Canada, whose borders corresponded roughly to those of today's Quebec, was French-speaking/Francophone, while Upper Canada was occupied by the recently established English Loyalists, who were given the majority of the power. After a rebellion by Francophone patriots, the Union Act made Canada a united province with the stated goal of assimilating these Francophone groups.

French Canadians were largely dominated by Anglophones until the 1960s, when they embarked on a "quiet revolution" that led to important reforms, including the separation of the state and the Catholic Church and the promotion of the French language, whose continued existence was under threat. In this context, the large waves of migration of the 1970s became an important issue for Francophones. In this context, the large waves of migration of the 1970s were an important issue for Francophones, and one of the goals of the nationalist movement leading the province was to change the ethnic conception of the Franco-Canadian identity into a Quebec identity that included all its inhabitants. The adoption of Bill 101 in 1977, which required newcomers to undertake their schooling in French, made it possible to integrate them into a society that claimed to be multicultural. As hip-hop developed with the post–101 law generations, "the diverse background of the 'new Francophones' enabled the extensive use of English and other languages—that is, Haitian Creole, Jamaican Creole, Spanish, Arabic—to be added into the mix, in Hip-Hop shows and recording" (Sarkar, Low, and Winer 2006,

354). The multilingualism of Quebec hip-hop therefore became a prominent feature of this process.

The Mela Sarkar–led research team at McGill University, which conducted several studies on the links between identity and language in Quebec hip-hop (Low and Sarkar 2012; 2014; Low, Sarkar, and Winer 2009; Sarkar 2008; Sarkar and Allen 2007), conceptualized this multilingualism in several ways. The concepts of *name-proclaiming*, *translanguaging*, *multilingual speaking*, and *third space* were particularly emphasized (Low and Sarkar 2014). Regardless of the concept used, their conclusions were always the same: the ways in which young people navigate between languages is representative of a fluid and multiple conception of identity that can combine, for example, an immigrant heritage and a Quebec experience. Nevertheless, this part of immigrant identity is rejected by the traditional narrative of Quebec identity, which, marked by "200 years of defensive withdrawal and linguistic survival," remains imbued with an ethnic and linguistic ideal (Lesacher 2015, 60, 66–75).[1] In addition, in the 2010s, the type of hip-hop that gained visibility in the media was personified by rappers who could all be associated with the majority group. Due to this visibility, multilingualism created tensions among numerous generalist commentators (Leclerc 2016; Lesacher 2015, 65–66). Thus, several groups, such as Dead Obies, Radio Radio, Alaclair Ensemble, and Loud Lary Ajust, who attracted a great deal of criticism due to their use of English, spoke out for recognition from their compatriots as Quebecois in their own right. In an open letter, a member of Dead Obies wrote,

> My bastardization shocks you? So be it. Your puritanism disgusts me. Some members of Dead Obies grew up with a Francophone mother and an Anglophone father, or vice versa. So, ask them what their vision of Quebec identity is. Because yes, despite the fact that they had an experience diametrically opposed to yours or even mine, they are Quebecois, just as much as you and I are. Should we exclude their Quebec-ness because it does not correspond to ours? (Mccan 2014)[2]

Faced with an ever-present protectionist reflex, the multilingualism of rappers is therefore "a call to social consciousness and a challenge to the 'received wisdom' of the 'histories' and sociopolitical structures in which the artists were embedded" (Low and Sarkar 2014, 121). In other words, it shows that not only do rappers not recognize themselves in the projected image of Quebec identity, but also the methods through which history is taught deeply disturb them, and this is also true among majority ethnic Francophone whites:

> [W]e see in these works of popular culture that "the history of Quebec [is] being transformed from a single narrative thread, the heroic survival of a

handful of French settlers, into a fabric woven from multiple migrations" (Green 2004, 17). . . . Loco Locass, Samian, and Webster use the didactic function of their art to appeal to a young audience with the hope of influencing a new generation of Quebecers to embrace the values of true knowledge, understanding, recognition and accommodation. (Ransom 2013, 26)

It is in this context that the members of the group Alaclair Ensemble, who are linked to the majority culture through their skin color, their accent, and their use of French as a main language, offer a rereading of Quebec history that integrates immigrants and defends an inclusive vision of "Quebec-icity." As Ransom, Low, Sarkar, Allen, and Lesacher concluded, this rewriting process operates through collective memory, but in this case the group uses a new method, that of uchronia.

UCHRONIA

The term *uchronia*, modeled on the word *utopia*, first appeared in 1876 in the title of the book *Uchronia (Utopia in History)* by Charles Renouvier (reprinted in 1988). If, etymologically speaking, utopia (*u-tópos*) is a non-place, uchronia is simply defined as a non-time (*u-chronos*), or a time that does not exist. Thus, the uchronia of Renouvier is the imaginary narrative of European history as it might have developed, from an apocryphal letter from Cassius to Marcus Aurelius. This missive causes a domino effect that leads to the banishment of Christians in the West and leads to considerable progress in the fields of arts and technology in Europe.

Often translated as *alternate history*, or *alternative history*, this genre has appealed to many literary people. Sometimes considered as a subgenre of science fiction, uchronia can also be dyschronia. Not only has it been used in cinema, comics and video games, it has also been used in advertising, architecture, philately, and numismatics, as well (Henriet 2009, 209–14). Finally, uchronia serves as a scientific research tool in such areas as economics (whose uchronic branch is called cliometrics) and history, in that it "allows the historian to perform mental experiments since laboratory experimentation is impossible" (Guiot 1981).[3]

For Picholle, who uses uchronia to test the importance of the cultural parameter in the history of quantum ideas,

One of the most common methodological errors in the history of scientific ideas is to adopt a continuist and finalist approach when using primary sources. . . . Playing with the possibility of alternative trajectories, to identify questions that no longer arise, or have never reached the stage of maturity for explicit formulation, is above all for the historian to increase his own sensitivity to these murmurs, to ideas not yet indexed. . . . A uchronia is above all a machine for asking unanswered questions. (Picholle 2016, 19)[4]

These exercises of imagination remind us that history is not a reality but a narrative that can diverge according to who tells it (Gobled and Campeis 2015; Henriet 2009, 34–38). In any case, it is not revisionist or negationist: While having fun modifying the course of the history, the authors do not try to contest that which is taught. It is worth mentioning that issues related to the sovereignty and survival of French occupy an important place in literary uchronias in Quebec, enough for Gobled and Campeis, Ransom, and Henriet to devote specific sections to them (Gobled and Campeis 2015, 62–63; Henriet 2004, 251–54; Henriet 2009, 128–30, 164–65; and Ransom 2001; 2006; 2012).

MUSIC AND UCHRONIA

In music, uchronia is easily spotted in song lyrics and staged video clips (Gobled and Campeis 2015, 361; Henriet 2004, 299–300; Henriet 2009, 211–12). Some literary uchronias also involve well-known composers. Mozart, for example, has received the uchronic treatment, reimagined variously as a woman, an investigator, or a creator of rock and roll (Henriet 2009, 132). The Belgian Thierry Van Roy pushed the idea further by creating a uchronic musical project, which he called "music-fiction," whose goal is

> re-writing history and, in doing so, creating a music which could have existed if history had decided it. . . . Unlike "world music" in its geographical and multicultural sense, "Music-Fiction" uses the vertical notion of time and history; the music of "The Black Slavics" was born from the imaginary meeting of the African and Slavonic cultures but in Russia in the 17th century. (Van Roy, n.d.)

By building a complete uchronic universe, the Alaclair Ensemble project is more like the one created by the German group Kraftwerk. Like them, the Quebecois group is reflecting on its identity by reinventing the historical fabric of its country. Moreover, if uchronia exists only in the reader's reception of it (Gobled and Campeis 2015, 18), fans of Alaclair Ensemble give us the best demonstration by participating willingly in it.

ALACLAIR ENSEMBLE AS UCHRONIC PERFORMANCE

The construction of a uchronia depends on a *founding event*, a real historical moment, one that is easily recognizable, credible, and consensual but one for which one imagines a different outcome. Often, these founding events involve the presence of a real person or a providential man. For example, Hitler, Napoleon, and Einstein have all had their share of uchronic stories written about them. The date of this founding event is known as the *point of divergence*.

In the uchronia proposed by Alaclair Ensemble, the point of divergence brings us back to 28 February 1838, when Robert Nelson pronounced the Declaration of Independence of Lower Canada. Although not well known elsewhere in the world, this event is of great interest to people from Quebec: "Because of the province's unique history of double colonization and the ambivalent position of its historical majority French-speakers as both colonizer and colonized, envisioning a better state of affairs and warning about how bad affairs could get if not changed has played a central role in the Quebec imaginary since the late-nineteenth and early-twentieth centuries" (Ransom 2006, 57). In fact, according to Patrice Houle's analysis, "Quebec uchronia is always political" (Houle 2010, 28).[5]

Let us begin by putting this into context. After a failed rebellion in 1837, a group of French-Canadian *Patriotes* exiled to the United States attempted a new invasion of Lower Canada. On 28 February, Robert Nelson was proclaimed president of the future republic by his comrades, with whom he distributed copies of the declaration of independence of Lower Canada. Official history tells us that British troops quickly pushed back the Patriots and that Lower Canada was forcibly joined to Upper Canada in 1840 by the Union Act, with the stated aim of assimilating the Francophone population, for whom some rights were revoked.

In the uchronia that concerns us here, the rebellion was a success, and the declaration was adopted, making Lower Canada a free republic. Since the program proposed by the Patriots led to real political change, including the separation of church and state, equal rights for Native Americans, access to education, the abolition of the death penalty, freedom of the press, and the equal use of the French and English languages, the adoption of the declaration could have led to a more inclusive society well before the Quiet Revolution.

Alaclair Ensemble's uchronia is visible in many aspects of their performance. In the scenography, one can recognize numerous Canadian symbols that have been distorted in such a way as to suggest that they had evolved in Lower Canada. Speeches by Robert Nelson and a Lower-Canadian national anthem punctuate their shows and records. Their website features music, a capital, a flag and national languages, the names of a president and a minister of culture, and a full reproduction of the 1838 Declaration of Independence of Lower Canada.

ARE ALACLAIR ENSEMBLE NATIONALISTS?

At first glance, the hijacking of Canadian images may seem sardonic. The new lyrics of the national anthem strip Canada of its traditionally narrated history, and the flag depicts a maple leaf with the stem angled upward toward the sky, which goes against the rules stipulating how the Canadian national flag must be deployed: "If hung horizontally, the upper part of the leaf (the points of the leaf) should be up and the stem down" (Government of Canada 2018). In addition, every Alaclair Ensemble record refers to Canadian politics in a conspicuous way, whether in the album sleeves, where former prime minister Steven Harper is depicted wearing a Superman costume and as the Queen of England, or by titles like *Les maigres blancs d'Amérique du Noir* (The Skinny Whites of Black America) and *Les frères cueilleurs* (The Gatherer Brothers), both of which refer to Canadian culture and history.

Then again, one must never take Alaclair Ensemble at face value. *Les maigres blancs d'Amérique du Noir*, which refers to the book *Nègres blancs d'Amérique* (White Negroes of America, 1968), written in prison by the separatist Pierre Vallières, is more like a tribute to the roots of hip-hop than a nationalist manifesto. In fact, in ridiculing the comparison that Vallières made between Quebecois and slaves, Alaclair seems to reverse the power relationships: North America becomes a black continent, and rappers as *maigres blancs* (skinny whites) are represented as a minority.

In short, by displaying so many national symbols, Alaclair Ensemble is not seeking to offend either Quebec or Canada but to shake up stereotypes and represent itself in a free and inclusive country: "Robert Nelson wanted Lower Canada to have its own identity, an identity that would not be based on a language or ethnicity, but rather on a series of common values and realities," said the rapper Ogden in an interview with the newspaper *La Presse* (Charette 2012).[6] A Facebook post from 12 November 2012 could not be clearer: "We want to remind everyone that Lower-Canada and its flag represent the union between FRANCOPHONES AND ANGLOPHONES who oppose monarchy and imperialism TOGETHER, and who share common civil and republican values. The nationalist ethnolinguistic identity has no place whatsoever in our discourse" (Alaclair Ensemble 2012).

In this sense, one could establish a link between this uchronia and the *third space* evoked by Sarkar and Allen: "[Homi K.] Bhabha (1990) describes this 'third space' as a positioning that 'displaces the histories that constitute it, and sets up new structures of authority, new political initiatives, which are inadequately understood through received wisdom' (p. 211)" (Sarkar and Allen 2007, 121). By evoking an imaginary country, Alaclair proposes an environment where Quebecois, indigenous people, and immigrants—whether they are French-speaking, English-speaking, or sign—are on an equal footing. "Without representing any cause, it was a given that we would seek to stir up some of the mainstream history, as it had been taught to us, in our music" confirms KenLo (Horth Gagné 2016).[7]

Alaclair Ensemble thus acknowledge and use Quebec's cultural history but want to mix it up. This also goes for the way they present themselves: Alaclair Ensemble does not claim to rap but to "post-rigodon." In the page devoted to the genre ("postrigodon," n.d.), the group gives five definitions that link traditional Quebec music (rigodon) and producer J Dilla's hip-hop. In other words, for Alaclair Ensemble, post-rigodon is a way of expressing an attachment to Quebec's oral tradition as well as to contemporary American music. The song "VARIETTE" offers a good example of this musical mix by combining a rigodon with an African rhythm (Genest 2014). It is also an "indexicality" of identity strategy (Bucholtz and Hall 2010): In an interview with the magazine *Paroles & Musique*, the group admits to having adopted this label in order to dissociate itself from the traditional Quebec hip-hop scene (Martel 2013). Several other contemporary groups have done the same: Dead Obies speak of "post-rap," and Loud Lary Ajust, of "hipster rap."

The allusion to rigodon is therefore an invitation to all: "A rigodon is a tune that everyone knows and everyone can sing, even if they sing badly" (Maybe Watson 2011).[8] This invitation is repeated in their innumerable references to Quebec's popular culture, which appeals to collective memory: "We are affirming the strength of our cultural difference through the poignancy of many of our references," says Ogden who, while having been born in Quebec, is the child of two Bosniac parents (Papineau 2013).[9]

THE NOD TO THE READER

If uchronias are normally meticulously studied so that the imagined sequences are believable down to their smallest details, Alaclair Ensemble's uchronia is not encumbered with historical plausibility and contains several anachronisms. Gobled and Campeis would describe it as a wide, literary, or romantic uchronia; a uchronia that "opens the field of possibilities to the maximum, even if the described universe becomes totally wacky or historically impossible" (2015, 43).[10] In any case, one could cancel out these anachronisms by imagining that the "Declaration of Independence of Lower Canada" was implemented and that the vast majority of political or cultural events occurred in the same way as in our universe. Thus, Steven Harper could have been born in 1959 even if Lower Canada had become a free republic, and the geographical and political proximity of Upper Canada could have justified a mention by Alaclair. Only Robert Nelson, a providential character, is really disconnected from temporality because, although born in 1793, he still goes onstage with the other members of the group, personified by Ogden.

By allowing anachronisms, Alaclair Ensemble can, at its leisure, insert innumerable nods to the reader, which is one of the favorite stylistic methods of uchronists:

> Nods to the reader are often obvious, especially when they involve famous people . . . ; however, this complicity between author and reader can go even further, especially in more sophisticated uchronias where the author addresses a smaller public that possesses, as he does, a deeper understanding of a certain field, and for whom the author includes an increasing number of hidden references. (Henriet 2009, 45)[11]

This is a game that greatly pleases Alaclair Ensemble, who take advantage of it to demonstrate their knowledge of hip-hop and thus legitimize themselves at a local and international level through a strategy of *adequation*. The most obvious "nods" are probably in the form of musical quotes; for example, "The Next Episode" by Dr. Dre in "Les infameux" (The Infamous) and "La Vi Ti-Neg" (Hard Life for the Young) of the Quebec group Muzion in "N'toun de Ipop Sué Lev" (A 'iphop Tune on M'Lips). More subtly, many lyrics parody parts of well-known rap songs. In "Les infameux," the rappers verbally respond to Snoop Dogg, the Pharcyde, Mobb Deep, and Dr. Dre, for example, by refusing their invitation to smoke marijuana. Moreover, Alaclair does not stop with rap. In addition to Khia, "Mon Cou" (My Neck) alludes to Black-Eyed Peas and Madonna, but international glamour references are replaced by popular Quebec references.

Other nods are hidden in the album sleeves—*Les frères cueilleurs* contains at least ten—and in the transfictional use of characters or elements of fiction, such as a fictional apocalypse in 2013 that is hidden in promotion discourses, lyrics, sleeve design, and number of tracks. Uchronia is about a time that does not exist, a space where the author can invent a dream world, and Alaclair Ensemble like to play with it (e.g., the group's preoccupation with the year 2013). Not even the Roman calendar is exempt: The group promoted the release of a record (Alaclair Ensemble 2013) for an invented date, April 34 (*sic*), then hid it in a kind of *deep-web* ("Deep Web" n.d.). To find the next record (Alaclair Ensemble 2014), the listener had to participate in a virtual treasure hunt at an IKEA store. Much like a piece of furniture but also intended as an invitation for people to remix it, the record had to be assembled, with the instrumental parts on one side and unaccompanied vocals on the other.

Conlang

At first sight, Alaclair Ensemble's conlang is quite hard to understand and could be perceived as an impassable form of coding. However, it can be more effectively understood as a conlang that is about "celebrating an attitude towards language which is also an attitude toward community and diversity," as Low, Sarkar, and Winer said of the multilingual practices of Montreal's hip-hop scene (2009, 77). The group gives all the information necessary for learning the dialect on its website but does so in a playful way by using very elusive definitions. Everybody can, therefore, understand that *pichasson* designates "a little boy from São Paulo with a mushroom cut" and that *brizasser les fizzoules* means "amincir le peup'" (to slim the peop' down), but this last example is still not very comprehensible.[12] One has to know that Alaclair Ensemble commonly take expressions that have been legitimated in the hip-hop scene and replace them by their opposite. So *mince* (thin) would in fact be translated as "big," which means something brilliant. Therefore, "amincir le peup" is listed as signifying "donner un spectacle" (put on a show), in the sense that a show would be a space where everybody can do something brilliant together ("Glossaire" n.d.). In addition to the glossary, many of the concepts used by Alaclair are developed in the section "Alaclair High," a kind of virtual college "dedicated to the perpetuation of post-rigodon" (Alaclair Ensemble 2016).[13] Alaclair makes sure that its conlang is accessible, which the group also does by subtitling its video "Fouette" for the benefit of French people who would not understand the Quebec dialect.

Language is an inherent part of utopia. As Marina Yaguello reminds us, utopia in literature includes "u-chronia, i.e. time that does not exist, [and] within this duality is inserted *u-glossie*, i.e. language that does not exist" (Yaguello 1984, 24).[14] Highly varied reasons, from scientific experimentation to the search for a universal language, justify the invention of a language, but a language created for purely artistic purposes, like Klingon, is known as conlang. Conlangs are rarely inserted in isolation; a culture, a grammar, a sound, and an aesthetic quality usually complete the picture.

In the same way, it is in order to create an alternative world in which words are uninhibited and stripped of their strict codes that Alaclair Ensemble invents this language. Let us remember that words have a concrete influence on our perception and our understanding of things (Cooper and Spolsky 1991). Thus, the deliberately amusing and childish sounds of their invented language invite us to take a more innocent look at things and create a *distinction* that sets them off from the street culture that is legitimized in hip-hop. The group does not hesitate to twist French words and to exaggerate the sounds of the Quebec *Joual*, thus offering a type of resistance to traditional French. For example, to invite users to download an album for free, they write, "Pour télélourder GRATISSEMENT cette soucoupe volante" (to download for FRII this flying saucer; Alaclair Ensemble 2013).[15] The postrigodon manifesto even refers to Roman Jakobson's linguistic notion (pragmatic axis > syntagmatic axis) to underline that Alaclair Ensemble's conlang is, above all, poetic.

Authentication

As we have seen, Alaclair Ensemble does not claim to come from a particularly difficult socioeconomic environment. In fact, an attempt to *authenticate* Alaclair Ensemble according to Cutler's seven dimensions would end up being a resounding failure (2010, 302). In addition to representing the majority white and Francophone population of Quebec (and, thus, the racial and political/economic dimensions), and addressing a general public rather than purists (the cultural dimension) they cultivate a gentleman-like image (the gender-sexual dimension). Maybe Watson goes so far as to proclaim himself "chef des gentils" (leader of the nice guys; Maybe Watson 2011), and his other pseudonym, "Produit Laitier" (Dairy Product), does not seem to have been chosen for the purpose of commanding respect either, in much the same way as the group's name cannot fail to evoke the nursery rhyme "À la claire fontaine" (At the Clear Fountain). Clearly, the rappers are not concerned about not having had the experiences or blood ties that could create an *adequation* (connection) with the black community nor whether this legitimizes their authenticity (the *partialness* principle). Instead, they prefer to follow the adage "Keep it real" in the personal sense.

The group's claim to authenticity thus seems to lie at the level of the talent/skills and social/locational dimensions, as outlined by Cutler. Moreover, by drawing on these two dimensions, Alaclair Ensemble validates its authenticity both locally and internationally (Terkourafi 2010, 7). With all group members having been on the scene for at least ten years, depicting Quebec reality and not hesitating to show their knowledge of the world of hip-hop and its codes, they have gained the status of elders, which gives them a certain legitimacy. This is confirmed when one recalls that, beyond their official releases, Alaclair Ensemble also produces, in pure hip-hop tradition, an innumerable quantity of mixtapes. Moreover, how could the hip-hop or linguistics purists possibly feel intimidated by a group that presents itself as "a Lower Canadian postrigodon troupe zigzagging between Quoibec and Mourial. Made up of graduates of Alaclair High, its goal is to slim the peop' down. Is Alaclair Ensemble for children?" (Alaclair Ensemble, n.d.).[16]

CONCLUSION: THE POWER OF UCHRONIA

Humor is not an innocent strategy. For the philosopher Simon Critchley, "it undermines our ordinary assumptions about the empirical world. It could be seen as arising from the gap between the actual state of things and the way this state is represented through the joke, between what is expected and what actually happens" (Critchley 2004, 9).[17] Humor, therefore, necessarily fulfills two functions: to challenge our norms and habits and to propose a positive change, an "amélioration du vivre ensemble" (improvement in how we live together; Cotte 2012, 11).

This brings us back to uchronia, which, by making us see a different world, reminds us that our perception of the Other sometimes rests on very little. In relation to the use of Robert Nelson's character and the universe of Lower Canada, Ogden affirms that

> there is always a double message: that of the presence of English in our culture, and that of the colonized people. I am very interested in delving into the gap that exists between English and French in Quebec. . . . I think that there is more truth to find in that than to camp on one side or the other. . . . The power that I have is to continue to tell the world that there are many things that make up Quebec society, such as English, history. (Lalande 2013)[18]

Serge Perraud states that "identity is linked to the historical consciousness of the individual, reinventing one's origins means creating oneself" (1995, 34).[19] In his thesis on Quebec science fiction, Patrice Houle explains the legacy of this idea: "He (the uchronian) inhabits an ideal epistemological position for his social reflection. . . . The author thus has immense power over the imaginary and symbolic representation of his people" (Houle 2010, 19).[20] This is how Alaclair Ensemble can, through their uchronic performance, reinvent themselves in a world where immigrants, native people, and French descendants—whether they speak French, English, Cree, or sign language—are included in Quebec's DNA. Their portrait of a multiple Québécois identity, painted outside the traditional canvas of hip-hop and framed by fiction, may legitimately invite us to leave aside obsessions with purity and authenticity.

REFERENCES

Alaclair Ensemble. "We Want to Remind Everyone That Lower-Canada and Its Flag Represent the Union between FRANCOPHONES AND ANGLOPHONES." *Facebook*, 12 November 2012. https://mbasic.facebook.com/alaclairensemble/photos/a.143529515683399.15964 .129504923752525/444081168961564/

———. "Alaclair Ensemble—1ère partie Les Gogetters." La Petite Église. N.d. http:// www.lapetiteeglise.com/profil/423-alaclairensemble.html

———. "Alaclair High." n.d. 24 May 2018. http://alaclair.com/alaclair-high/

Bucholtz, Mary, and Kira Hall. "Identity and Interaction: A Sociocultural Linguistic Approach." *Discourse Studies* 7, nos. 4–5 (2005): 585–614. http://doi.org/10.1177/1461445605054407

———. "Locating Identity in Language." In *Language and Identities*, edited by Carmen Llamas and Dominic Watt, 18–28. Edinburgh: Edinburgh University Press, 2010.

Chamberland, Roger. "The Cultural Paradox of Rap Made in Quebec." In *Black, Blanc, Beur: Rap Music and Hip-Hop Culture in the Francophone World*, edited by Alain-Philippe Durand, 124–37. Lanham, MD: Scarecrow Press, 2002.

Charette, Didier. "Portrait d'un artiste engagé: Ogden, le refus de l'étiquette." *Quartier L!bre*, 7 February 2012. http://quartierlibre.ca/portrait-dun-artiste-engage-ogden-le-refus-de-letiquette/

Cooper, Robert L., and Bernard Spolsky. "Introduction." In *The Influence of Language on Culture and Thought: Essays in Honor of Joshua A. Fishman's Sixty-Fifth Birthday*, edited by Robert L. Cooper and Bernard Spolsky, 1–6. Berlin: Mouton de Gruyter, 1991.

Cotte, Jérôme. "L'humour et le rire comme outils politiques d'émancipation?" M.A. thesis, Université du Québec à Montréal, 2012.

Critchley, Simon. *De l'humour*. Translated by Nicolas Pinet. Paris: Kimé, 2004.

Cutler, Cecelia. " 'She's so Hood': Ghetto Authenticity on the White Rapper Show." In *Languages of Global Hip-Hop*, edited by Marina Terkourafi, 300–328. New York: Continuum, 2010.

"Deep Web." Alaclair Ensemble. N.d. http://alaclair.com/deep-web/

Duncan, Andy. "Alternate History." In *The Cambridge Companion to Science Fiction*, edited by Edward James and Farah Mendlesohn, 209–18. Cambridge: Cambridge University Press, 2003.

Entwisle, Stephen. "La Chanson Goes Hip-Hop: Local Identity, Globalization, and Contemporary Music in Quebec Nationalism." M.A. thesis, University of Calgary, 1999.

Fraley, Todd. "I Got a Natural Skill . . . : Hip-Hop, Authenticity, and Whiteness." *Howard Journal of Communications* 20, no. 1 (2009): 37–54. https://doi.org/10.1080/10646170802664979

Genest, Catherine. "Party Envol et Macadam de la St-Jean/Alaclair Ensemble: Vive le Bas-Canada Libre!" *Voir*, 19 June 2014. https://voir.ca/musique/2014/06/19/party-envol-et-macadam-de-la-st-jean-alaclair-ensemble-vive-le-bas-canada-libre/

"Glossaire." Alaclair Ensemble. N.d. http://alaclair.com/glossaire

Gobled, Karine, and Bertrand Campeis. *Le guide de l'uchronie*. Arles: Éditions ActuSF, 2015.

Government of Canada. "Rules for Flying the National Flag of Canada." 19 September 2018. https://www.canada.ca/en/canadian-heritage/services/flag-canada-etiquette/flying-rules.html

Green, Mary Jean. "Transcultural Identities: Many Ways of Being Québécois." In *Textualizing the Immigrant Experience in Contemporary Quebec*, edited by Susan Ireland and Patrice J. Proulx, 11–22. Westport, CT: Praeger, 2004.

Guiot, Denis. "Faire de l'uchronie." *Mouvance*, no. 5 (1981): 77–86.

Henriet, Éric B. *L'histoire revisitée: Panorama de l'uchronie sous toutes ses formes*. Paris: Encrage, 2004.

———. *L'uchronie*. Paris: Klincksieck, 2009.

Horth Gagné, Mathieu. "Alaclair Ensemble: Postrigodon en évolution." *Métro*, 1 September 2016. http://journalmetro.com/culture/1016960/alaclair-ensemble-post-rigodon-en-evolution/

Houle, Patrice. "Paradigme Québec, la science-fiction québécoise." M.A. thesis, Université du Québec à Montréal, 2010.

Jakobson, Roman. "Closing Statement: Linguistics and Poetics." In *Style in Language*, edited by Thomas A. Sebeok, 350–77. New York: Wiley, 1960.

Lalande, Olivier. "Six questions aux champions hip-hop Alaclair Ensemble. " *Nightlife.ca*, 3 May 2013. http://www.nightlife.ca/2013/05/03/six-questions-aux-champions-hip-hop-alaclair-ensemble

Leclerc, Catherine. "Radio Radio à Montréal: 'La right side of the wrong.'" *Revue de l'Université de Moncton* 47, no. 2 (2016): 95–128.

Lee, Katja. "Reconsidering Rap's 'I': Eminem's Autobiographical Postures and the Construction of Identity Authenticity." *Canadian Review of American Studies* 38, no. 3 (Winter 2008): 351–73.

Lesacher, Claire. "Le rap comme activité(s) sociale(s): Dynamiques discursives et genre à Montréal (approche sociolinguistique)." Ph.D. diss., Université Rennes 2, 2015.

Low, Bronwen, and Mela Sarkar. "Le plurilinguisme dans les cultures populaires, un terrain inexploré? L'étude du langage mixte du rap montréalais en guise d'exemple." *Kinephanos* 3, no. 1 (2012): 20–47.

———. "Translanguaging in the Multilingual Montreal Hip-Hop Community: Everyday Poetics as Counter to the Myths of the Monolingual Classroom." In *Heteroglossia as Practice and Pedagogy*, edited by Adrian Blackledge and Angela Creese, 99–118. Dordrecht: Springer, 2014. https://doi.org/10.1007/978-94-007-7856-6_6

Low, Bronwen, Mela Sarkar, and Lise Winer. "'Ch'us mon propre Bescherelle': Challenges from the Hip-Hop Nation to the Quebec Nation." *Journal of Sociolinguistics* 13, no. 1 (2009): 59–82.

Martel, Stéphane. "Alaclair Ensemble." *Paroles & Musique*, 29 July 2013. https://www.magazinesocan.ca/features/features-music-creators/alaclair-ensemble-gang-guys/

Mccan, Yes. "Dead Obies et le Franglais: la réplique aux offusqués." *Voir*, 23 July 2014. https://voir.ca/jepenseque/2014/07/23/la-replique-aux-offusques/

Papineau, Philippe. "Alaclair, la drôle de bête." *Le Devoir*, 4 May 2013. https://www.ledevoir.com/culture/musique/377348/alcair-la-drole-de-bete

Perraud, Serge. "L'uchronie: pour une histoire différente." *Présence d'esprit*, no. 7 (1995): 34–38.

Picholle, Eric. "Un laser uchronique pour questioner l'histoire des idées quantiques?" *Espaces et temps: Actes des Quatrième Journées Enseignement et Science-fiction de l'ESPE* (2016). https://hal.archives-ouvertes.fr/hal-01427115

Ransom, Amy J. "New Maps of Hell: Postcolonial Utopia and Esther Rochon's Les Chroniques infernales." *Spaces of Utopia: An Electronic Journal* 2nd series, no. 1 (2012): 56–87.

———. "Oppositional Postcolonialism in Québécois Science Fiction." *Science Fiction Studies* 33, no. 2 (2006): 291–312.

———. "'Québec History X': Re-Visioning the Past through Rap." *American Review of Canadian Studies* 43, no. 1 (2013): 12–29.

———. "'Territoires hors du commun.' La souveraineté nationale et l'identité individuelle dans la science-fiction québécoise contemporaine." *Solaris* 138 (2001): 133–60.

Renouvier, Charles. *Uchronie, 1876*. Paris: Fayard, (1857) 1988.

Sarkar, Mela. "'Ousqu'on chill à soir?' Pratiques multilingues comme stratégies identitaires dans la communauté hip-hop montréalaise." *Diversité urbaine*, no. hors-série (2008): 27–44.

Sarkar, Mela, and Dawn Allen. "Hybrid Identities in Quebec Hip-Hop: Language, Territory, and Ethnicity in the Mix." *Journal of Language, Identity, and Education* 6, no. 2 (2007): 117–30.

Sarkar, Mela, Bronwen Low, and Lise Winer. "'Pour connecter avec le Peeps': Québéquicité and the Quebec Hip-Hop Community." In *Identity and Second Language Learning: Culture, Inquiry, and Dialogic Activity in Educational Contexts*, edited by Miguel Mantero, 351–72. Charlotte, NC: Information Age, 2006.

Terkourafi, Marina, ed. *Languages of Global Hip-Hop*. New York: Continuum, 2010.

Vallières, Pierre. *Nègres blancs d'Amérique*. Quebec: Éditions Parti Pris, 1968.

Van Roy, Thierry. "The Black Slavics." N.d. http://users.skynet.be/sky77600/blackslavics/Black%20Slavics%20angl.htm

Yaguello, Marina. *Les fous du langage: Des langues imaginaires et de leurs inventeurs*. Paris: Éditions du Seuil, 1984.**[ED: The entries for the bib on this page (above) are messed up and I am unable to get the tabs correct for them.]**

DISCOGRAPHY

Alaclair Ensemble. *4,99*. Indépendant, compact disc. Originally released in 2010.

———. *Postrigodon*. Indépendant, compact disc. Originally released in 2011.

———. *Les maigres blancs d'Amérique du Noir*. Indépendant, compact disc. Originally released in 2013.

———. *TOUTE EST IMPOSSIBLE*. Indépendant, compact disc. Originally released in 2014.

———. *Alaclair High*. Disques 7ième Ciel, compact disc. Originally released in 2016.

———. *Les frères cueilleurs*. Disques 7ième Ciel, compact disc. Originally released in 2017.

Dr. Dre. *The Next Episode*. Aftermath/Interscope, compact disc. Originally released in 2000.

Khia. *My Neck, My Back (Lick It)*. Artemis, compact disc. Originally released in 2002.

Maybe Watson. *Maybe Watson*. Indépendant, compact disc. Originally released in 2011.

Muzion. *La vi ti nèg*. Vik Recordings, compact disc. Originally released in 1999.

Notes

FOREWORD

1. Afrika Bambaataa of the Zulu Nation introduced "knowledge" as the fifth element of hip-hop, though some argue that it is beat boxing (vocal percussion). See Price (2006) and Chang (2005) for further discussion.
2. In Grandmaster Flash and the Furious 5's "The Message."
3. Hiphop Archive and Research Institute (HARI). http://hiphoparchive.org.
4. Ibid.
5. For example, *blouson*, the French word for "jacket," would be *zomblou*. *Verlan* is used widely in the suburbs of Paris and also incorporates Arabic slang.
6. Paris. MC Solaar: *Ça fait longtemps qu'on n'a pas vu Guru Gangstarr. Ça serait pas cool s'il revenait à Paris?* Friend: *Ouais.* MC Solaar: *On va essayer de l'appeler.*

INTRODUCTION

1. According to the *Encyclopedia Britannica* (2019), hip-hop "refers to a complex culture comprising four elements: deejaying or 'turntabling'; rapping, also known as 'MCing' or 'rhyming'; graffiti painting, also known as 'graf' or 'writing'; and 'B-boying,' which encompasses hip-hop dance, style, and attitude. . . . (A fifth element, 'knowledge of self-consciousness,' is sometimes added to the list of hip-hop elements, particularly by socially conscious hip-hop artists and scholars)."
2. For a discussion of the difference between "post-colonialism" and "postcolonialism," see Puig (2019, pp. 101–10).

1. FORTY YEARS OF FRENCH RAP

1. "Incitent à la haine, à la violence et bafouent les valeurs républicaines de la France."
2. "Incitation à blesser et tuer les fonctionnaires de police et représentants de l'État."
3. "Renforcer le contrôle des provocations à la discrimination, à la haine ou à la violence."

4. I would like to thank Emmanuelle Carinos and Emily Shuman for their feedback. The title of this chapter is a reference to Rocé's album *Identité en crescendo*, released in 2006 and written in collaboration with Raqual le Requin. The full discography of this chapter can be found on my blog: http://surunsonrap.hypotheses.org/3614.

2. HIP-HOP MUSIC AND RAP IN CITIES IN CRISIS

1. Rap is especially present in the working-class suburbs of the north and south of Paris.
2. Since 1999, Billboard distinguishes "Hot R&B/Hip-Hop Songs" and "Hot Rap Songs" in the United States. The rap songs often have explicit lyrics. In France, there is not a strong distinction between these two musical trends, even if hip-hop refers to a musical content (Pirenne 2011, 637–38).
3. In France, the Ministry of Culture's last major survey on French cultural practices was in 2008. Rap and hip-hop were the second-favorite musical trend of French youth, after international variety songs.
4. Marseille's unemployment rate today is 11.8 percent versus 9.2 percent in all of France, according to official statistics (INSEE 2018).
5. See Sheila Crane (2011) and Minayo Nasiali (2016) for histories of urban developments in Marseille in the twentieth century.
6. See Ted Swedenburg (2002).
7. Nearly 50 percent of the people who settled in Marseille from 2001 to 2006 came from regions other than Provence (Gasquet-Cyrus and Trimaille 2017, 88). Marseille had 861,635 inhabitants on January 1, 2018, according to the latest census of INSEE (https://www.insee.fr/fr/statistiques/fichier/2525755/dep13.pdf).
8. Arles in particular, where, after the Guggenheim Foundation of Bilbao, the architect Frank Gehry is now building the headquarters of the Luma Foundation.
9. The municipality decided to restructure the square to reduce the size of the market, prohibit the large free parking that allowed the people of Marseille to go out at night to the restaurants of this spirited neighborhood, and close a lively space that hosted café terraces and music groups. In October 2018, they banned the market, cut the trees, and surrounded the square with an eight-foot concrete wall to protect the construction site. Many protests took place by inhabitants of the neighborhood, shopkeepers, and city residents who were shocked by the local government's violent approach, but they did not succeed in stopping the project.

3. "FEAR OF A BLACK PLANET"

1. The term *banlieue* resists simple translation into English. Its literal meaning is "suburb," but in fact, it is a term much more fraught with controversy and which carries deeply racialized and classed connotations (Stovall 2003; Tissot 2007, 2008).
2. Translated from the French by the author: "la préfecture qui voulait interdire le concert à cause de toute l'ampleur donnée par les medias" Unless otherwise noted, all translations in the chapter are the author's.
3. Translated from the French: "Il y avait des débats en permanence à la radio, à la télé, les rumeurs circulaient comme quoi le concert allait être interdit aux blancs, ce genre de choses. On était dans le délire total. Le *summum* de la connerie, ça a été Guillaume Durand sur la 5. Le mec était en duplex depuis le Zénith en mode 'reporter de guerre' et faisait un compte-rendu toutes les dix minutes au journal télévisé, pour savoir ce qu'il se passait, si un blanc s'était fait tuer, si un pigeon s'était fait écraser par une voiture noire. [Rires] C'était limite ça, franchement. Mais c'était la folie, il y avait des cordons de CRS devant le Zénith et même des types sur les toits de la salle pour pouvoir tout surveiller!"

4. Translated from the French: "Public Enemy en concert au Zénith à Paris. C'est un événement attendu et redouté. . . . Chez Public Enemy, le message est clair et les symboles efficaces."

5. Translated from the French: "C'est pour eux qu'ils sont venus jouer, mais c'est aux journalistes qu'ils se sont d'abord adressés à une heure du concert."

6. Translated from the French: (First anchor, Paul Amar): "On craignait le pire hier soir à Paris, mais le pire ne s'est pas produit." (Second anchor, Élise Lucet): "Non, Paris n'a pas du tout été à feu."

7. Translated from the French: "'Pas un blanc sera accepté dans la salle.' Toute la journée, la folle rumeur avait couru. Il faut dire que Public Enemy a une sale reputation. Aux États-Unis, ce groupe est numéro un du Rap, une musique issue des ghettos et qui scande un cri de révolte contre la misère et le désespoir. Sur scène, Public Enemy multiplie les provocations et prône la défense de la race noire contre les blancs. Ils sont 'racistes, haineux, et anti-sémites,' affirment leurs détracteurs. . . . Hier, le concert avait dégonflé la rumeur: public jeune, beaucoup de noirs, mais il y avait des blancs. Ambience décontracté. Pas le moindre incident."

8. Translated from the French: "Le rap débarque en Europe. Ce mouvement musical noir américain né il y a quelques années dans les quartiers pauvres de New York s'est étendu aux principales villes des États-Unis et maintenant, il arrive chez nous. Le rap s'oppose fermement à l'*establishment* de blancs, et quelques fois, il va très loin dans cette direction. . . . Hier, il s'est produit au Zénith à Paris, et Bernard Gely a pu mesurer son impact."

9. Translated from the French: "Un sens certain de la publicité, et un discours qui dérange aux États-Unis. Fer de lance du rap, Public Enemy touche notre pays plus par la force de sa musique que par celle de ces propos délivrés en américain. Mais globalement, le message passe."

10. Translated from the French: "Ce que réclame Public Enemy, c'est une reconnaisance de l'identité 'Noire' et un monde sans exclusion."

11. Translated from the French: "Public Enemy, c'est un groupe de rap estampillé 'Black Power,' qui réanime la mentalité Black Panther et qui en fait l'historique. . . . Les jeunes à Paris arborent fièrement leur collier 'Afrique.' . . . On se sentait représentés par leur musique qui nous faisait vibrer."

12. From very early on, Afrika Bambaataa encouraged aspiring French artists to rap in their own language and about their own experiences. Many followed his advice, including one of the best-known French rappers, MC Solaar. See Desse and SBG 1993, 49.

13. For more on *verlan*, see Fagyal 2007 and 2010 and Doran 2002.

14. See Bigeault 2005; Bocquet and Pierre-Adolphe 1996, 64–66; and Cachin 2012, 10 and 50.

15. Stomy Bugsy, freestyle rap on Radio Nova (101.5 FM), *Deenastyle* radio show, 1989. For background on the prevalence of skinheads in Paris in the 1980s, see Louis and Prinaz 1990.

16. For more on the Five Percent Nation of Gods and Earths, see Knight 2007; and Miyakawa 2005; Nuruddin 1994; and O'Connor 2006.

17. Translated from the French: "Comme une mode? . . . Afrique ou pas, ce qu'on vit ici, c'est qu'on est vus comme des nègres par des keufs qui nous coursent. Et ça, on ne peut pas l'oublier."

18. Translated from the French: "Parce qu'on voit bien à quel point il faut dans les banlieues . . . renouer avec notre savoir. À l'école, on ne nous a rien appris de l'histoire africaine. Rien. . . . On a commencé à s'énerver quand on s'est aperçus que même en Afrique, ils enseignaient aussi peu notre histoire."

19. Translated from the French: "Tu revendiques l'Amérique/Tes origines viennent d'Afrique/Ta mère t'appelle Mamadou/Tu prends le nom de Andrew."

20. For background on the compilation, see Cachin 2012.

21. Translated from the French: "Paris imiterait-il New-York où les gangs se disputent le macadam et le marché de la drogue à coups de .357 Magnum?"

22. Translated from the French: "le risque existe car ces gamins de plus en plus nombreux vivent sur une étrange planète, quelque part entre Manhattan, Dakar et Argenteuil. Ils jouent les guerriers de Harlem à Cergy-Pontoise, s'inventent des Central Park à Evry."

23. Translated from the French: "Souvent livrés à eux-mêmes au sein de familles disloquées (notamment pour les Guadeloupéens), ces fils métissés de l'Afrique et du Bronx, qui arborent bijoux brillants, casquettes à visières et jeans très amples, se rêvent aussi charmeurs qu'Eddie Murphy et plus forts que Myke [*sic*] Tyson."

24. Translated from the French: "Les halls commencent à ressembler au métro new-yorkais . . . en moyenne une aggression tous les deux jours."

25. Translated from the French: "Les administrations publiques ont en effet mis en œuvre un ensemble de dispositifs à destination du hip-hop, dans la mesure où la majorité de ses pratiquants—des jeunes qui habitant en banlieue, souvent issus de l'immigration (notamment africaine et maghrébine)—ont des caractéristiques sociologiques qui les définissent comme une 'population à problèmes,' et donc comme une cible potentielle pour l'action publique."

26. Translated from the French: "Musique, graffitis, mode, la rage du rap a conquis nos lycées et nos banlieues. Enquête sur ce phénomène venu des trottoirs de New York."

27. Translated from the French: "à l'heure où le fossé Nord–Sud s'approfondit . . . la culture est un moyen de dialogue essentiel."

28. Translated from the French: "provoque des rencontres entre les deux 'camps'; mais aussi entre des pays ou des villes qui ont le même problème, comme la violence urbaine, par exemple. New York, la ville du rap, la ville la plus ouverte du monde qui est aussi celle de tous les ghettos, paraissait à cet égard toute indiquée."

29. Translated from the French: "Notre objectif est double: sensibiliser, créer le dialogue entre différents acteurs (créateurs, responsables de l'action sociale, élus, etc.), puis l'enraciner dans la durée. Un exemple: après ce voyage, il y aura un travail avec des policiers (un cycle de formation de huit mois), avec le FAS, la Délégation interministérielle à la Ville et la Rue-de-Valois. Les institutions ont du mal à travailler transversalement, on est là pour les y aider."

30. For example, Angelo and Jean-Marie Gopée continued building their concert booking organization, and in recent years Angelo has served as managing director of Live Nation France, the French subsidiary of the American live entertainment company; the rapper Rockin' Squat of the group Assassin returned many times to New York to record songs and collaborate with American artists; and Christophe Lacroix went back often, as well, first as simply a hip-hop enthusiast and then as an urban marketing consultant.

4. GHETTO PATRIMONY

1. For general discussions and analysis of the 2005 confrontations, see Bloom 2009; Lapeyronnie 2009; Le Goaziou and Mucchielli 2006; Mbembe 2009, and the essays collected on the SSRC discussion forum on "Riots in France": riotsfrance.ssrc.org. My discussion of the violence and its larger context draws on Paul Silverstein and Chantal Tetreault 2005.

2. In pejorative French slang, cops are often called "chickens." "Sacrifice de poulets" appeared on an album of rap songs solicited to accompany the 1995 release of Mathieu Kassovitz's film *La Haine*, which explicitly treated the subject of police violence in the *cités*. The rappers were forced to pay a heavy fine, and subsequently the group concentrated their efforts on their individual careers and to the direction of a musical production cooperative, Secteur Ä, from their native Sarcelles.

3. "FranSSe" appeared on the 2004 album *Politikment incorrekt*. The case was subsequently thrown out, as the court determined that Deputy Mach had suffered no personal injury since his own children were no longer minors.

4. NTM was accused of "outrage par paroles à l'autorité de l'ordre public" (verbal abuse against public authority) for a 1995 Bastille Day performance of their 1993 hit "Police," in which the police are decried as a "veritable gang" of "écervelés mandatés par la justice" (brainless ones empowered by the law), and one of the characters dreams of hunting down *keufs* (cops) in the subway. The incident occurred during a larger "Liberty Concert" held in the southern town of La Seyne-sur-Mer to protest the Front National's recent mayoral victories in neighboring Toulon and Orange, and during the performance the rappers called on the audience to "nique la police" (fuck the police), apparently indicating the security guards working at the

concert. The group's two members were sentenced to six months in prison (reduced to two months suspended on appeal), plus a 50,000-francs fine and a six-month ban on all professional activity. For further discussion of the *affaire*, see Dély and Renault 1996; Hélénon 1998; Prévos 1998, 2001, 2002; and Silverstein 2002.

5. Then–Interior Minister Nicolas Sarkozy prosecuted Hamé for "délit de diffamation publique envers une administration publique" (public defamation against a public administration) for an April 2002 article that appeared in La Rumeur's self-published fanzine that accompanied the release of their debut album. In the article—a sophisticated, hard-hitting analysis of the state production of "insecurity" in France's *cités*—Hamé maintained that "Les rapports du ministre de l'Intérieur ne feront jamais état de lieu des centaines de nos frères abattus par les forces de la police sans qu'aucun des assassins n'ait été inquiété" (The Ministry of Interior's reports will never mention the hundreds of our brothers killed by the police force without any of the murderers being investigated). After several rounds of prosecutorial appeal, the Cour de Cassation (Court of Appeal) eventually dismissed the case on the grounds that the offending remarks did not refer to a single action or event that could be disproved. For a collection of documents related to the *affaire*, as well as a republication of Hamé's text, see http://sitecon.free.fr/rumeur.htm (last accessed 5 February 2019). For an analysis, see Tshimanga 2009, 258.

6. Interior Minister Dominique de Villepin prosecuted the trio Sniper for having "incité à blesser et tuer les fonctionnaires de police et représentants de l'État" (incited the attacking and killing of police officers and state representatives) following a 28 April 2004 concert performance in Rouen of their 2001 hit "La France," in which the rappers sang that they wanted to see the police hang for their crimes. The case and its appeal were both dismissed, with the judges opining that the lyrics merely expressed "la désolation et le mal de vivre des jeunes de banlieue" (the desolation and hopelessness of the *banlieue* youth; Kessous 2006).

7. Sarkozy's threats followed from a series of complaints against Sniper from far-right militants, police unions, and the Jewish watchdog Ligue internationale contre le Racisme et l'Antisémitisme (LICRA, International League against Racism and Anti-Semitism). The complaints referenced not only the song "La France" (*Du rire aux larmes*; From Laughter to Tears) but also "Jeteur de pierres" (Stone Thrower) on *Gravé dans la roche* (Carved in Stone), a 2003 song about the Israeli-Palestinian conflict in which the Intifada is presented as justified resistance against a "puissance colonisatrice" (colonizing power).

8. "Brise[r] le tabou du racisme anti-Blanc de certains rappeurs."

9. See Désir 1985, and Parti Socialiste 1981.

10. "Manifeste 'contre le nouvel antisémitisme,'" *Le Parisien*, 21 April 2018.

11. Throughout the chapter I use "hardcore" and "gangsta" interchangeably to reference a set of French hip-hop artists identifiable by their musical poetics (in particular their harshness of vocal flow and complex layering of samples used) and thematic content (their focus on racism and violence) that distinguish them from the more laid-back flows and less aggressive lyrics of MC Solaar or TTC, as well as from the crossover styles of FFF or Raggasonic or the Sufi rap of Abd Al Malik—all of which may nonetheless engage in sociopolitical critique. The distinction Adam Krims makes between "gangsta" and "conscious" genres in French hip-hop—which to a large extent replicate a prior U.S. folk classification between West Coast and East Coast styles—no longer appears to apply, if it ever did (Krims 2000, 155). For a further discussion of the hardcore style, see Mucchielli 1999, 60–66; and Silverstein 2002, 60. For a contrast between hardcore and Sufi rap, see Silverstein 2018.

12. The term "ghettocentricity" comes from Robin D. G. Kelley's discussion of American gangsta rap (Kelley 1996). In using this rubric, I am by no means claiming an equivalence of the lived experience in French *cités* with the racially segregated inner-city areas of the United States known popularly as "ghettos" (Wacquant 1992, 2008). Rather, I am echoing rap artists' own deployment of a language of "ghettos," as explicitly appropriated from the African American hip-hop lexicon.

13. *Caillera* is a back-slang (*verlan*) rendition of *racaille*, or "scum," a term of insult that has been ambivalently appropriated by some young *cité* men and particularly gangsta rappers of the 1990s and early 2000s.

14. For longer discussions of the roles of sports and music in French colonial and postcolonial civilizing missions, see Bancel and Gayman 2002; Darby 2002; Deville-Danthu 1997; Dubois 2010, 241–66; and Silverstein 2008, 23–25.

15. The public controversy over Zinedine Zidane's *coup de boule* (headbutt) during the championship match of the 2006 soccer World Cup must be understood in this light. The singular moment of personal retribution, the last act in what was presented as an otherwise glorious career, challenged the heroic legacy charted for Zidane by the state and the mainstream media. He was immediately criticized in the editorial pages of *Le Monde* for the example he was setting for other children of immigrants like himself growing up in the *cités* (Caussé 2006), after which he publicly expressed regret for his action and was formally forgiven by President Jacques Chirac. For an analysis, see Dubois 2010, 241–66; Guénif-Souilamas 2009; and Silverstein 2008, 23–25.

16. For a history of French hip-hop, see Bazin 1995; Cachin 1996; Cannon 1997; Gross, McMurray, and Swedenburg 1994; Meghelli 2004; and Prévos 1998, 2001, 2002.

17. Swedenburg (1992) offers a parallel discussion of the "commodification of insubordination" in American rap.

18. See Suprême NTM, "L'Argent pourrit les gens" (Money Rots People) (*Authentik*, 1991).

19. See 113, "Marginal" (*113 degrés*, 2005), and "Les Evadés" (The Escapees) and "C'est ici que la vie commence" (Here Is Where Life Begins) on *Ni barreaux, ni barrières, ni frontières* (Neither Prison Bars, Barriers, nor Borders, 1998).

20. See Hobsbawm 1959 and 1969.

21. In 2007, *banlieue* filmmaker Jean-François Richet—known for his previous work on *cité* violence, including *Ma 6-T va crack-er* (1997)—directed a two-part film on the life of Mesrine. Mesrine is played by Vincent Cassel, who made his name playing *cité* toughs in the films of Mathieu Kassovitz and is perhaps most identified with his portrayal of Vinz in *La Haine* (1995)—a character who threatens to avenge the police killing of his friend Abdel but who in the final scene is himself the victim of police violence. Cassel's brother was one of the founding members of the rap group Assassin, rapping under the name Rockin' Squat.

22. Monsieur R's composition recapitulates earlier efforts by the French hard-rock band Trust, whose 1980 track "Instinct de mort" (Death Instinct) draws on Mesrine's autobiography of the same name. In general, French hardcore rappers do not tend to draw directly on prior histories of French musical politics (e.g., the 1950s œuvre of chanson singer Georges Brassens) that similarly lionize rebellious marginality and violence against the state.

23. NTM's 1998 eponymous comeback album commences provocatively with a continuation of the introductory fantasy from the offending hit "Police," a mock conversation between two police officers fearing the return of the group. Sniper's retrospective track "La France (itinéraire d'une polémique)" (France [Itinerary of a Controversy]) replays the refrain from the original song in slightly altered form, with the offending reference to France as a "garce" (bitch) who has cheated on them, changed to France as a "farce" that has betrayed them. It continues by reprimanding the prosecutors for confusing an "appel au secours" (cry for help) with a call for murder and reminds the audience that the Marseillaise national hymn also explicitly incites violence. Monsieur R's 2006 *Black Album*, released before the conclusion of his civil court case, indexes the censorship to which the artist had been subject by featuring a black, wordless cover and no images throughout the CD booklet.

24. On parkour as a mode of urban appropriation, see Bloom 2009 and Silverstein, *Postcolonial France* 2018, 115–29.

25. The term "patrimoine du ghetto" comes from a 2005 collaborative track released by Mac Tyer and Kery James. On urban policing, see Fassin 2013 and Jobard and Lévy 2009.

26. See 113, "Main dans la main" (Hand in Hand), *Les Princes de la ville* (Princes of the City, 1999); Lunatic, "HLM3" (Housing Project no. 3), *Mauvais œil* (Evil Eye, 2000); Sinik, "Si proche des miens" (So Close to My People), *Sang froid* (Cold Blood, 2006).

27. See La Clinique, "Est-ce ça la France?" (Is This France?), *Sachons dire non* (Know How to Say "No," 1998).

28. See La Rumeur, "On m'a demandé d'oublier" (I Was Asked to Forget), *Volet 2: Le franc-tireur* (Part 2: The Sharpshooter, 1998); and "Predateur isolé" (Isolated Predator), *L'Ombre sur la mesure* (The Shadow on the Beat, 2002).

29. See Sinik, "Si proche des miens," *Sang froid* (2006); and Various Artists, *Urban Peace* (2002).

30. See 113, "Les Evadés," *Ni barreaux, ni barrières, ni frontières* (1998).

31. See Assassin, "Kique ta merde" (Kick Your Shit), *Le Futur que nous réserve-t-il?* (What Does the Future Hold for Us? 1992); and Cannon 1997, 162–63.

32. Monieur R, "J'accuse" (I Accuse), *Sachons dire non* (1998).

33. Fonky Family, "Sans faire couler le sang" (Without Shedding Blood), *Si Dieu veut . . .* (If God Wants, 1998).

34. See Kery James and Mac Tyer, "Patrimoine du ghetto," *Patrimoine du ghetto* (2005); and Sniper, "La France," *Du rire aux larmes* (2001).

35. See Rockin' Squat and Supernatural, "Undaground Connection" (*Le Flow: The Definitive French Hip Hop Compilation*, 1998); see Aidi 1985; Meghelli 2004; and Stovall 1996.

36. On the 1983 march, see Hajjat 2013. For detailed oral histories of the "Beur movement" of the early 1980s, see Aïchoune 1985; Bouamama, Sad-Saoud, and Djerdoubi 1994; Boubeker and Hajjat 1993; Derderian 2004; and Silverstein 2004. For a documentary history of the *indigènes*, see Bouteldja and Khiari 2012.

37. See Afrodiziac, "Combien de temps" (How Long), *Sachons dire non* (1998).

38. See 113, "C'est ici que la vie commence," *Ni barreaux, ni barrières, ni frontières* (1998); Ministère AMER, "Sacrifice de poulets" (Various Artists 1995); Sniper, "Brûle" (Burn), *Trait pour trait* (2006).

39. Contemporary rappers like La Rumeur and Youssoupha (who cut an album entitled *NGRTD* [2015], a shortening of *négritude*) trace their intellectual lineage to earlier writers like Aimé Césaire and Léopold Senghor and engage in a similar critique of colonialism and racism as both historical and ongoing. Sufi rapper and slam poet Abd Al Malik composed a trans-African oratory to Aimé Césaire on the occasion of his death in 2008.

40. *Hejira* refers to the prophet Muhammad's migration from Mecca to Medina in 622 but has come to stand in for broader pious mobility within the Islamic tradition. See Lunatic, "HLM3" and "Avertisseurs" (Admonishers), *Mauvais œil* (2000).

41. See 113, "Les Evadés," *Ni barreaux, ni barrières, ni frontières* (1998); Suprême NTM, "Blanc et noir" (White and Black), *Authentik* (1991).

42. Kery James, " Y'a pas de couleur" (There Is No Color), *Si c'était à refaire* (If I Had to Do It Again, 2001).

43. See, for instance, the album art of Mac Kregor and Hematom Concept's 2006 compilation *Insurrection*. For an analysis of this evocation of racialized citizenship, see Silverstein 2008.

44. On the affective politics of postcolonial love in France, see Silverstein, *Postcolonial France*, 2018; and Silverstein, "Sounds of Love and Hate," 2018.

45. Monsieur R, "Quoi ma gueule," *Sachons dire non 2* (2001).

5. RAP MUSIC IN GUADELOUPE, AN OVERSEAS FRENCH DEPARTMENT IN THE CARIBBEAN

1. This recording was a self-produced mixtape that was never mastered nor distributed by a record company.

2. Kandia passed away in 2013.

3. The Zulu Nation is the first hip-hop association that was created in New York City by Afrika Bambaataa (real name Kevin Donovan) in 1973.

4. The first uses of this nickname to make reference to Guadeloupe incidentally came out of the urban environments. According to Erka, the members of NAT were the first to use this designation that has become so popular today.

5. Distributed by Declic Communication, it received positive reviews in the specialized-Francophone press.

6. "Slas," as he was known, quickly became a reference in video directing. He went on to work with the future director of Neg' Marrons, Jean-Claude Flamand Barny, directing and producing several works in various formats: albums, compilations, and mixtapes. Mixtapes are compilations of songs recorded in a specific order with both previously recorded and original musical compositions. They are generally produced by a deejay or a rap artist and reflect their musical tastes. The phenomenon was especially prevalent in the 1990s. It competed with the official albums produced by the record industry and allowed independent artists to make their work known.

7. GGDN is the acronym for Grand Genre de Nègre, a black man in the West Indies who has style and who commands respect.

8. Compas or Kompa is a popular Haitian music that is rooted in Haitian meringue of the 1950s. Today this style represents a central aspect of the country's musical identity.

9. This site is no longer available.

10. This clash took place due to rather conventional reasons in this particular case: a problem between individuals that ended up in a rap song that itself produced responses, and so on.

11. The Société des auteurs, compositeurs et éditeurs de musique (SACEM) is an organization tasked with protecting authors' rights and with collecting the payment of those that make use of their productions.

12. In memory of the first deejay in the history of hip-hop in Guadeloupe, DJ Kandia, who died in 2013. Thanks for the interviews and information: Bronx B, Trafyk Jam, Star Jee, Exxòs, Tysmé, Khyla, Sista Flo, Nèg Lyrical, Duspee, Fuckly, Bugfu, DJ Gunshot, Osteel, Edson X, Brother Jimmy, Erka, and DJ Phonie. All interviews were conducted in person between 2008 and 2011.

6. FRENCH RAPPER-WRITERS AND ACTIVISM

1. See the success of the tour "L'Âge d'or du rap français" (Golden Age of French Rap) (Aïnouz 2016).

2. Even though the literal translation of *banlieue* is "suburb," an area geographically located at the periphery of a large city, the word is now also understood as "ghetto" and has become a euphemism for the racial other, as the outskirts of Paris and Marseille, the two largest French cities, have been populated mostly by immigrants from North Africa or sub-Saharan Africa.

3. "La France a des problèmes de mémoire/Elle connaît Malcolm X mais pas Frantz Fanon, pas le FLN."

4. See Disiz's interview with *Good Morning Cefran* (Disiz, 15 May 2015).

5. Translation mine. "Ce que montraient les medias n'était pas nos référentiels, nos modèles. Ailleurs, il y avait heureusement des Noirs qui émergeaient et nous servaient d'exemple. Je parle bien sûr de Nelson Mandela, . . . Steve Biko, Kwame Nkrumah, Aimé Césaire, ou Frantz Fanon aux Antilles. . . . Malcolm X, Martin Luther King, Mohamed Ali montraient avec fierté que l'homme noir n'était pas moins capable qu'un autre."

6. "Dans cette réflexion, tu es assez inspiré par les luttes américaines? Ça m'influence beaucoup parce qu'adolescent, j'étais dans une crise identitaire car j'avais l'impression d'être noir. Je me retrouvais donc beaucoup plus dans les questions de luttes des Noirs américains que dans celle des Noirs en France. Je trouve qu'ici cette histoire est tue. On ne connaît pas l'histoire des migrations antillaises ou africaines en France, ni des philosophes, écrivains ou musiciens noirs. Les Américains ont la faculté de créer du mythe tout de suite. Angela Davis, Malcolm X, Martin Luther King, ça me faisait rêver alors j'ai puisé dans cette histoire-là."

7. "Le trait de départ, c'était Malcolm X. Ce qui nous intéresse, c'est son cursus. Son parcours peut encore exister à notre époque."

8. "Mes modèles en politique, ce sont Martin Luther King et Malcolm X."

9. "Il avait déjà tout compris Barack Obama: c'est à nous de nous structurer, de faire émerger nos propres leaders. Alors oui, il y a des tentatives d'organisation ici ou là comme la marche pour l'égalité en 1983. . . . Aucune de ces initiatives n'a été vaine, c'est certain.

Malheureusement, elles restent encore trop timides ou, en tous cas, politiquement inoffen-sives."

10. "Je ne parle pas que de mon quartier, je parle du futur de mon pays. Et j'aurais pu parler de la même manière des projects aux États-Unis, des favelas au Brésil ou des townships en Afrique du Sud." For more on Malik, see Bourderionnet 2011; Sayare 2012; and Spieser-Landes 2015.

11. "Malcolm X, une pointure; Biko et Fanon: connais pas."

12. "Un homme libre, ivre d'égalité et de fraternité."

13. "Du haut de mon hip hop je ne vois qu'avec le cœur. . . . / Mon frère, fais comme Malcolm pour être mieux."

14. "Appelle-moi Malcolm X avec un gilet pare-balle."

15. https://twitter.com/parisblackpride?lang=en

16. On their website, one reads, "Afrofeminism *does not come from the United States* [their emphasis]. This kind of idea shows the extent to which women are forgotten in our History, and even more so if they are non-white" (L'afroféminisme ne prend [pas] ses racines aux États-Unis. Ce type d'idée reçue montre à quel point les femmes sont oubliées de l'Histoire et plus encore si elles racisées). https://mwasicollectif.com/histoire-des-luttes-des-femmes-noires?

7. NEW MEDIA, NEW VOICES

1. For a history of Skyrock's programming and marketing decisions, see Hammou (2016).

2. Compagnies Républicaines de Sécurité (CRS), or elite general reserve police officers known primarily for controlling crowds and policing during demonstrations and riots.

3. "Numéro 1 sans coke ni sky."

4. "Pour que les petits puissent dormir chez leur mère." For a detailed account of this event, see Miclet (2017).

5. "Porte-parole, ce n'est pas pour moi. Haut-parleur, pourquoi pas."

6. See, for example, Hélénon (1998) and Kleppinger (2016).

7. "Il y a un album, il y a des affaires, on va commencer par les affaires. Vous étiez il y a quelques jours à la barre correctionnelle du tribunal de Bobigny, accusé d'avoir bloqué pendant plusieurs minutes l'autoroute A3."

8. "J'ai fait une connerie, je l'assume, et j'espère ne pas trop donner de mauvaises idées."

9. "Vous flippez?"

10. "Je réponds de mes actes, j'assumerai les conséquences."

11. *Rebeu* is a term in French backslang, or *verlan*, often used to designate youth of North African heritage, while *bougnoule* is an extremely offensive and racist term designating North Africans in France. "Je ne fais pas France Inter ou BFM TV parce qu'ils veulent juste un rebeu qui sait aligner plus de trois syllabes. Le bougnoule de service, c'est pas moi. Et puis je veux aussi parler de musique. T'imagines causer de mon album sur BFM Grand Angle? J'ai très peur de la récupération politique, d'un milliard de trucs. Il y a des pièges devant moi."

12. "J'ai parfois le sentiment qu'on souhaite me faire passer pour une bête de foire. Lor-squ'on cite successivement *La Nouvelle Revue française* puis mes pires punchlines, je sais qu'on veut me faire passer pour un con."

13. "Je n'ai pas envie de m'enfermer dans les stéréotypes que les médias veulent coller sur moi. Je n'ai pas envie de dire, 'Je suis français.' Non, je ne me sens pas plus français qu'un autre. Demain si je veux, je pars en Thaïlande. Je ne serai jamais le porte-parole des banlieues. Les politiques parlent tout le temps d'intégration dans leurs discours mais tu penses vraiment que dans le XVIe arrondissement de Paris, les gens ont envie d'avoir une famille de Maliens sur leur palier?"

14. "Ça va être un gros média qui va réunir toutes les nouveautés musicales mais aussi culturelles. . . . Ce que personne ne fait, on va le faire à notre sauce comme il se doit."

15. "Je souhaite ouvrir une vraie plateforme pour que la nouvelle génération ne soit pas confrontée aux problèmes que j'ai connus: la difficulté de signer en maison de disque, de passer en radio, etc. Sur OKLM, il n'y a pas de piston. Si tu es fort, on poste ta vidéo ou ton son. C'est

méritocratique. . . . Pour moi c'est une révolution car ça permet d'éliminer tous les carcans des maisons de disque, toutes les logiques de piston à la Laurent Bouneau."

16. "OKLM.com c'est un moyen pour toi de contrer la vision du rap défendue par Sky-rock?"; "Le but c'est de récupérer ce qu'on nous a volé."

17. "Sur la grosse radio de rap qu'est Skyrock on ne découvre rien, on passe des sons qui ont déjà fait leurs preuves, qui ont des millions de vues. . . . Ils ne prennent aucun risque."

18. "Être un rappeur, c'est loin d'être une fin en soi pour moi. Je voulais comprendre la chaîne de la musique du stylo sur la feuille jusqu'à la mise en bacs de l'album."

19. "J'ai créé mes propres connections dans *JesuispasséchezSo*, il y a des mecs qu'on a entendus pour la première fois dans *JesuispasséchezSo*, il y a des mecs qui commençaient à peine à faire des reseaux que j'ai invités à venir faire quelques millions de vues avec moi et qu'on retrouve dans mon projet d'ailleurs, et j'en suis très content."

20. "C'est le seul endroit où on peut voir un total inconnu qui sort de son parking venir faire un freestyle passer juste derrière un disque diamant qui est à la une de tous les magazines en ce moment. C'est un échange, c'est un partage."

21. "Pendant longtemps, la majorité des gens, moi le premier, pensait que les radios n'avaient plus d'intérêt à l'ère Internet. Après tout, pourquoi aurait-on encore besoin d'un média qui nous dit quoi écouter à telle heure alors que le web nous offre une possibilité infinie de sons? Cela dit, je pense que les gens ont commencé à en avoir assez des playlists, et cherchent désormais des professionnels capables d'épurer le travail pour eux."

22. "Skyrock n'a plus à jouer le rôle de prescripteur. Ce travail est déjà amplement fait sur Internet. Nous, on est là pour permettre aux artistes de passer une nouvelle étape dans leur carrière en les diffusant à nos quatre millions d'auditeurs quotidiens. On est un média populaire et on se tromperait de cible si on était toujours dans la découverte."

23. "Booba est devenu une légende dans le milieu du rap français parce qu'il a réussi à faire deux disques d'or sans l'aide de Skyrock,' explique un proche. 'Aujourd'hui, il est dans une guerre ouverte avec cette station car il estime que c'est pas à elle de raconter l'histoire de cette culture vu le comportement qu'elle a eue avec lui."

24. "Notre grande phrase est de répéter que le rap est la musique qui vend le plus en France. Mais qui en profite? Plus les patrons issus du milieu se multiplient, plus on garde le contrôle et on se réapproprie les retombées de notre musique."

25. "Ça permet une liberté de création."

26. "On est un microcosme un peu particulier, on est la musique qui vend le plus en France, et je pense qu'on est celle qui est la moins présentée médiatiquement. . . . Une fois que la lumière est sur vous, il faut l'assumer."

27. "Quoi qu'il fasse ou rappe, le geste s'inscrit presque systématiquement dans une straté-gie marketing."

28. "Il se positionne en grand frère du rap. OKLM lui permet de mettre en avant une démarche positive: 'J'aide les autres, je partage,' en opposition avec son image plutôt sulfu-reuse. C'est aussi un moyen de développer sa productivité."

29. "Je pense qu'il s'agit avant tout d'une posture. Booba est extrêmement malin. Il a très bien compris l'existence d'un système anti-Skyrock dans le rap français et il a su se positionner en fonction de ça."

8. HIP-HOP BASED EDUCATION (HHBE) IN PARIS AND ITS SUBURBS

1. Contrary to the United States, residents of suburbs in France (and most of the rest of the world) are more likely to be economically, socially, and spatially marginalized than those living within the city limits, where there are more resources and opportunities. Refer to note 8 for additional historical information related to Paris.

2. Among others, there were high-profile riots and conflicts in Marseille and Les Minguettes (1981), Venissieux (1983), Vaulx-en-Velin (1979, 1991), Sartrouville (1991), and Mantes-la-Jolie (1991) (Burbach, Soto, and Kagarlitsky 1997; Prévos 2002).

3. Translation of Lafargue de Grangeneuve's French text is done by Norton; here is the original passage: "Au tournant des années 1980 et 1990, une politique publique du hip-hop se met donc en place: la mise sur agenda du hip-hop est principalement la conséquence de l'émergence renouvelée des banlieues comme problème public."

4. According to McKechnie (2008), *participant observation* is "a method of data collection in which the researcher takes part in everyday activities related to an area of social life in order to study an aspect of that life through the observation of events observed in their natural context" (599–600). *Ethnographic interviewing* is defined by Spradley (2016) as a qualitative research method that uses data from participant observation to inform and guide one-on-one interviews with research partners.

5. Translation of Puma's French text is done by Norton: "Le rap est la première musique populaire française créée dans ce milieu social, pour une fois triomphante. Tandis que des générations entières de professeurs se sont battus en vain pour essayer d'intéresser les enfants à la littérature, il a suffi d'une paire de tubes, signés par MC Solaar ou IAM pour qu'une génération entière se passionne pour l'écriture de rimes et la consultation fréquente du dictionnaire!"

6. Formerly known as the Palais Omnisport de Bercy and Bercy Arena, with a seating capacity of 20,300, the AccorHotels Arena is one of the largest venues for performing arts in Paris: accorhotelsarena.com.

7. https://www.onetwothreerap.com/partenaires

8. Although they are often located not far from the city limits, many suburbs (or *banlieues*) are not well connected to the city's physical and economic infrastructures (i.e., public transportation, employment and educational opportunities, etc.). In France, many *banlieues* were first populated by temporary migrant workers from France's former colonies, recruited by the French government to rebuild Paris and other urban areas after World War II. These government recruiters intentionally selected people from the most marginalized groups and areas of former colonies (e.g., Amazighs from the Kabylie region of Algeria and the Atlas Mountains of Morocco), thinking they would be easier to exploit for their labor and send home once the projects were completed. Some of the HLMs (*Habitation à loyer modéré*, or rent-controlled housing similar to public housing projects in the United States) in Parisian *banlieues* are hastily converted dormitories previously used to house postwar migrant workers and lack running water to this day. For more information about this topic, see Yamina Benguigui's 1997 documentary *Mémoires d'immigrés*, which can be streamed for free here: https://www.youtube.com/watch?v=71XX3YmLJzk

9. For an excellent personal account of Faye's career trajectory and artistic motivations, listen to the song "QWERTY." The lyrics can be found here: https://genius.com/Gael-faye-qwerty-lyrics.

10. https://www.youtube.com/watch?v=ObQZzLiQw1g

11. For a nuanced visual account of Faye's personal history and social outreach in France and Rwanda, see Bozino and Sangaré (2014).

12. Faye's comments were translated from French by Norton: "C'est vrai que j'ai de plus en plus envie de m'investir et de m'impliquer dans le développement de la culture surtout au Rwanda . . . pouvoir faire des ponts et les liens entre la France et le Rwanda. . . . Par exemple des choses très banales ici, mais qui là-bas ce sont tout de suite des projets qui demandent beaucoup de volonté politique et associative. Comme avoir une salle de concert, comme avoir des ingénieurs du son, pouvoir permettre à des artistes de venir, de faire une tournée au pays, pas juste venir à Kigali, pouvoir aller dans d'autres villes. . . . Et moi, disons que mon ancrage en ce moment en France, dans mon métier je rencontre du monde et je me dis que c'est important à un moment donné que je puisse commencer à utiliser ces contacts que j'ai ici pour développer aussi là-bas."

13. For more information and photos of the Tour Paris 13, see: https://www.huffingtonpost.com/jaime-rojo-steven-harrington/la-tour-paris-13_b_4306128.html.

10. "BEATS WORKING"

1. French hip-hop dance has been protected, sponsored, commissioned, and developed with French state and regional public monies. During Jack Lang's tenure as minister of culture during Mitterrand's presidency, the overall culture budget reached a symbolic 1 percent of expenditures in the national budget and can be as high as 10 percent or 11 percent in local and regional government budgets today.

2. See the catalogue for the exhibition *HIP HOP du Bronx aux rues arabes* (HIP HOP, from the Bronx to the Streets of Arab Nations), Institut du Monde Arabe (28 April–26 July 2015), tracing the history of hip-hop in France. With Jack Lang as its current director, the IMA exhibit and catalogue traced how French hip-hop responded to the United States, to black and Latino youth, and to so-called Anglo-Saxon conceptions of minority identity. But hip-hop is also shown as a multicultural movement in France, mobilizing communities of North African and sub-Saharan African heritage, as well as their communities of origin.

3. Some of them have gone off to championships and remained active in *soirées* (parties) and battles with deejays; some, like Les Twins, have moved into more commercial forms and venues. However, some—sometimes the same ones—have also moved toward careers as professional dancers on French stages reserved for contemporary dance.

4. *Le Monde* reported Macron as having said that he "would concede nothing to the do-nothings, cynics, or extremists" opposing economic reforms ("ne céderait rien, ni aux fainéants, ni aux cyniques, ni aux extrêmes"; de Royer 2017).

5. "I made the mistake of saying that the Congress operates on a French work week," Jeb Bush was reported as saying (Anonymous 2015). The *BBC News* article included a table of OECD data, "Average annual hours worked per person," in which France came in seventh place, above Denmark and Germany and following Mexico, Greece, the United States, Japan, Spain, and the United Kingdom.

6. In spite of the stereotypes, France takes *performance* very seriously, as a quantitative concept that extends to the world of the performing arts, which, unlike American "show business," is part of a strategic *politique culturelle* and a line in the national budget. The word "performance" resonates differently in French: representing both substance and excellence. Bernard Stiegler (2004) gives the history of the word "performance" in French as a way to measure and calculate potential. There is also a French history of productivity linked to ergonomics as well as exploitation. In *Dancing Machines: Choreographies of the Age of Mechanical Reproduction* (McCarren 2003), I discuss this conflictual history in the work of Jules Amar, whose *Le Moteur humain* (1923) is still celebrated on a wall in the courtyard of the former school of the Arts et Métiers in Paris. French productivity has also recently been defended by socialist economist Thomas Piketty (2017).

7. Reproductions of the strip, referred to as "Beats Working" and in which Gladys Knight and her group—her brother Merald "Bubba" Knight, Eddie Patten, and William Guest—are not named, can be found, for example, at https://www.flickr.com/photos/deathtogutenberg/ 3442959270.

8. In an interview on France Ô television (15 April 2019), Mourad Merzouki emphasized the two dancers' desire to turn away from the violence or stereotypes of rap at the beginning of their careers, as revealed in archival footage from France Ô television in 1993 shown during the program *Clair Obscur* (interview with Sebastien Folin, 15 April 2019). Merzouki spoke about the "endurance of hip hop dance" in France in the numerous projects proposed to his dance center by young choreographers.

9. Attou continues, "New York city, the Queen of Diversity, fascinates and inspires me." The breakthrough choreography *Récital* (1998) by Merzouki's Compagnie Käfig, that included Attou, staged the figure of a classical music "conductor" leading the dancers. Attou has taken up classical music again in *Un Break à Mozart* (in 2016, including Mischel in the cast) and *Un Break à Mozart 1.1* (in 2017, with classical musicians onstage with the dancers).

10. Many dancers in Paris who would all have other jobs if they were working in New York (second or third jobs; part-time jobs) live on a combination of salaried performances and state unemployment insurance.

11. The status of *intermittent du spectacle*, created for technicians and performers working first in cinema and later in television, allowed workers to string along short-term contracts and receive benefits when not employed. The sector has depended on these workers who might not complete a full workweek every week but who need to be ready to work extra hours when called. In spite of abuses of the system by employers, the *régime d'intermittence*, although often described as being in danger, remains solidly in place because of the power of the media that most need and use it. French employers might offer a part-time contract (*contrat à durée déterminée*, or CDD) rather than a full-time one (*contrat à durée indéterminée*, or CDI) in the knowledge that a worker declared as part-time will get unemployment compensation and health care even if she is, effectively, working full-time for the media. In media with part-ownership by the state, employer abuses of the system are well known. But because the media need *intermittents*, they have served as the most powerful lobby for them.

12. Some movements seem close to *flexing* or *electro* but with a different movement quality, less tension, or bound-flow.

13. From the perspective of the dancers, there is admiration on both sides: In Europe, they admire the American energy in popular dances, and in the United States, dancers envy the European valorization of the stage and over the past two decades have sought funding there. One example is the rapper M. Sayyid (Maurice Greene) of ANTIPOP CONSORTIUM who was touring in the summer of 2018 to regional French theaters with a program called "Grace and the Color of Sound" that included a French hip-hop dancer.

14. See, for example, the text of a lecture by Renaud Donnedieu de Vabres quoted at length in my *French Moves: The Cultural Politics of le Hip Hop* (McCarren 2013). According to this former French and European minister of culture, dance figured among those arts that define Europe and that would create and promote a fraternity amid a changing demographic. In this mission created for dance, there is a clear reference to its bodily representations and to the representation of diversity among dancers—in particular, in *le hip hop*.

15. "Est-ce une nouvelle forme de travail ou une nouvelle forme d'embauche? L'intermittence présente deux visages, l'un libertaire, l'autre ultralibéral. Le régime de l'intermittence balaye tout l'espace entre 'je travaille quand je veux, où je veux, comme je veux' et 'je travaille quand je peux, où ils veulent, comme ils veulent'" (70). Corsani and Lazzarato reported in 2008 that 50 percent of dance artists earn an annual salary of less than 7,900 euros. From a U.S. perspective, this would be seen as "free money"—imagine giving a dancer $10,000 a year just because she or he is a dancer, whether or not she or he performs. "Beats working!" we would say. But the logic of the French system is to support the "invisible work" that makes performance possible. Hip-hop dance becomes emblematic of that *work* that they argue is done outside of *employment*—the ongoing, constant preparation that is training, choreographic development, and rehearsing.

16. "À tout ce qui est visible, la partie émergée de l'iceberg, ce qu'on donne en représentation, vient s'ajouter toute la partie invisible, immergée qui est souvent plus importante que la précédente. C'est à l'intérieur de celle-ci qu'il y a les temps de conception, de préparation, de documentation . . . et ils sont dans la majeure partie des cas peu ou non rémunérés. Comment peut-on évaluer le travail de l'artiste pour juger de ce qui est relatif à son exigence propre et ce qui est vraiment nécessaire à l'aboutissement de son travail? Il me semble que l'une et l'autre sont indissociables, de la même manière qu'un chercheur en médecine, en physique, en littérature, n'est pas payé à sa ou ses découvertes, mais à son temps de recherche" (59). This "time for research," the status of dance *as* research, seems foreign to our conception of the performing arts in the United States. Workshops or residencies in the United States might allow a choreographer such time but would invariably be sponsored by an employer, by private support, and only occasionally by a fellowship or public monies. While creative invention continues to happen in U.S. street dance—one recent example is the Jookin' of dancer Charles Riley (Lil'Buck)—the French ensemble process is less about exceptional choreographic "genius" and more about reflective, sustainable creation.

17. The Opéra has long housed under one roof the impoverished *rats* (young students and apprentices) of the ballet school and the *étoiles* (star dancers who became wealthy). On the entrepreneurial practice of nineteenth-century Paris Opéra director (and later *député*) Louis-

Désiré Véron, see McCarren (1998). In hip-hop dance, however, there has been "protection" from the market that makes this kind of crossover commercial activity unusual.

18. Other hip-hoppers recruited over to acting or film include Stomy Bugsy (Gilles Duarte), an early break-dancer better known as a rapper and actor who earned new recognition with his leading role in *Aliker* (2009). The reception of *La Haine* (1995) also brought filmmaker-actor Mathieu Kassovitz romantic leading roles in mainstream French films (*Amélie*, 2001) and brand sponsorship/advertisement for a men's fragrance, although the cases are not exactly comparable.

19. Benyamina's film speaks to, and helps to create, a public for whom "hip-hop dancer" or dance instructor is becoming more mainstream. In the 2016 film *Polina, danser sa vie*, Paris Opéra Ballet *étoile* Jérémie Bélingard improbably plays a hip-hop dance instructor working with urban disadvantaged youth and liberating a young Russian ballerina from her movement complexes. As an inner-city Belgian dance teacher, his character delivers "association" rhetoric: "I do improv dance to help young people with integrating." At the same time, Bélingard was making commercials for Hermès and taking bows in his final year at the Palais Garnier.

20. In an interview online with *YARD*, however, Benyamina emphasized that she brought her students and interns to Cannes and to luxury hotels, for example, to prepare them for the social and class challenges they would face. And she found them up to the challenge: "Le luxe calme," she says ("luxury has a calming effect"; Benyamina 2016).

21. Dounia can dance, but she does not have the time, the idea, or the *opportunity* to develop into an artist. Yet to play Dounia, Oulaya Amamra, already trained in ballet, was asked by Benyamina to train in parkour for a year: Her character's struggle is represented physically as well as verbally in the film.

22. With a new vocabulary, a new orientation in line with the young *cadres* who in the 1960s and 1970s took over management positions in industries formerly controlled by families; or, somewhat later, in the new city defined by the term "project" to describe a range of work that masks important class differences. Thus, an NGO association for hip-hop dance such as Hip Hop Citoyens (Hip Hop Citizens) has a *project* to help residents move toward citizenship while dancing hip-hop, but a real estate developer also has a *project* for turning urban space into marketable housing. Amamra's discourse echoes that of her character; she is not critiquing a mentality of "money, money, money" but sees it as the only way to advance in a system that does nothing for the population she represents (Boltanski and Chiapello 2018).

23. In parallel to the question of the "invisible work" that makes dance performance possible, there are myths about the work done in training for a film. Dancers have crossed over into acting, but an actor called upon to play a dancer in a film is still acting and—as was the case for Natalie Portman in Darren Aronofsky's *Black Swan* (2010)—faces concerns about body doubles, acknowledged or unacknowledged. Thirty years after *Flashdance* (1983), the "entertainment world" celebrated break-dancer Richard Colón of the Rock Steady Crew for his headspins doubling for lead actress Jennifer Beals. But while it was broadly known at the time of the movie's release that "Crazy Legs" had done her break-dance moves, it was not the case for French dancer Marine Jahan, who was her stand-in for the rest of her dancing (Meriah 2013).

24. This variation on dancer-choreographer Martha Graham's well-known and much-contested statement that "the body never lies" is proposed here in a gendered economy in which Djigui can "cash in" on his talent, whereas Dounia cannot.

25. Even before Macron's election, Fleur Pellerin, minister of small and medium-sized enterprises, innovation, and the digital economy (2012–2014), and minister of culture and communication (2014–2016), was tasked with focusing on new markets and monetization for French culture.

26. Just as *The Roots* explored the limits of high performance, with gestural allusions to *le burnout* and a recent series of work-related suicides at France Télécom, so the 2018 feature *Break*, directed by former B-boy Marc Fouchard and starring Mischel as a dancer returning to work from prison, explores the sociology of work-related risks for dancers. In radio and television interviews at the time of the film's release, Fouchard promoted it as *entertainment*, liberating its French performers to be "multicasquettes" (multitasking) in the American way rather than classified as dancer, actor, or singer. However, French cinema itself represents a "cultural exception," supported in its production and protected in its release.

27. I have argued in "Somebody or Anybody? Hip Hop Choreography and the Cultural Economy" that dance is productive of this kind of surplus value, even without necessarily producing any particular thing, as in Post-Fordist virtuosity (2018). But it does not follow a script, and it does not involve linguistic competencies, so it suggests a different model than that of "services" or politics. It stands for that invisible work that creates and supports such performance.

11. ILLEGAL MURAL EXPRESSIONS

1. "Retournement sur le moi de la libido retirée de ses investissements objectaux."
2. "Qui sème le vent, récolte la tempête."
3. "Donnez-leur un mur, ils ne feront pas des chefs-d'œuvre, ils créeront un style."
4. "Le graffiti est et doit rester un mot merdeux, une insulte aux constipés de l'esprit."
5. RATP stands for the Régie Autonome des Transports Parisiens, or Autonomous Operator of Parisian Transports, and is a state-owned public transportation functionary stationed in Paris, France, and in charge of most of the transport in Paris and the Ile-de-France region.
6. Beginning in 1988, the far-right Front National party in France began scheduling its annual march honoring their symbol Jeanne d'Arc on May 1.

12. OF MELODY, MARKETS, AND MOBILIZATION

1. My observations here draw on intermittent ethnographic engagement in Dakar's hip-hop scene that began in 2007 and was most concentrated in 2011 and 2012, including oral histories, immersion in the hip-hop scene with a core group of rappers and hip-hop heads, and general awareness of continuing issues and debates in Senegalese hip-hop in the intervening years based on personal conversations, news sources, and social media.
2. This type of slang is known as *verlan*.
3. Senegalese hip-hoppers generally cite two rappers, MC Lida and Mbacké Dioum, as having separately released the first original Senegalese hip-hop tracks.
4. An egotrip is a self-aggrandizing song.
5. *Griot* is a French-language invention that refers to hereditary musicians who perform oral histories, epic poetry, social commentary, and praise-singing and genealogies in the stratified social organizations of many West African societies.
6. For more on the development of urban Wolof, see McLaughlin 2009; Swigart 1994.

13. RAP MUSIC IN QUEBEC

1. Quebec City, Sherbrooke, as well as Limoilou, a true "sacred place for Quebecois hip hop," according to Olivier Boisvert-Magnen who writes for the magazine *Voir* (Boisvert-Magnen 30 March 2018).
2. Sans Pression's and Yvon Krevé's first recordings came from this label, as well as independent French rap classics *Si Dieu Veut* (If God Wants) by the Fonky Family and *Dans la lumière* (In the Light) by Zoxea.
3. Notably interviews by Jam (de Brown), Farfadet, Cédric Morgan, or Benoît Beaudry from the show *Ghetto Erudit* with Philippe Papineau in an article for the magazine *Le Devoir*.
4. A few examples include Sans Pression and Akhenaton of IAM on "La Tendance se maintient" (The Tendency Remains Stable) and Dubmatique and les 2Bal on "Authentiques."

5. Created by DJ "Noji Mzilikazi" Jam Patrol, *Up Front* was the first Quebecois/Canadian hip-hop magazine.

6. In January 2008, the group Kourtrajmé (Kim Chapiron, Toumani Sangaré, and Romain Gavras), starting off with clips from French rappers Rocé, Oxmo Puccino, and Mafia K'1 Fry, even made a documentary about him: *Les Mathématiques du Roi Heenok* (King Heenok's Mathematics; Gavras and Mazouz 2008).

7. Their success in 2013 is notable: After the album *Montréal $ud*, they published a work describing their vocabulary.

8. For example, the duo DawaMafia mixed up dance hall and rap ("D'où je viens"; Where I Come From), Obia le Chef gave Afropop a try, while Loud collaborated with the singer Cœur de Pirate.

9. This can be seen in "Ten" (acronym of "Tout est noir," or All Is Black), in which Obia le Chef criticizes segregation, and "Devenir immortel (et puis mourir)," in which Loud attacks Quebec rappers for dropping their accents and regional character in order to blend into French or European markets.

14. ALACLAIR ENSEMBLE'S "POSTRIGODON"

1. "200 ans de repli défensif et de survivance linguistique."

2. "Ma bâtardisation vous choque? Soit. Votre puritanisme me dégoûte. Certains membres de Dead Obies ont grandi avec une mère francophone et un père anglo, ou vice-versa. Demandez-leur donc c'est quoi, leur vision de l'identité québécoise. Parce que oui, malgré le fait qu'ils aient vécu une expérience diamétralement opposée à la vôtre ou même à la mienne, ils sont Québécois, tout autant que vous et moi. Devrait-on exclure leur québécité parce qu'elle ne correspond pas à la nôtre?"

3. "Permet à l'historien de réaliser des expériences mentales puisque l'expérimentation en laboratoire lui est impossible."

4. "[L]'une des erreurs méthodologiques les plus courantes en histoire des idées scientifiques est d'aborder les sources primaires dans une approche continuiste et finaliste. . . . Jouer avec la possibilité de trajectoires alternatives, identifier des questions qui ne se posent plus, voire n'ont jamais atteint le stade de maturité de la formulation explicite, c'est d'abord pour l'historien accroître sa propre sensibilité à ces frémissements, à des idées non encore répertoriées. . . . [U]ne uchronie est avant tout une machine à poser des questions sans réponse."

5. "[L]'uchronie québécoise est toujours politique."

6. "Robert Nelson voulait que le Bas-Canada ait sa propre identité, une identité qui ne serait pas basée sur une langue ou une ethnie, mais plutôt sur une série de valeurs et de réalités communes."

7. "Sans représenter aucune cause, fouetter un peu l'histoire *mainstream* telle qu'elle nous a été enseignée allait de soi dans notre musique."

8. "Un rigodon, c'est une toune que tout le monde connaît et que tout le monde peut chanter même s'il chante mal."

9. "On est en train d'affirmer la force de notre différence culturelle à travers le pathétique de plusieurs de nos références."

10. "Ouvre au maximum le champ des possibles même si l'univers décrit en devient totalement farfelu ou historiquement impossible."

11. "Le clin d'œil au lecteur est souvent évident, en particulier lorsqu'il fait intervenir des personnages illustres . . . ; toutefois, cette connivence entre l'auteur et son lecteur peut se prolonger, en particulier dans des uchronies plus savantes où l'auteur s'adresse alors à un public plus restreint mais comme lui très cultivé dans un certain domaine et à l'attention duquel il multiplie les clins d'œil cachés."

12. "Un petit garçon de São Paulo avec une coupe champignon."

13. "Dédié à la perpétuation du postrigodon."

14. "L'u-chronie, le temps qui n'existe pas [et] au sein de cette dualité vient s'insérer l'u-glossie, la langue qui n'existe pas."

15. "Soucoupe volante" is being used to denote a disc-shaped object, i.e., a CD in this case. There is also a pun on "GRATISSEMENT," *gratis* meaning "free of charge" in French slang.

16. "Une troupe postrigodon bas-canadienne zigzaguant entre Quoibec et Mourial. Moyen-née par les gradués du Alaclair High, sa fin est le brizassage de fizzoules. Alaclair Ensemble, c'est pour les enfants?" "Quoibec" and "Mourial" are amusing phonetic distortions of the cities of "Quebec" and "Montreal."

17. "Vient ébranler nos affirmations ordinaires sur le monde empirique. On pourrait consi-dérer qu'il surgit de l'écart entre l'état réel des choses et la façon dont cet état est représenté dans la blague, entre attente et occurrence."

18. "[Y]'a toujours un double message: celui de la présence de l'anglais dans notre culture, et celui du peuple colonisé. Moi, ça m'intéresse beaucoup, d'aller creuser dans le gap qui existe entre l'anglais et le français au Québec. . . . Je pense qu'il y a plus de vérité à trouver là-dedans qu'en se campant d'un bord ou de l'autre. . . . Le pouvoir que j'ai, c'est de continuer de dire au monde qu'il y a plusieurs choses qui font la société québécoise, comme l'anglais, l'histoire."

19. "L'identité étant liée à la conscience historique de l'individu, réinventer ses origines, c'est se créer soi-même."

20. "Il s'inscrit dans une position épistémologique idéale pour sa réflexion sociale. . . . L'auteur détient ainsi un pouvoir immense sur la représentation imaginaire et symbolique de son peuple."

Index

About the Editor, Contributors, and Translators

Alain-Philippe Durand is dean of the College of Humanities, professor of French, Honors College Distinguished Fellow, and affiliated faculty in Africana Studies, Latin American Studies, LGBT Studies, and Public and Applied Humanities at the University of Arizona. He is the author and editor of the books *Black, Blanc, Beur: Rap Music and Hip-Hop Culture in the Francophone World* (Scarecrow Press, 2002); *Un Monde Techno: Nouveaux espaces électroniques dans le roman français des années 1980 et 1990* (preface by Marc Augé, Weidler, 2004); *Novels of the Contemporary Extreme* (coedited with Naomi Mandel, Continuum, 2006); and *Frédéric Beigbeder et ses doubles* (Rodopi, 2008). He has published chapters and articles in such journals as *PMLA*, *The French Review*, *Romance Notes*, *Contemporary French Civilization*, *L'Esprit créateur*, *Romance Quarterly*, *Contemporary French & Francophone Studies: SITES*, *L'Atelier du Roman*, and *ADFL Bulletin*, among others. He is associate editor of the journal *Contemporary French Civilization*. In 2013, he launched the minor in Hip-Hop Studies at the University of Arizona.

* * *

Catherine M. Appert is an ethnomusicologist and assistant professor in the Department of Music at Cornell University, where she teaches courses on African and African diasporic music, ethnographic theory and methods, and global hip-hop. Her recent book, *In Hip Hop Time: Music, Memory, and Social Change in Urban Senegal* (Oxford University Press, 2018), examines the dynamic relationships between popular music, historical memory, and diasporic belonging in urban Senegal. Her research has been supported by the Fulbright-Hays Program and the American Council for Learned Societies with the Mellon Foundation. She has published articles in *Ethnomusicology*, *Africa*, and *New Literary History* and has presented her research at numerous annual meetings of the Society for Ethnomusicology, the American Anthropological Association, the African Studies Association, and the International Association for the Study of Popular Music.

Hugues Bazin has been an independent researcher in social sciences since 1993, director of the Laboratory of Social Innovation by Research-Action, an associate researcher at the *Maison des Sciences de l'Homme* in Paris-Nord and the National Institute of Youth and Popular Education. Former director of the magazine *Paroles et Pratiques Sociales* in the 1980s and graduate of the *École des Hautes Études en Sciences Sociales* in anthropology and sociology, he synthesizes the social and scientific in his career. This articulation is best illustrated in a research-action approach with populations and social spaces whose challenges often remain in the "shadow archive" of knowledge. From popular neighborhoods to urban practices, he was among the first in the 1980s and 1990s to organize meetings and to write about hip-hop cultural expression, notably through the book *Hip-hop Culture* (Desclée de Brouwer, 1995). These critical encounters with a generation of young social and cultural actors contributed to the work *Espaces populaires de création culturelle: Stakes of Situational Action Research* (INJEP, 2006). This exposure of a network of actor-researchers questioning the role of the social sciences prompted the creation of the Laboratory of Social Innovation through Research-Action in 2009. It continues to be attentive to the forms of emergencies and interstitial spaces of creativity and, more generally, to the stakes of a "work of culture" between popular education and cultural action. As an associate researcher, he runs seminars on social and cultural practices, informal education, the contemporary city, special practices, and eco-development.

Maxime Delcourt is associate editor in chief of *Jack*, the musical site of *Canal+*. He is also a freelance journalist who writes for various French culture magazines (*Les Inrockuptibles*, *Noisey*, *Slate*) and has authored special editions of *Le Mot et le Reste*, such as *2Pac, Me against the World*.

Steve Gadet is a university lecturer in American Civilization at the Université des Antilles, Schoelcher Campus, Martinique, France. He is also an active rapper and author of several books.

Ariane Gruet-Pelchat has been deeply involved in the underground Québécois scene for fifteen years, both as a musician and as a music journalist. Her research looks at discourses on music, the dynamics at play in the Montreal underground scene, and the boundaries between the alternative and commercial scenes. She plays violin in the group Groenland as well as in other lesser-known bands.

Karim Hammou is a researcher at the National Center for Scientific Research (Centre national de la recherche scientifique or CNRS) and is a member of the team Urban Cultures and Societies (Cultures et sociétés urbaines or CSU) at the Sociological and Political Research Center of Paris (Centre de Recherches Sociologiques et Politiques de Paris, CRESPPA). Host of the research blog entitled *Sur un son rap*, he is also the author of the book *Une histoire du rap en France* (La Découverte, 2012) and one of the administrators of H-Herc, a LISTSERV on hip-hop in teaching, research, and culture. In 2016, he co-organized the international colloquium Built to Last: Francophone Perspectives on Hip-Hop Music ("Conçues pour durer. Perspectives francophones sur les musiques hip-hop"). His work links sociology from artistic worlds and sociology from power relationships in the study of cultural industries. His current research projects focus notably on the logic behind musical categorizations, the commercial exploitation of minority attributes in the cultural industries, and the history of racialized music in France. He recently published "Mainstreaming French Rap Music: Commodification and Artistic Legitimation of Other Cultural Goods," *Poetics* 59 (December 2016): 67–81.

Jean-Marie Jacono has been associate professor of musicology (Laboratoire d'études en sciences des arts, LESA) at Aix-Marseille University (AMU) since 1992. His work, in the fields of music sociology and semiotics, has been dedicated to Russian music (a doctoral thesis on the revisions of Mussorgsky's opera *Boris Godunov*) but also modern popular music (song and rap). The first musicologist to have studied French rap, Jean-Marie Jacono has written many articles about rap in Marseille and the group IAM. He is a cofounder, alongside Perle Abbrugiati and Joël July, of the international network Chanson: Les ondes du monde (Song: The Waves of the World) that organized the first biannual international workshops of contemporary song in 2017 in Aix, Marseille (MuCEM), and Lens (Louvre). He codirects the "chants—sons" (Song—Sounds) collection at Provence University Press. In addition to numerous articles and chapters on rap and other themes, he is the coauthor (with Lionel Pons) of *Henri Tomasi, du lyrisme méditerranéen à la conscience révoltée* (Presses de l'Université de Provence, 2015).

Kathryn Kleppinger is associate professor of French and Francophone studies at George Washington University. She has published journal articles on the works of Alain Mabanckou and Léonora Miano, the sociology of "beur" publishing, the Littérature-Monde manifesto, and the terrorist attacks on

Charlie Hebdo. Her work has appeared in such journals as *Contemporary French and Francophone Studies: SITES* and *Contemporary French Civilization.* She is also the author of *Branding the Beur Author: Minority Authors and the Media, 1983–2013* (Liverpool University Press, 2015) and the coeditor of *French Cultural Studies for the 21st Century* (Delaware University Press, 2017) and *Post-Migratory Cultures in Postcolonial France* (Liverpool University Press, 2018).

Felicia McCarren is professor of French at Tulane University in New Orleans and was a resident fellow at the Paris Institute for Advanced Study from 2016 to 2017, researching the natural and cultural history of gender and diversity on French stages. McCarren is the author of *Dance Pathologies: Performance, Poetics, Medicine* (Stanford Writing Science Series,1998); *Dancing Machines: Choreographies of the Age of Mechanical Reproduction* (Stanford 2003; reprinted 2015); and *French Moves : The Cultural Politics of le hip hop* (Oxford, 2013). She was awarded the De la Torre Bueno Prize by the Society of Dance History Scholars and the Outstanding Publication of the Year 2014 from the Congress on Research in Dance. McCarren has presented and published archival and ethnographic work on the Moroccan south, with National Endowment for the Humanities (NEH) startup funding (2011). Recent articles include "Dancing D-Day" in the *Oxford Handbook of Dance and Politics*; "Minority Visibility and Hip Hop Choreography: France 2015" in *Contemporary Choreography: A Critical Reader* (forthcoming from Routledge); and "Somebody or Anybody? Postcolonial Choreography and the Cultural Economy" in *Post-Migratory Cultures in Post-Colonial France*, edited by Kathryn Kleppinger and Laura Reeck (Liverpool University Press, 2018).

Samir Meghelli is a historian and museum curator in Washington, D.C. He received his B.A. (magna cum laude) from the University of Pennsylvania, and his M.A., M.Phil., and Ph.D. in history from Columbia University. He was previously a professor at the University of Illinois at Urbana-Champaign, as well as a visiting scholar at Northeastern University and Sciences Po. He is the coauthor of *The Global Cipha: Hip Hop Culture and Consciousness* (2006) and coeditor of *New Perspectives on Marcus Garvey, the U.N.I.A., and the African Diaspora* (2011), and his writings have appeared in *The New York Times*, *Black Arts Quarterly*, and *Western Journal of Black Studies*, among other places. He is currently completing a book about the transatlantic history of hip-hop between the United States and France.

Alain Milon is professor of philosophy at the University of West Paris-Nanterre. His research focuses on the intersection of philosophy, literature, and contemporary poetry, and specializations on authors like Blanchot, Artaud, Ponge, and Michaux. He also explores social issues, such as urban development and the relationship between man and nature. His publications include *La Communauté en archipel: La place de l'Étranger* (Presses Paris Nanterre, 2018); *Sous la langue, Artaud: La réalité en folie* (Les Belles Lettres, 2016); *Pour une critique de la raison écologique: Le plan de nature* (Circé, 2014); *Cartes inconnues: Approche critique de l'espace* (Les Belles Lettres, 2013); *La Fêlure du cri: Violence et écriture* (Les Belles Lettres, 2010); and *Bacon, l'effroyable viande* (Les Belles Lettres, 2008).

Marcyliena Morgan is a professor in the Department of African and African American Studies at Harvard University and the director of the Hiphop Archive and Research Institute. Professor Morgan founded the Hiphop Archive at the W. E. B. Du Bois Institute for Afro-American Research at Harvard University in 2002. She earned both her B.A. and her M.A. degrees at the University of Illinois in Chicago. She obtained an additional M.A. at the University of Essex, England, and her Ph.D. through the Graduate School of Education at the University of Pennsylvania. She has conducted field research on the African diaspora, identity, and language in the United States, England, and the Caribbean. She has received major grants from the Ford Foundation and from the Centers for Disease Control and Prevention (CDC). She is the author of many works that focus on youth, gender, racism, language, culture, identity, sociolinguistics, discourse, and interaction, including the *Daedulus* publication "Hip-Hop and the Global Imprint of a Black Cultural Form" (with Dionne Bennett; 2011); *Language, Discourse, and Power in African American Culture* (Cambridge University Press, 2002); and her book *The Real Hiphop: Battling for Knowledge, Power, and Respect in the LA Underground* (Duke University Press, 2008). Her most recent book publication is *Speech Communities* with Cambridge University Press (2014).

Charles Norton is a Ph.D. candidate in aesthetics at the University of West Paris-Nanterre, where his dissertation examines how hip-hop cultures are being used globally for education and social justice. Beyond research, he works as a language consultant for the Seattle Sounders Football Club and teaches in the Hip-Hop Studies program at the University of Arizona. Additionally, Norton is a co-organizer of the annual Tucson Hip-Hop Festival and has facilitated free Hip-Hop Based Education workshops for youth in France, the United States, and Morocco.

Stève Puig holds a Ph.D. in French from the City University of New York, and he is currently assistant professor at St. John's University in New York, where he is doing research on French Caribbean literature and urban culture in metropolitan France. His latest publications include an article for *Women in French* on Audrey Pulvar's novel *L'Enfant-bois* and an online publication on urban literature and dystopia for *Itinéraires*. He is also interested in representations of New York in contemporary French literature.

Paul A. Silverstein is professor of anthropology at Reed College (Portland, USA). He is author of *Algeria in France: Transpolitics, Race, and Nation* (Indiana University Press, 2004) and coeditor of *Bourdieu in Algeria: Colonial Politics, Ethnographic Practices, Theoretical Developments* (University of Nebraska Press, 2009). His writings on racial politics and popular culture among Franco-Maghrebis have appeared in *Social Text*, *Ethnography*, and *Patterns of Prejudice*, among other venues, and in a forthcoming book, *Postcolonial France* (Polity Press).

* * *

Katie B. Angus is associate professor of French and second language acquisition in the Department of Foreign Languages and Literatures at the University of Southern Mississippi, where she teaches courses online and face-to-face to undergraduate students of French and graduate students enrolled in the M.A. in the Teaching of Languages (MATL) program. Her research interests lie in L2 teacher development, technology, and literacy-based teaching.

Patricia Frederick is professor of French and chair of the Department of Global Languages and Cultures at Northern Arizona University, where she has taught French language, culture, literature, and film for more than twenty years. Her publications include critical studies and literary translations, and her scholarly interests also comprise issues in contemporary culture.

Sarah Glasco is associate professor of French and coordinator of the Women's, Gender, and Sexualities Studies Interdisciplinary Minor Program at Elon University. Her publications include *Parody and Palimpsest: Intertextuality, Language, and the Ludic in the Novels of Jean-Philippe Toussaint* (Peter Lang, 2015), a multiplicity of reviews for the *French Review*, as well as articles in *Expressions Maghrébines* and *CUR-Quarterly*. Her current research includes the role of faculty in global learning, teaching French through the lens of social justice, and Yé-Yé and feminism in France in the 1960s.

Richard J. Gray II is associate professor of French at Ashland University. His fields of study include interdisciplinary approaches to French literary studies, postcolonial studies, and Francophone studies. His newest book is a translation of forensic pathologist Philippe Charlier's anthropological study of zombies in Haiti entitled *Zombies: An Anthropological Investigation of the*

Living Dead (University Press of Florida, 2017). He is also the author of *Francophone African Poetry and Drama: A Cultural History Since the 1960s* (McFarland, 2014) and of numerous articles and book reviews.

Matthew Kemp currently teaches at the University of Rhode Island. He received his Ph.D. in French from Florida State University in 2006. His dissertation looks at official and intellectual discourses emanating from France and the United States in the aftermath of 9/11 and the Iraq War. He has published several articles on this topic. From 2007 to 2014, he worked at Kent State University, where he taught courses in French language, literature, and culture.

André Pettman is a doctoral student in French at Columbia University. He received his M.A. in French from the University of Arizona. He studies twentieth- and twenty-first-century French and Francophone literature and is currently working on a master's thesis on *Rose poussière* by Jean-Jacques Schuhl.